Testimonies

for the Church

Vol. 7

Ellen G. White

Copyright Notice

Copyright © 2022 by Waymark Books

Published by Waymark Books

All rights reserved. No part of this publication may be reproduced, distributed, or transmitted in any form or by any means, including photocopying, recording, or other electronic or mechanical methods, without the prior written permission of the publisher, except in the case of brief quotations embodied in critical reviews and certain other noncommercial uses permitted by copyright law. For permission requests, contact the publisher, addressed "Attention: Permissions Coordinator," at this address: WaymarkBooks@gmail.com.

TABLE OF CONTENTS

Section 1: Acceptable Service
1. The Work of Soulsaving 5
2. The Signal of Advance 8
   An Ever-Widening Work 9
3. Work for Church Members 11
   The Waste Places of the Earth 14
   Self-Supporting Missionaries 15
4. Workers from the Ranks 16
5. Extending Triumphs of the Cross 19
   The Work of the Church 20
   The Holy Spirit our Efficiency 20
   Power Given the Apostles 21
   The Same Power to be Revealed 21
6. The Work in the Cities 23
7. The Work in Greater New York 25
8. Delay No Longer 27
9. Family Worship 28
10. Responsibilities of Married Life 31

Section 2: Our Sanitarium Work
11. Extent of the Work 36
    New York City 39
    The Southern States 40
    In All Lands 41
12. Knowledge of Health Principles 44
13. Calling of Sanitarium Workers 48
14. A Message to Our Physicians 51
15. The Value of Outdoor Life 54

16. Out of the Cities 57
17. In the Country 60
18. Not Among the Wealthy 62
19. Consideration in Buildings 64
20. Not for Pleasure Seekers 68
21. Centralization 71
22. The Sign of our Order 74

Section 3: Health Foods
23. Medical Missionaries in Cities 79
24. The Restaurant Work 82
    Care of the Helpers 84
    Closing Restaurants on Sabbath 87
25. Healthful Foods 89
26. Manufacture of Health Foods 91
    To Our Brethren in All Lands 92
    An Evil Work 93
27. Educate the People 95

Section 4: The Publishing Work
28. God's Purpose in Publishing 100
    Witnesses for Truth 100
    Demonstrating Christian Principles ... 103
    Missionary Agencies 105
    Training Schools for Workers 107
    God's Purpose Fulfilled 108
29. Our Denominational Literature ... 109
    The Object of our Publications 110

    Personal Experience Needed......... 111
    Matter for Publication 113
    Unity... 114
    Items of Experience 114
    The Message for this Time........... 115
    Publication of Books..................... 116
    Prices 116
    Translations 117
30. Commercial Work...................... 118
    Opportunities in Commercial Work... 118
    Not to Stand First 119
    Prices 120
    Demoralizing Literature 120
31. Publishing in Foreign Fields 124
32. Publishing House Relations 125
    Consolidation................................ 126
    Rivalry.. 127
    Co-operation 128
33. The Canvasser 128
34. The Author................................. 129
35. Church & Publishing House........... 133
    Duty of Church to Publishing House 133
    Duty of Publishing House to Church 137
36. Sacredness of God's Instruments..... 140
37. Dependence on God................... 142
38. Co-operation 144
39. Self-Control and Fidelity 145
40. Danger from Improper Reading... 148
41. Avoid Debt................................. 150
42. Faith and Courage 153
43. Self-Sacrifice.............................. 157

Section 5: In the Southern Field
44. Needs of the Southern Field....... 161
    An Appeal for the Colored Race ... 162
    A Call from the Colored Race....... 163
    A Gospel for the Poor.................... 165
    What Can be Done 166
45. Centers of Influence 169
    Nashville as a Center 170
46. Instruction to Workers 172
47. Be of Good Courage................... 177

Section 6: Counsels to Burden Bearers
48. Ministers & Business Matters 180
    Educate Men in Business Lines 181
    Right Principles Essential 182
49. Take Time to Talk with God..... 183
50. The Work of the Ministry.......... 186
51. Committee Meetings.................. 187
    Diet and Board Meetings 188
52. Church Discipline....................... 190
53. "Consider One Another" 193
54. To Teachers in Our Schools....... 195
    Aggressive Effort 196
    Christ's Greeting to the World 196
    The Outlook.................................. 198
    Power from on High..................... 199
55. Those Struggling with Difficulties ..202
    Unwise Changes 204
    A Call to Service........................... 205
56. A Wise Distribution of Means ... 207
57. Our Aged Pioneer Workers........ 209
58. Care for Workers....................... 212
    Workers Neglected 213
    Providing Homes for Workers 213
    Our Sanitariums a Refuge............. 214
    A Worker's Fund.......................... 215

— Section 1 —

Acceptable Service

"Be not conformed to this world: but be ye transformed by the renewing of your mind, that ye may prove what is that good, and acceptable, and perfect will of God." Romans 12:2.

1. The Work of Soulsaving

God has given me a message for His people. They must awake, spread their tents, and enlarge their borders. My brethren and sisters, you have been bought with a price, and all that you have and are is to be used to the glory of God and for the good of your fellow men. Christ died on the cross to save the world from perishing in sin. He asks your co-operation in this work. You are to be His helping hand. With earnest, unwearying effort you are to seek to save the lost. Remember that it was your sins that made the cross necessary. When you accepted Christ as your Saviour you pledged yourself to unite with Him in bearing the cross. For life and for death you are bound up with Him, a part of the great plan of redemption.

The transforming power of Christ's grace molds the one who gives himself to God's service. Imbued with the Spirit of the Redeemer, he is ready to deny self, ready to take up the cross, ready to make any sacrifice for the Master. No longer can he be indifferent to the souls perishing around him. He is lifted above self-serving.

He has been created anew in Christ, and self-serving has no place in his life. He realizes that every part of his being belongs to Christ, who has redeemed him from the slavery of sin; that every moment of his future has been bought with the precious lifeblood of God's only-begotten Son.

Have you so deep an appreciation of the sacrifice made on Calvary that you are willing to make every other interest subordinate to the work of saving souls? The same intensity of desire to save sinners that marked the life of the Saviour marks the life of His true follower. The Christian has no desire to live for self. He delights to consecrate all that he has and is to the Master's service. He is moved by an inexpressible desire to win souls to Christ. Those who have nothing of this desire might better be concerned for their own salvation. Let them pray for the spirit of service.

How can I best glorify Him whose I am by creation and by redemption? This is to be the question that we are to ask ourselves. With anxious solicitude the one who is truly converted seeks to rescue those who are still in Satan's power. He refuses to do anything that would hinder him in his work. If he has children he realizes that his work must begin in his own family. His children are exceedingly precious to him. Remembering that they are the younger members of the Lord's family, he strives with all his power to place them where they will stand on the Lord's side. He has pledged himself to serve, honor, and obey Christ; and he puts forth patient, untiring effort so to train his children that they will never be hostile to the Saviour.

On fathers and mothers, God has placed the responsibility of saving their children from the power of the enemy. This is their work, a work that they should on no account neglect. Those parents who have a living connection with Christ will not rest until they see their children safe in the fold. They will make this the burden of their life.

Parents, do not neglect the work waiting for you in the church in your own family. This is your first field of missionary effort. The most important work you can do is to place your children on the Lord's side. When they err, deal with them tenderly, yet firmly. Let them unite with you in opposing the evil by which Satan seeks to destroy the souls and bodies of human beings. Share with them the secret of the cross, the secret that to you means sanctification, redemption, and eternal victory. As you take your children with you into the service of the Lord, what a victory you gain.

If the families around you are opposed to the truth, strive to lead them to yield to the claims of Christ. Work patiently, wisely, considerately, winning your way by the tender ministry of love. Present the truth in such a way that it will be seen in all its beauty, exerting an influence that cannot be resisted. Thus the walls of prejudice will be broken down.

If this work were faithfully done, if fathers and mothers would work for the members of their own families, and then for those around them, uplifting Christ by a godly life, thousands of souls would be saved. When God's people are truly converted, when they realize the obligation resting on them to labor for those within their reach, when they leave no means untried to rescue sinners from the power of the enemy, the reproach will be removed from our churches.

We have now only a little time in which to prepare for eternity. May the Lord open the closed eyes of His people and quicken their dulled senses, that they may realize that the gospel is the power of God unto salvation to them that believe. May they see the importance of giving so pure and righteous a representation of God that the world shall see Him in His beauty. May they be so filled with the Spirit that dwells in Him that the world will have no power to divert them from the work of presenting to men the wonderful possibilities before every soul who receives Christ.

In all lines of our work there is need of greater earnestness. Time is passing. God's servants are to be "not slothful in business; fervent in spirit; serving the Lord." People need the truth, and by earnest, faithful effort it is to be communicated to them. Souls are to be sought for, prayed for, labored for. Earnest appeals are to be made. Fervent prayers are to be offered. Our tame, spiritless petitions are to be changed into petitions of intense earnestness. God's word declares: The effectual fervent prayer of a righteous man availeth much.

The world is our field of missionary toil, and we are to go forth to labor surrounded with the atmosphere of Gethsemane and Calvary.

2. The Signal of Advance

It is an eternal law of Jehovah that he who accepts the truth that the world needs is to make it his first work to proclaim this truth. But who is there that makes the burden of perishing sinners his own? As I look upon the professed people of God, and see their unwillingness to serve Him, my heart is filled with a pain that I cannot express. How few are heart to heart with God in His solemn, closing work. There are thousands to be warned, yet how few consecrate themselves wholly to the work, willing to be or to do anything if only they may win souls to Christ. Jesus died to save the world. In humility, in lowliness, in unselfishness, He worked and is working for sinners. But many of those who ought to co-operate with Him are self-sufficient and indifferent.

Among God's people today there is a fearful lack of the sympathy that should be felt for souls unsaved. We talk of Christian missions. The sound of our voices is heard; but do we feel Christ's tender heart longing for those outside the fold? And unless our hearts beat in union with the heart of Christ, how can we understand the sacredness and importance of the work to which we are called by the words: "Watch for ... souls, as they that must give account"? Hebrews 13:17.

God is waiting for men and women to awake to their responsibilities. He is waiting for them to link themselves with Him. Let them mark the signal of advance, and no longer be laggards in working out the will of the Lord.

Do we realize how large a number in the world are watching our movements? From quarters where we least expect will come voices urging us forward in the work of giving to the world the last message of mercy. Ministers and people, wake up! Be quick to recognize and seize every opportunity and advantage offered in the turning of the wheel of providence. God and Christ and the heavenly angels are working with intense activity to hold in check the fierceness of Satan's wrath, that God's plans may not be thwarted. God lives and reigns. He is conducting the affairs of the universe. Let His soldiers move forward to victory. Let there be perfect unity in their ranks. Let them press the battle to the gates. As a mighty Conqueror, the Lord will work for them.

Section 1: Acceptable Service

Let the gospel message ring through our churches, summoning them to universal action. Let the members of the church have increased faith, gaining zeal from their unseen, heavenly allies, from a knowledge of their exhaustless resources, from the greatness of the enterprise in which they are engaged, and from the power of their Leader. Those who place themselves under God's control, to be led and guided by Him, will catch the steady tread of the events ordained by Him to take place. Inspired with the Spirit of Him who gave His life for the life of the world, they will no longer stand still in impotency, pointing to what they cannot do. Putting on the armor of heaven, they will go forth to the warfare, willing to do and dare for God, knowing that His omnipotence will supply their need.

- **An Ever-Widening Work**

God's servants are to make use of every resource for enlarging His kingdom. The apostle Paul declares that it is "good and acceptable in the sight of God our Saviour; who will have all men to be saved, and to come unto the knowledge of the truth," that "supplications, prayers, intercessions, and giving of thanks, be made for all men." 1 Timothy 2:3,4,1. And James says: "Let him know, that he which converteth the sinner from the error of his way shall save a soul from death, and shall hide a multitude of sins." James 5:20. Every believer is pledged to unite with his brethren in giving the invitation, "Come; for all things are now ready." Luke 14:17. Each is to encourage the others in doing wholehearted work. Earnest invitations will be given by a living church. Thirsty souls will be led to the water of life.

The apostles carried a weight of responsibility to enlarge their sphere of labor, to proclaim the gospel in the regions beyond. From their example we learn that there are to be no idlers in the Lord's vineyard. His servants are constantly to enlarge the circle of their efforts. Constantly they are to do more, never less. The Lord's work is to widen and broaden until it encircles the world.

After making a missionary tour, Paul and Barnabas retraced their steps, visiting the churches they had raised up and selecting men to unite with them in the work. Thus God's servants are to labor today, selecting and training worthy young men as colaborers. God help us to sanctify ourselves, that by our example others may be sanctified, enabled to do successful work in winning souls to Christ.

We are nearing the close of this earth's history; soon we shall stand before the great white throne. Soon your time for work will be forever past. Watch for opportunities to speak a word in season to those with whom you come in contact. Do not wait to become acquainted before you offer them the priceless treasures of truth. Go to work, and ways will open before you.

At the day of judgment there comes to the lost a full realization of the meaning of the sacrifice made on Calvary. They see what they have lost by refusing to be loyal. They think of the high, pure association it was their privilege to gain. But it is too late. The last call has been made. The wail is heard: "The harvest is past, the summer is ended, and we are not saved." Jeremiah 8:20.

Upon us rests the weighty responsibility of warning the world of its coming doom. From every direction, from far and near, are coming calls for help. God calls upon His church to arise and clothe herself with power. Immortal crowns are to be won; the kingdom of heaven is to be gained; the world, perishing in ignorance, is to be enlightened.

The world will be convinced, not by what the pulpit teaches, but by what the church lives. The minister in the desk announces the theory of the gospel; the practical piety of the church demonstrates its power.

Enfeebled and defective, needing constantly to be warned and counseled, the church is nevertheless the object of Christ's supreme regard. He is making experiments of grace on human hearts and is effecting such transformations of character that angels are amazed and express their joy in songs of praise. They rejoice to think that sinful, erring human beings can be so transformed.

As the third angel's message swells into a loud cry, great power and glory will attend its proclamation. The faces of God's people will shine with the light of heaven.

The Lord will fit men and women—yes, and children, as He did Samuel—for His work, making them His messengers. He who never slumbers or sleeps watches over each worker, choosing his sphere of labor. All heaven is watching the warfare which, under apparently discouraging circumstances, God's servants are carrying on. New conquests are being achieved, new honors won, as the Lord's servants, rallying round the banner of their Redeemer, go forth to fight the good fight of faith. All the heavenly angels are at the service of the humble, believing people of God; and as the Lord's army of workers here below sing their songs of praise, the choir above join with them in thanksgiving, ascribing praise to God and to His Son.

Nothing is apparently more helpless, yet really more invincible, than the soul that feels its nothingness and relies wholly on the merits of the Saviour. God would send every angel in heaven to the aid of such a one, rather than allow him to be overcome.

The battle cry is sounding along the line. Let every soldier of the cross push to the front, not in self-sufficiency, but in meekness and lowliness, and with firm faith in God. Your work, my work, will not cease with this life. For a little while we may rest in the grave, but, when the call comes, we shall, in the kingdom of God, take up our work once more.

3. Work for Church Members

We have a message from the Lord to bear to the world, a message that is to be borne in the rich fullness of the Spirit's power. Let our ministers see the need of seeking to save the lost. Direct appeals are to be made to the unconverted. "Why eateth your Master with publicans and sinners?" the Pharisees asked Christ's disciples. And the Saviour responded: "I am not come to call the righteous, but sinners to repentance." Matthew 9:11, 13. This is the work He has given us. And never was there greater need of it than at the present time.

God has not given His ministers the work of setting the churches right. No sooner is this work done, apparently, than it has to be done over again. Church members that are thus looked after and labored for become religious weaklings. If nine tenths of the effort that has been put forth for those who know the truth had been put forth for those who have never heard the truth, how much greater would have been the advancement made! God has withheld His blessings because His people have not worked in harmony with His directions.

It weakens those who know the truth for our ministers to expend on them the time and talent that should be given to the unconverted. In many of our churches in the cities the minister preaches Sabbath after Sabbath, and Sabbath after Sabbath the church members come to the house of God with no words to tell of blessings received because of blessings imparted. They have not worked during the week to carry out the instruction given them on the Sabbath. So long as church members make no effort to give to others the help given them, great spiritual feebleness must result.

The greatest help that can be given our people is to teach them to work for God, and to depend on Him, not on the ministers. Let them learn to work as Christ worked. Let them join His army of workers and do faithful service for Him.

There are times when it is fitting for our ministers to give on the Sabbath, in our churches, short discourses, full of the life and love of Christ. But the church members are not to expect a sermon every Sabbath.

Let us remember that we are pilgrims and strangers on this earth, seeking a better country, even a heavenly. Let us work with such earnestness, such devotion, that sinners will be drawn to Christ. Those who have united with the Lord in the covenant of service are under bonds to unite with Him in the great, grand work of soul saving. Let church members, during the week, act their part faithfully, and on the Sabbath relate their experience. The meeting will then be as meat in due season, bringing to all present new life and fresh vigor. When God's people see the great need of working as Christ worked for the conversion of sinners, the testimonies borne by them in the Sabbath service will be filled with power. With joy they will tell of the precious experience they have gained in working for others.

Our ministers are not to spend their time laboring for those who have already accepted the truth. With Christ's love burning in their hearts, they are to go forth to win sinners to the Saviour. Beside all waters they are to sow the seeds of truth. Place after place is to be visited; church after church is to be raised up. Those who take their stand for the truth are to be organized into churches, and then the minister is to pass on to other equally important fields.

Just as soon as a church is organized, let the minister set the members at work. They will need to be taught how to labor successfully. Let the minister

Section 1: Acceptable Service

devote more of his time to educating than to preaching. Let him teach the people how to give to others the knowledge they have received. While the new converts should be taught to ask counsel from those more experienced in the work, they should also be taught not to put the minister in the place of God. Ministers are but human beings, men compassed with infirmities. Christ is the One to whom we are to look for guidance. "The Word was made flesh, and dwelt among us, ... full of grace and truth." "And of His fullness have all we received, and grace for grace." John 1:14,16.

The power of the gospel is to come upon the companies raised up, fitting them for service. Some of the new converts will be so filled with the power of God that they will at once enter the work. They will labor so diligently that they will have neither time nor disposition to weaken the hands of their brethren by unkind criticism. Their one desire will be to carry the truth to the regions beyond.

The Lord has presented before me the work that must be done in our cities. The believers in these cities can work for God in the neighborhood of their homes. They are to labor quietly and in humility, carrying with them wherever they go the atmosphere of heaven. If they keep self out of sight, pointing always to Christ, the power of their influence will be felt.

As a worker gives himself unreservedly to the service of the Lord, he gains an experience that enables him to labor more and more successfully for the Master. The influence that drew him to Christ helps him to draw others to Christ. The work of a public speaker may never be laid upon him, but he is nonetheless a minister for God, and his work testifies that he is born of God.

It is not the Lord's purpose that ministers should be left to do the greatest part of the work of sowing the seeds of truth. Men who are not called to the ministry are to be encouraged to labor for the Master according to their several ability. Hundreds of men and women now idle could do acceptable service. By carrying the truth into the homes of their friends and neighbors, they could do a great work for the Master. God is no respecter of persons. He will use humble, devoted Christians, even if they have not received so thorough an education as some others. Let such ones engage in service for Him by doing house-to-house work. Sitting by the fireside, they can— if humble, discreet, and godly—do more to meet the real needs of families than could an ordained minister.

Why do not believers feel a deeper, more earnest concern for those who are out of Christ? Why do not two or three meet together and plead with God for the salvation of some special one, and then for still another? In our churches let companies be formed for service. Let different ones unite in labor as fishers of men. Let them seek to gather souls from the corruption of the world into the saving purity of Christ's love.

The formation of small companies as a basis of Christian effort has been presented to me by One who cannot err. If there is a large number in the church, let the members be formed into small companies, to work not only for the church members, but for unbelievers. If in one place there are only two or three who know the truth, let them form themselves into a band of workers. Let them keep their bond of union unbroken, pressing together in love and unity, encouraging one another to advance, each gaining courage and strength from the assistance of the others.

Let them reveal Christlike forbearance and patience, speaking no hasty words, using the talent of speech to build one another up in the most holy faith. Let them labor in Christlike love for those outside the fold, forgetting self in their endeavor to help others. As they work and pray in Christ's name, their numbers will increase; for the Saviour says: "If two of you shall agree on earth as touching anything that they shall ask, it shall be done for them of My Father which is in heaven." Matthew 18:19.

• The Waste Places of the Earth

In humble dependence upon God, families are to settle in the waste places of His vineyard. Consecrated men and women are needed to stand as fruit-bearing trees of righteousness in the desert places of the earth. As the reward of their self-sacrificing efforts to sow the seeds of truth, they will reap a rich harvest. As they visit family after family, opening the Scriptures to those in spiritual darkness, many hearts will be touched.

In fields where the conditions are so objectionable and disheartening that many workers refuse to go to them, most remarkable changes for the better may be brought about by the efforts of self-sacrificing lay members. These humble workers will accomplish much because they put forth patient, persevering effort, not relying upon human power, but upon God, who gives them His favor. The amount of good that these workers accomplish will never be known in this world.

• Self-Supporting Missionaries

Self-supporting missionaries are often very successful. Beginning in a small, humble way, their work enlarges as they move forward under the guidance of the Spirit of God. Let two or more start out together in evangelistic work. They may not receive any particular encouragement from those at the head of the work that they will be given financial support; nevertheless let them go forward, praying, singing, teaching, living the truth. They may take up the work of canvassing, and in this way introduce the truth into many families.

As they move forward in their work they gain a blessed experience. They are humbled by a sense of their helplessness, but the Lord goes before them, and among the wealthy and the poor they find favor and help. Even the poverty of these devoted missionaries is a means of finding access to the people. As they pass on their way they are helped in many ways by those to whom they bring spiritual food. They bear the message God gives them, and their efforts are crowned with success. Many will be brought to a knowledge of the truth who, but for these humble teachers, would never have been won to Christ.

God calls for workers to enter the whitening harvest field. Shall we wait because the treasury is exhausted, because there is scarcely sufficient to sustain the workers now in the field? Go forth in faith, and God will be with you. The promise is: "He that goeth forth and weepeth, bearing precious seed, shall doubtless come again with rejoicing, bringing his sheaves with him." Psalm 126:6.

Nothing is so successful as success. Let this be secured by persevering effort, and the work will move forward. New fields will be opened. Many souls will be brought to a knowledge of the truth. What is needed is increased faith in God.

Our people have received great light, yet much of the ministerial force has been spent on the churches, teaching those who should be teachers; enlightening those who should be "the light of the world;" watering those from whom should flow rivers of living water; enriching those who might be mines of precious truth; repeating the gospel invitation to those who, scattered to the uttermost parts of the earth, should be giving the message of heaven to those who have not heard; feeding those who should be in the highways and byways giving the call: "Come; for all things are now ready."

Those for whom the fetters of sin have been broken, who have sought the Lord with brokenness of heart and have obtained answer to their yearning request for righteousness, are never cold and spiritless. Their hearts are filled with unselfish love for sinners. They put away from them all worldly ambition, all self-seeking. Contact with the deep things of God makes them more and more like their Saviour. They exult in His triumphs; they are filled with His joy. Day by day they are growing unto the full stature of men and women in Christ.

4. Workers from the Ranks

With intense interest God is looking on this world. He has noted the capacity of human beings for service. Looking down the ages, He has counted His workers, both men and women, and has prepared the way before them, saying: "I will send My messengers to them, and they shall see great light shining amid the darkness. Won to the service of Christ, they will use their talents to the glory of My name. They will go forth to work for Me with zeal and devotion. Through their efforts the truth will appeal to thousands in a most forcible manner, and men spiritually blind will receive sight and will see of My salvation. Truth will be made so prominent that he who runs may read. Ways will be devised to reach hearts. Some of the methods used in this work will be different from the methods used in the past, but let no one, because of this, block the way by criticism."

Section 1: Acceptable Service

Those whom God chooses as workers are not always talented, in the estimation of the world. Sometimes He selects unlearned men. To these He gives a special work. They reach a class to whom others could not obtain access. Opening the heart to the truth, they are made wise in and through Christ. Their lives inhale and exhale the fragrance of godliness. Their words are thoughtfully considered before they are spoken. They strive to promote the well-being of their fellow men. They take relief and happiness to the needy and distressed. They realize the necessity of ever remaining under Christ's training, that they may work in harmony with God's will. They study how best to follow the Saviour's example of cross bearing and self-denial. They are God's witnesses, revealing His compassion and love, and ascribing all the glory to Him whom they love and serve.

Constantly they are learning of the Great Teacher, and constantly they reach higher degrees of excellence, yet all the time feeling a sense of their weakness and inefficiency. They are drawn upward by their strong, loving admiration for Christ. They practice His virtues; for their life is assimilated to His. Ever they move onward and upward, a blessing to the world and an honor to their Redeemer. Of them Christ says: "Blessed are the meek: for they shall inherit the earth." Matthew 5:5.

Such workers are to be encouraged. Their work is done, not to be seen of men, but to glorify God. And it will bear His inspection. The Lord brings these workers into connection with those of more marked ability, to fill the gaps they leave. He is well pleased when they are appreciated, for they are links in His chain of service.

Men who are self-important, who are filled with the thought of their own superior abilities, overlook these humble, contrite workers; but not for one moment does God lose sight of them. He marks all that they do to help those in need of help. In the heavenly courts, when the redeemed are gathered home, they will stand nearest the Son of God. They will shine brightly in the courts of the Lord, honored by Him because they have felt it an honor to minister to those for whom He gave His life.

God will move upon men in humble positions to declare the message of present truth. Many such will be seen hastening hither and thither, constrained by the Spirit of God to give the light to those in darkness. The truth is as a fire in their bones, filling them with a burning desire to enlighten those who sit in darkness. Many, even among the uneducated, will proclaim the word of the Lord. Children will be impelled by the Holy Spirit to go forth to declare the message of heaven. The Spirit will be poured out upon those who yield to His promptings. Casting off man's binding rules and cautious movements, they will join the army of the Lord.

In the future, men in the common walks of life will be impressed by the Spirit of the Lord to leave their ordinary employment and go forth to proclaim the last message of mercy. As rapidly as possible they are to be prepared for labor, that success may crown their efforts. They co-operate with heavenly agencies, for they are willing to spend and be spent in the service of the Master. No one is authorized to hinder these workers. They are to be bidden Godspeed as they go forth to fulfill the great commission. No taunting word is to be spoken of them as in the rough places of the earth they sow the gospel seed.

Life's best things—simplicity, honesty, truthfulness, purity, unsullied integrity—cannot be bought or sold; they are as free to the ignorant as to the educated, to the black man as to the white man, to the humble peasant as to the king upon his throne. Humble workers, who do not trust in their own strength, but who labor in simplicity, trusting always in God, will share in the joy of the Saviour. Their persevering prayers will bring souls to the cross. In co-operation with their self-sacrificing efforts Jesus will move upon hearts, working miracles in the conversion of souls. Men and women will be gathered into church fellowship. Meetinghouses will be built and schools established. The hearts of the workers will be filled with joy as they see the salvation of God.

When the redeemed stand in the presence of God, they will see how shortsighted were their conclusions as to what heaven records as success. As they review their efforts to achieve success they will see how foolish were their plans, how petty their supposed trials, how unreasonable their doubts. They will see how often they brought failure to their work by not taking God at His word. And one truth will stand out in clear lines: that position does not prepare a man for entrance into the heavenly courts. They will see, too, that the honor given to man is due to God alone, that to Him belongs all the glory. From the lips of the angelic choir and the redeemed host will peal forth the chorus: "Great and marvelous are Thy works, Lord God Almighty; just and true are Thy ways, Thou King of saints. Who shall not fear Thee, O Lord, and glorify Thy name? for Thou only art holy." Revelation 15:3, 4.

5. Extending the Triumphs of the Cross

"He that spared not His own Son, but delivered Him up for us all, how shall He not with Him also freely give us all things?" Romans 8:32.

As this wonderful, priceless Gift was bestowed, the whole heavenly universe was mightily stirred in an effort to understand God's unfathomable love, stirred to awaken in human hearts a gratitude proportionate to the value of the Gift. Shall we, for whom Christ has given His life, halt between two opinions? Shall we return to God only a mite of the capabilities and powers lent us by Him? How can we do this while we know that He who was Commander of all heaven laid aside His royal robe and kingly crown, and, realizing the helplessness of the fallen race, came to this earth in human nature to make it possible for us to unite our humanity to His divinity? He became poor that we might come into possession of the heavenly treasure, "a far more exceeding and eternal weight of glory." 2 Corinthians 4:17.

To rescue us He descended from one humiliation to another until He, the divine-human, suffering Christ, was uplifted on the cross to draw all men to Himself. The Son of God could not have shown greater condescension than He did; He could not have stooped lower.

This is the mystery of godliness, the mystery that has inspired heavenly agencies so to minister through fallen humanity that in the world an intense interest will be aroused in the plan of salvation. This is the mystery that has stirred all heaven to unite with man in carrying out God's great plan for the salvation of a ruined world.

- **The Work of the Church**

To human agencies is committed the work of extending the triumphs of the cross from point to point. As the Head of the church, Christ is authoritatively calling upon everyone who claims to believe on Him to follow His example of self-denial and self-sacrifice in working for the conversion of those whom Satan and his vast army are exerting every power to destroy. God's people are called upon to rally without delay under the bloodstained banner of Christ Jesus. Unceasingly they are to continue their warfare against the enemy, pressing the battle even to the gates. And everyone who is added to the ranks by conversion is to be assigned his post of duty. Everyone should be willing to be or to do anything in this warfare. When church members put forth earnest efforts to advance the message, they will live in the joy of the Lord and will meet with success. Triumph always follows decided effort.

- **The Holy Spirit our Efficiency**

Christ, in His mediatorial capacity, gives to His servants the presence of the Holy Spirit. It is the efficiency of the Spirit that enables human agencies to be representatives of the Redeemer in the work of soul saving. That we may unite with Christ in this work we should place ourselves under the molding influence of His Spirit. Through the power thus imparted we may co-operate with the Lord in the bonds of unity as laborers together with Him in the salvation of souls. To everyone who offers himself to the Lord for service, withholding nothing, is given power for the attainment of measureless results.

The Lord God is bound by an eternal pledge to supply power and grace to everyone who is sanctified through obedience to the truth. Christ, to whom is given all power in heaven and on earth, co-operates in sympathy with His instrumentalities—the earnest souls who day by day partake of the living bread, "which cometh down from heaven." John 6:50. The church on earth, united with the church in heaven, can accomplish all things.

Section 1: Acceptable Service

- **Power Given the Apostles**

On the Day of Pentecost the Infinite One revealed Himself in power to the church. By His Holy Spirit He descended from the heights of heaven as a rushing, mighty wind, to the room in which the disciples were assembled. It was as if for ages this influence had been held in restraint, and now heaven rejoiced in being able to pour upon the church the riches of the Spirit's power.

And, under the influence of the Spirit, words of penitence and confession were mingled with songs of praise for sins forgiven. Words of thanksgiving and of prophecy were heard. All heaven bent low to behold and to adore the wisdom of matchless, incomprehensible Love. Lost in wonder, the apostles and disciples exclaimed: "Herein is love." 1 John 4:10. They grasped the imparted gift. And what followed? Thousands were converted in a day. The sword of the Spirit, newly edged with power and bathed in the lightnings of heaven, cut its way through unbelief.

The hearts of the disciples were surcharged with a benevolence so full, so deep, so far-reaching, that it impelled them to go to the ends of the earth testifying: God forbid that we should glory, save in the cross of our Lord Jesus Christ. They were filled with an intense longing to add to the church of such as should be saved. They called on the believers to arouse and do their part, that all nations might hear the truth and the earth be filled with the glory of the Lord.

- **The Same Power to be Revealed Today**

By the grace of Christ the apostles were made what they were. It was sincere devotion and humble, earnest prayer that brought them into close communion with Him. They sat together with Him in heavenly places. They realized the greatness of their debt to Him. By earnest, persevering prayer they obtained the endowment of the Holy Spirit, and then they went forth, weighted with the burden of saving souls, filled with zeal to extend the triumphs of the cross. And under their labors many souls were brought from darkness to light, and many churches were raised up.

Shall we be less earnest than were the apostles? Shall we not by living faith claim the promises that moved them to the depths of their being to call upon the Lord Jesus for the fulfillment of His word: "Ask, and ye shall receive"? John 16:24. Is not the Spirit of God to come today in answer to earnest, persevering prayer, and fill men with power? Is not God saying today to His praying, trusting, believing workers, who are opening the Scriptures to those ignorant of the precious truth they contain: "Lo, I am with you alway, even unto the end of the world"? Matthew 28:20. Why, then, is the church so weak and spiritless?

As the disciples, filled with the power of the Spirit, went forth to proclaim the gospel, so God's servants are to go forth today. Filled with an unselfish desire to give the message of mercy to those who are in the darkness of error and unbelief, we are to take up the Lord's work.

He gives us our part to do in co-operation with Him, and He will also move on the hearts of unbelievers to carry forward His work in the regions beyond. Already many are receiving the Holy Spirit, and no longer will the way be blocked by listless indifference.

Why has the history of the work of the disciples, as they labored with holy zeal, animated and vitalized by the Holy Spirit, been recorded, if it is not that from this record the Lord's people today are to gain an inspiration to work earnestly for Him? What the Lord did for His people in that time, it is just as essential, and more so, that He do for His people today. All that the apostles did, every church member today is to do. And we are to work with as much more fervor, to be accompanied by the Holy Spirit in as much greater measure, as the increase of wickedness demands a more decided call to repentance.

Everyone on whom is shining the light of present truth is to be stirred with compassion for those who are in darkness. From all believers, light is to be reflected in clear, distinct rays. A work similar to that which the Lord did through His delegated messengers after the Day of Pentecost He is waiting to do today. At this time, when the end of all things is at hand, should not the zeal of the church exceed even that of the early church? Zeal for the glory of God moved the disciples to bear witness to the truth with mighty power. Should not this zeal fire our hearts with a longing to tell the story of redeeming love, of Christ and Him crucified? Should not the power of God be even more mightily revealed today than in the time of the apostles?

6. The Work in the Cities

Oakland, California, April 1, 1874.

I dreamed that several of our brethren were in counsel considering plans of labor for this season. They thought it best not to enter the large cities, but to begin work in small places, remote from the cities; here they would meet less opposition from the clergy and would avoid great expense. They reasoned that our ministers, being few in number, could not be spared to instruct and care for those who might accept the truth in the cities, and who, because of the greater opposition they would there meet, would need more help than would the churches in small country places. Thus the fruit of giving a course of lectures in the city would, in a great measure, be lost.

Again, it was urged that, because of our limited means, and because of the many changes from moving that might be expected from a church in a large city, it would be difficult to build up a church that would be a strength to the cause. My husband was urging the brethren to make broader plans without delay and put forth, in our large cities, extended and thorough effort that would better correspond to the character of our message. One worker related incidents of his experience in the cities, showing that the work was nearly a failure, but he testified to better success in the small places.

One of dignity and authority—One who is present in all our council meetings—was listening with deepest interest to every word. He spoke with deliberation and perfect assurance. "The whole world," He said, "is God's great vineyard. The cities and villages constitute a part of that vineyard. These must be worked. Satan will try to interpose himself and discourage the workers, so as to prevent them from giving the message of light and warning in the more prominent as well as in the more secluded places. Desperate efforts will be made to turn the people from truth to falsehood. Angels of heaven are commissioned to co-operate with the efforts of God's appointed messengers on earth. Ministers must encourage and maintain an unwavering faith and hope, as did Christ, their living Head. They must keep humble and contrite in heart before God."

God designs that His precious word, with its messages of warning and encouragement, shall come to those who are in darkness and are ignorant of our faith. It is to be given to all, and will be to them a witness, whether they will hear, or whether they will forbear. Do not feel that the responsibility rests upon you to convict and convert the hearers. The power of God alone can soften the hearts of the people. You are to hold forth the word of life, that all may have an opportunity of receiving the truth if they will. If they turn from the truth of heavenly origin, it will be their condemnation.

We must not hide the truth in the corners of the earth. It must be made known; it must shine in our large cities. Christ in His labors took His position by the lakeside and in the great thoroughfares of travel where He could meet people from all parts of the world. He was giving the true light; He was sowing the gospel seed; He was rescuing truth from its companionship with error, and presenting it in its original simplicity and clearness, so that men could comprehend it.

The heavenly Messenger who was with us said: "Never lose sight of the fact that the message you are bearing is a world-wide message. It is to be given to all cities, to all villages; it is to be proclaimed in the highways and the byways. You are not to localize the proclamation of the message." In the parable of the sower, Christ gave an illustration of His own work and that of His servants. The seed fell upon all kinds of soil. Some seed fell upon poor soil, yet the sower did not therefore cease his work. You are to sow the seeds of truth in every place. Wherever you can gain access, hold forth the word of God. Sow beside all waters. You may not at once see the result of your labors, but be not discouraged. Speak the words that Christ gives you. Work in His lines. Go forth everywhere as He did during His ministry on the earth.

The world's Redeemer had many hearers, but few followers. Noah preached one hundred and twenty years to the people before the Flood, and yet there were few who appreciated this precious, probationary time. Save Noah and his family, not one was numbered with the believers and entered into the ark. Of all the inhabitants of the earth, only eight souls received the message; but that message condemned the world. The light was given in order that they might believe; their rejection of the light proved their ruin. Our message to the world will be a savor of life unto life to all who accept it, and of condemnation to all who reject it.

The Messenger turned to one present and said: "Your ideas of the work for this time are altogether too limited. Your light must not be confined to a small compass, put under a bushel, or under a bed; it must be placed on a candlestick, that it may give light to all that are in God's house—the world. You must take broader views of the work than you have taken."

7. The Work in Greater New York

St. Helena, California, September 1, 1902.

The time has come to make decided efforts to proclaim the truth in our large cities. The message is to be given with such power that the hearers shall be convinced. God will raise up laborers to do this work. Let no one hinder these men of God's appointment. Forbid them not. God has given them their work. They will occupy peculiar spheres of influence and will carry the truth to the most unpromising places. Some who were once enemies will become valuable helpers, advancing the work with their means and their influence.

In these large cities missions should be established where workers can be trained to present to the people the special message for this time. There is need of all the instruction that these missions can give.

Under the direction of God the mission in New York City has been started. This work should be continued in the power of the same Spirit that led to its establishment. Those who bear the burden of the work in Greater New York should have the help of the best workers that can be secured. Here let a center for God's work be made, and let all that is done be a symbol of the work the Lord desires to see done in the world.

If in this great center medical missionary work could be established by men and women of experience, those who would give a correct representation of true medical missionary principles, it would have great power in making a right impression on the people.

In every city that is entered a solid foundation is to be laid for permanent work. The Lord's methods are to be followed. By doing house-to-house work, by giving Bible readings in families, the worker may gain access to many who are seeking for truth. By opening the Scriptures, by prayer, by exercising faith, he is to teach the people the way of the Lord.

In Greater New York the Lord has many precious souls who have not bowed the knee to Baal, and there are those who through ignorance have walked in the ways of error. On these the light of truth is to shine, that they may see Christ as the Way, the Truth, and the Life.

We are to present the truth in the love of Christ. No extravagance or display should attend the work. It is to be done after Christ's order. It is to be carried forward in humility, in the simplicity of the gospel. Let not the workers be intimidated by outward appearances, how ever forbidding. Teach the word, and the Lord by His Holy Spirit will send conviction to the hearers.

After the truth has made an impression on hearts, and men and women have accepted it, they are to be treated as the property of Christ, not as the property of man. No human being should seek to bind others to himself as if he were to control them, telling them to do this and forbidding them to do that, commanding, dictating, acting like an officer over a company of soldiers. This is the way that the priests and rulers did in Christ's day, but it is not the right way. The workers are to press together in Christian unity, but no unwise authority is to be exercised over those who accept the truth. The meekness of Christ should appear in all that is said and done.

Let the worker show his growth in grace by submission to the will of God. Thus he will gain a rich experience. As in faith he receives, believes, and obeys Christ's words, there will be an intensity of effort; there will be cherished a faith that works by love and purifies the soul. The fruit of the Spirit will be seen in the life, and the efficiency of the Spirit will be seen in the work.

Christ is our example, our inspiration, our exceeding great reward. "Ye are God's husbandry, ye are God's building." 1 Corinthians 3:9. God is the Master Builder, but man has a part to act. He is to co-operate with God. "We are laborers together with God." Verse 9. Never forget the words, "together with God."

Remember that working with Christ as your personal Saviour is your strength and your victory. This is the part that all are to act. To those who do this comes the assurance: "As many as received Him, to them gave He power to become the sons of God." John 1:12. Christ declares: "Without Me ye can do nothing." John 15:5. And the humble, believing soul responds: "I can do all things through Christ which strengtheneth me." Philippians 4:13.

Christ is the sympathetic, compassionate Redeemer. He has given His commission: "Go ye into all the world." Mark 1:15. All must hear the message of warning. A prize of richest value is held up before those who are running the Christian race. Those who run with patience will receive a crown of life that fadeth not away.

8. Delay No Longer

Our workers are not reaching out as they should. Our leading men are not awake to the work that must be accomplished. When I think of the cities in which so little has been done, in which there are so many thousands to be warned of the soon coming of the Saviour, I feel an intensity of desire to see men and women going forth to the work in the power of the Spirit, filled with Christ's love for perishing souls.

Those in our cities—living within the shadow of our doors—have been strangely neglected. Organized effort should now be put forth to give them the message of present truth. A new song is to be put into their mouths. They are to go forth to impart to others now in darkness the light of the third angel's message.

We all need to be wide awake, that, as the way opens, we may advance the work in the large cities. We are far behind in following the light given to enter these cities and erect memorials for God. Step by step we are to lead souls into the full light of truth. And we are to continue the work until a church is organized and a humble house of worship built. I am greatly encouraged to believe that many not of our faith will help considerably by their means. The light given me is that in many places, especially in the great cities of America, help will be given by such persons.

Workers in cities should read carefully the tenth and eleventh chapters of Hebrews and appropriate to themselves the instruction that this scripture contains. The eleventh chapter is a record of the experiences of the faithful. Those who work for God in the cities must go forward in faith, doing their very best. As they watch and work and pray, God will hear and answer their petitions. They will obtain an experience that will be invaluable to them in their after work. "Faith is the substance of things hoped for, the evidence of things not seen." Hebrews 11:1.

My mind is deeply stirred. In every city there is work to be done. Laborers are to go into our large cities and hold camp meetings. In these meetings the very best talent is to be employed, that the truth may be proclaimed with power. Men of varied gifts are to take part. One man has not all the gifts required for the work. To make a camp meeting successful, several workers are needed. No one man should feel it his prerogative to do all the important work.

As in these meetings the speakers proclaim the truth in the power of the Spirit, hearts will be reached. The love of Christ, received into the heart, will banish the love of error.

There is need of camp meetings like those held in the early stages of the work, camp meetings separate from the business work of the conference. At a camp meeting the workers should be free to give the knowledge of the truth to those who attend from outside.

At our camp meetings arrangements should be made so that the poor can obtain wholesome, well-prepared food as cheaply as possible. There should also be a restaurant in which healthful dishes are prepared and served in an inviting manner. This will prove an education to many not of our faith. Let not this line of work be looked upon as separate from other lines of camp meeting work. Each line of God's work is closely united with every other line, and all are to advance in perfect harmony.

9. Family Worship

If ever there was a time when every house should be a house of prayer, it is now. Infidelity and skepticism prevail. Iniquity abounds. Corruption flows in the vital currents of the soul, and rebellion against God breaks out in the life. Enslaved by sin, the moral powers are under the tyranny of Satan. The soul is made the sport of his temptations; and unless some mighty arm is stretched out to rescue him, man goes where the arch-rebel leads the way.

And yet, in this time of fearful peril, some who profess to be Christians have no family worship. They do not honor God in the home; they do not teach their children to love and fear Him. Many have separated themselves so far from Him that they feel under condemnation in approaching Him. They cannot "come boldly unto the throne of grace," "lifting up holy hands, without wrath and doubting." Hebrews 4:16; 1 Timothy 2:8. They have not a living connection with God. Theirs is a form of godliness without the power.

The idea that prayer is not essential is one of Satan's most successful devices to ruin souls. Prayer is communion with God, the Fountain of wisdom, the Source of strength, and peace, and happiness. Jesus prayed to the Father "with strong crying and tears." Paul exhorts believers to "pray without ceasing," in everything, by prayer and supplication, with thanksgiving, making known their requests to God. "Pray one for another," James says. "The effectual fervent prayer of a righteous man availeth much." Hebrews 5:7; 1 Thessalonians 5:17; James 5:16.

By sincere, earnest prayer parents should make a hedge about their children. They should pray with full faith that God will abide with them and that holy angels will guard them and their children from Satan's cruel power.

In every family there should be a fixed time for morning and evening worship. How appropriate it is for parents to gather their children about them before the fast is broken, to thank the heavenly Father for His protection during the night, and to ask Him for His help and guidance and watchcare during the day! How fitting, also, when evening comes, for parents and children to gather once more before Him and thank Him for the blessings of the day that is past!

The father, or, in his absence, the mother, should conduct the worship, selecting a portion of Scripture that is interesting and easily understood. The service should be short. When a long chapter is read and a long prayer offered, the service is made wearisome, and at its close a sense of relief is felt. God is dishonored when the hour of worship is made dry and irksome, when it is so tedious, so lacking in interest, that the children dread it.

Fathers and mothers, make the hour of worship intensely interesting. There is no reason why this hour should not be the most pleasant and enjoyable of the day. A little thought given to preparation for it will enable you to make it full of interest and profit. From time to time let the service be varied. Questions may be asked on the portion of Scripture read, and a few earnest, timely remarks may be made. A song of praise may be sung. The prayer offered should be short and pointed. In simple, earnest words let the one who leads in prayer praise God for His goodness and ask Him for help. As circumstances permit, let the children join in the reading and the prayer.

Eternity alone will reveal the good with which such seasons of worship are fraught.

The life of Abraham, the friend of God, was a life of prayer. Wherever he pitched his tent, close beside it was built an altar, upon which were offered the morning and the evening sacrifice. When his tent was removed, the altar remained. And the roving Canaanite, as he came to that altar, knew who had been there. When he had pitched his tent he repaired the altar and worshiped the living God.

So the homes of Christians should be lights in the world. From them, morning and evening, prayer should ascend to God as sweet incense. And as the morning dew, His mercies and blessings will descend upon the suppliants.

Fathers and mothers, each morning and evening gather your children around you, and in humble supplication lift the heart to God for help. Your dear ones are exposed to temptation. Daily annoyances beset the path of young and old. Those who would live patient, loving, cheerful lives must pray. Only by receiving constant help from God can we gain the victory over self.

Each morning consecrate yourselves and your children to God for that day. Make no calculation for months or years; these are not yours. One brief day is given you. As if it were your last on earth, work during its hours for the Master. Lay all your plans before God, to be carried out or given up, as His providence shall indicate. Accept His plans instead of your own, even though their acceptance requires the abandonment of cherished projects. "Thus the life will be molded more and more after the divine example; and the peace of God, which passeth all understanding, shall keep your hearts and minds through Christ Jesus." Philippians 4:7.

10. Responsibilities of Married Life

My Dear Brother and Sister: You have united in a lifelong covenant. Your education in married life has begun. The first year of married life is a year of experience, a year in which husband and wife learn each other's different traits of character, as a child learns lessons in school. In this, the first year of your married life, let there be no chapters that will mar your future happiness.

To gain a proper understanding of the marriage relation is the work of a lifetime. Those who marry enter a school from which they are never in this life to be graduated.

My brother, your wife's time and strength and happiness are now bound up with yours. Your influence over her may be a savor of life unto life or of death unto death. Be very careful not to spoil her life.

My sister, you are now to learn your first practical lessons in regard to the responsibilities of married life. Be sure to learn these lessons faithfully day by day. Do not give way to discontent or moodiness. Do not long for a life of ease and inactivity. Guard constantly against giving way to selfishness.

In your life union your affections are to be tributary to each other's happiness. Each is to minister to the happiness of the other. This is the will of God concerning you. But while you are to blend as one, neither of you is to lose his or her individuality in the other. God is the owner of your individuality. Of Him you are to ask: What is right? What is wrong? How may I best fulfill the purpose of my creation? "Ye are not your own; for ye are bought with a price: therefore glorify God in your body, and in your spirit, which are God's." 1 Corinthians 6:19, 20. Your love for that which is human is to be secondary to your love for God. The wealth of your affection is to flow forth to Him who gave His life for you. Living for God, the soul sends forth to Him its best and highest affections. Is the greatest outflow of your love toward Him who died for you? If it is, your love for each other will be after heaven's order.

Affection may be as clear as crystal and beauteous in its purity, yet it may be shallow because it has not been tested and tried. Make Christ first and last and best in everything. Constantly behold Him, and your love for Him will daily become deeper and stronger as it is submitted to the test of trial. And as your love for Him increases, your love for each other will grow deeper and stronger. "We all, with open face beholding as in a glass the glory of the Lord, are changed into the same image from glory to glory." 2 Corinthians 3:18.

You now have duties to perform that before your marriage you did not have. "Put on therefore, ... kindness, humbleness of mind, meekness, longsuffering." "Walk in love, as Christ also hath loved us." Give careful study to the following instruction: "Wives, submit yourselves unto your own husbands, as unto the Lord. For the husband is the head of the wife, even as Christ is the head of the church...Therefore as the church is subject unto Christ, so let the wives be to their own husbands in everything. Husbands, love your wives, even as Christ also loved the church, and gave Himself for it." Colossians 3:12; Ephesians 5:2, 22-25.

Marriage, a union for life, is a symbol of the union between Christ and His church. The spirit that Christ manifests toward the church is the spirit that husband and wife are to manifest toward each other.

Neither husband nor wife is to make a plea for rulership. The Lord has laid down the principle that is to guide in this matter. The husband is to cherish his wife as Christ cherishes the church. And the wife is to respect and love her husband. Both are to cultivate the spirit of kindness, being determined never to grieve or injure the other.

My brother and sister, both of you have strong will power. You may make this power a great blessing or a great curse to yourselves and to those with whom you come in contact. Do not try to compel each other to do as you wish. You cannot do this and retain each other's love. Manifestations of self-will destroy the peace and happiness of the home. Let not your married life be one of contention. If you do you will both be unhappy. Be kind in speech and gentle in action, giving up your own wishes. Watch well your words, for they have a powerful influence for good or for ill. Allow no sharpness to come into your voices. Bring into your united life the fragrance of Christlikeness.

Before a man enters a union as close as the marriage relation, he should learn how to control himself and how to deal with others.

In the training of a child there are times when the firm, matured will of the mother meets the unreasoning, undisciplined will of the child. At such times there is need of great wisdom on the part of the mother. By unwise management, by stern compulsion, great harm may be done the child.

Whenever possible, this crisis should be avoided; for it means a severe struggle for both mother and child. But once such a crisis is entered into, the child must be led to yield its will to the wiser will of the parent.

The mother should keep herself under perfect control, doing nothing that will arouse in the child a spirit of defiance. She is to give no loud-voiced commands. She will gain much by keeping the voice low and gentle. She is to deal with the child in a way that will draw him to Jesus. She is to realize that God is her Helper; love, her power. If she is a wise Christian she does not attempt to force the child to submit.

She prays earnestly that the enemy shall not obtain the victory, and, as she prays, she is conscious of a renewal of spiritual life. She sees that the same power that is working in her is working also in the child. He becomes more gentle, more submissive. The battle is won. Her patience, her kindness, her words of wise restraint, have done their work. There is peace after the storm, like the shining of the sun after rain. And the angels, who have been watching the scene, break forth into songs of joy.

These crises come also in the life of husband and wife, who, unless controlled by the Spirit of God, will at such times manifest the impulsive, unreasoning spirit so often manifested by children. As flint striking flint will be the conflict of will with will.

My brother, be kind, patient, forbearing. Remember that your wife accepted you as her husband, not that you might rule over her, but that you might be her helper. Never be overbearing and dictatorial. Do not exert your strong will power to compel your wife to do as you wish. Remember that she has a will and that she may wish to have her way as much as you wish to have yours. Remember, too, that you have the advantage of your wider experience. Be considerate and courteous. "The wisdom that is from above is first pure, then peaceable, gentle, and easy to be entreated, full of mercy and good fruits." James 3:17.

One victory it is positively essential for you both to gain, the victory over the stubborn will. In this struggle you can conquer only by the aid of Christ. You may struggle hard and long to subdue self, but you will fail unless you receive strength from on high. By the grace of Christ you can gain the victory over self and selfishness. As you live His life, showing self-sacrifice at every step, constantly revealing a stronger sympathy for those in need of help, you will gain victory after victory. Day by day you will learn better how to conquer self and how to strengthen your weak points of character. The Lord Jesus will be your light, your strength, your crown of rejoicing, because you yield your will to His will.

Men and women may reach God's ideal for them if they will take Christ as their Helper. Make an unreserved surrender to God. To know that you are striving for eternal life will strengthen and comfort you. Christ can give you power to overcome. By His help you can utterly destroy the root of selfishness.

Christ died that the life of man might be bound up with His life in the union of divinity and humanity. He came to our world and lived a divine-human life, in order that the lives of men and women might be as harmonious as God designs them to be. The Saviour calls upon you to deny self and take up the cross. Then nothing will prevent the development of the whole being. The daily experience will reveal healthy, harmonious action.

Remember, my dear brother and sister, that God is love and that by His grace you can succeed in making each other happy, as in your marriage pledge you promised to do. And in the strength of the Redeemer you can work with wisdom and power to help some crooked life to be straight in God. What is there that Christ cannot do? He is perfect in wisdom, in righteousness, in love. Do not shut yourselves up to yourselves, satisfied to pour out all your affection upon each other. Seize every opportunity to contribute to the happiness of those around you, sharing with them your affection.

Words of kindness, looks of sympathy, expressions of appreciation, would to many a struggling, lonely one be as a cup of cold water to a thirsty soul. A word of cheer, an act of kindness, would go far to lighten the burdens that are resting heavily upon weary shoulders. It is in unselfish ministry that true happiness is found. And every word and deed of such service is recorded in the books of heaven as done for Christ. "Inasmuch as ye have done it unto one of the least of these My brethren," He declares, "ye have done it unto Me." Matthew 25:40.

Live in the sunshine of the Saviour's love. Then your influence will bless the world. Let the Spirit of Christ control you. Let the law of kindness be ever on your lips. Forbearance and unselfishness mark the words and actions of those who are born again, to live the new life in Christ.

"None of us liveth to himself." The character will manifest itself. The looks, the tone of the voice, the actions,—all have their influence in making or marring the happiness of the domestic circle. They are molding the temper and character of the children; they are inspiring or tending to destroy confidence and love. All are made either better or worse, happy or miserable, by these influences. We owe our families the knowledge of the word brought into practical life. All that it is possible for us to be to purify, enlighten, comfort, and encourage those connected with us in family relation should be done.

Section 2

Our Sanitarium Work

"Beloved, I wish above all things that thou mayest prosper and be in health, even as thy soul prospereth." 3 John 2

11. Extent of the Work

God has qualified His people to enlighten the world. He has entrusted them with faculties by which they are to extend His work until it shall encircle the globe. In all parts of the earth they are to establish sanitariums, schools, publishing houses, and kindred facilities for the accomplishment of His work.

The closing message of the gospel is to be carried to "every nation, and kindred, and tongue, and people." Revelation 14:6. In foreign countries many enterprises for the advancement of this message must yet be begun and carried forward. The opening of hygienic restaurants and treatment rooms, and the establishment of sanitariums for the care of the sick and the suffering, is just as necessary in Europe as in America. In many lands medical missions are to be established to act as God's helping hand in ministering to the afflicted.

Christ co-operates with those who engage in medical missionary work. Men and women who unselfishly do what they can to establish sanitariums and treatment rooms in many lands will be richly rewarded. Those who visit these institutions will be benefited physically, mentally, and spiritually—the weary will be refreshed, the sick restored to health, the sin-burdened relieved.

In far-off countries, from those whose hearts are by these agencies turned from the service of sin unto righteousness, will be heard thanksgiving and the voice of melody. By their songs of grateful praise a testimony will be borne that will win others to allegiance to and fellowship with Christ.

The conversion of souls to God is the greatest, the noblest work in which human beings can have a part. In this work are revealed God's power, His holiness, His forbearance, and His unbounded love. Every true conversion glorifies Him and causes the angels to break forth into singing.

We are nearing the end of this earth's history, and the different lines of God's work are to be carried forward with much more self-sacrifice than is at present manifest. The work for these last days is in a special sense a missionary work. The presentation of present truth, from the first letter of its alphabet to the last, means missionary effort. The work to be done calls for sacrifice at every advance step. From this unselfish service the workers will come forth purified and refined as gold tried in the fire.

The sight of souls perishing in sin should arouse us to put forth greater effort to give the light of present truth to those who are in darkness, and especially to those in fields where as yet very little has been done to establish memorials for God. In all parts of the world a work that should have been done long ago is now to be entered upon and carried forward to completion.

Our brethren generally have not taken the interest that they ought in the establishment of sanitariums in the European countries. In the work in these countries, the most perplexing questions will arise because of the circumstances peculiar to the various fields. But from the light given me, institutions will be established which, though at first small, will, by God's blessing, become larger and stronger.

Our institutions for any land are not to be crowded together in one locality. God never designed that the light of truth should be thus restricted. For a time the Jewish nation was required to worship at Jerusalem. But Jesus said to the Samaritan woman: "Believe Me, the hour cometh, when ye shall neither in this mountain, nor yet at Jerusalem, worship the Father." "The hour cometh, and now is, when the true worshipers shall worship the Father in spirit and in truth: for the Father seeketh such to worship Him. God is a Spirit: and they that worship Him must worship Him in spirit and in truth." John 4:21, 23, 24. Truth is to be planted in every place to which we can possibly gain access. It is to be carried to regions that are barren of the knowledge of God. Men will be blessed in receiving the One in whom their hopes of eternal life are centered. The acceptance of the truth as it is in Jesus will fill their hearts with melody to God.

To absorb a large amount of means in a few places is contrary to Christian principles. Every building is to be erected with reference to the need for similar buildings in other places. God calls upon men in positions of trust in His work not to block the way of advance by selfishly using in a few favored places, or in one or two lines of work, all the means that can be secured.

In the early days of the message very many of our people possessed the spirit of self-denial and self-sacrifice. Thus a right beginning was made, and success attended the efforts put forth. But the work has not developed as it should have developed. Too much has been centered in Battle Creek and in Oakland and in a few other places. Our brethren should never have built so largely in any one place as they have in Battle Creek.

The Lord has signified that His work should be carried forward in the same spirit in which it was begun. The world is to be warned. Field after field is to be entered. The command given us is: "Add new territory; add new territory." Shall we not as a people, by our business arrangements, by our attitude toward a world unsaved, bear a testimony even more clear and decisive than that borne by us twenty or thirty years ago?

Upon us has shone great light in regard to the last days of this earth's history. Let not our lack of wisdom and energy give evidence of spiritual blindness. God's messengers must be clothed with power. They must have for the truth an elevating reverence that they do not now possess. The Lord's solemn, sacred message of warning must be proclaimed in the most difficult fields and in the most sinful cities—in every place where the light of the third angel's message has not yet dawned. To everyone is to be given the last call to the marriage supper of the Lamb.

In proclaiming the message, God's servants will be called upon to wrestle with numerous perplexities and to surmount many obstacles. Sometimes the work will go hard, as it did when the pioneers were establishing the institutions in Battle Creek, in Oakland, and in other places. But let all do their best, making the Lord their strength, avoiding all selfishness, and blessing others by their good works.

- **New York City**

While in New York in the winter of 1901, I received light in regard to the work in that great city. Night after night the course that our brethren should pursue passed before me. In Greater New York the message is to go forth as a lamp that burneth. God will raise up laborers for this work, and His angels will go before them. Though our large cities are fast reaching a condition similar to the condition of the world before the Flood, though they are as Sodom for wickedness, yet there are in them many honest souls, who, as they listen to the startling truths of the advent message, will feel the conviction of the Spirit. New York is ready to be worked. In that great city the message of truth will be given with the power of God. The Lord calls for workmen. He calls upon those who have gained an experience in the cause to take up and carry forward in His fear the work to be done in New York and in other large cities of America. He calls also for means to be used in this work.

It was presented to me that we should not rest satisfied because we have a vegetarian restaurant in Brooklyn, but that others should be established in other sections of the city. The people living in one part of Greater New York do not know what is going on in other parts of that great city. Men and women who eat at the restaurants established in different places will become conscious of an improvement in health. Their confidence once gained, they will be more ready to accept God's special message of truth.

Wherever medical missionary work is carried on in our large cities, cooking schools should be held; and wherever a strong educational missionary work is in progress, a hygienic restaurant of some sort should be established, which shall give a practical illustration of the proper selection and the healthful preparation of foods.

When in Los Angeles I was instructed that not only in various sections of that city, but in San Diego and in other tourist resorts of Southern California, health restaurants and treatment rooms should be established.

Our efforts in these lines should include the great seaside resorts. As the voice of John the Baptist was heard in the wilderness, "Prepare ye the way of the Lord," so must the voice of the Lord's messengers be heard in the great tourist and seaside resorts.

- **The Southern States**

I have a message to bear in regard to the Southern field. We have a great work to do in this field. Its condition is a condemnation of our professed Christianity. Look at its destitution of ministers, teachers, and medical missionaries. Consider the ignorance, the poverty, the misery, the distress, of many of the people. And yet this field lies close at our doors. How selfish, how inattentive, we have been to our neighbors! We have heartlessly passed them by, doing little to relieve their sufferings. If the gospel commission had been studied and obeyed by our people, the South would have received its proportionate share of ministry. If those who have received the light had walked in the light, they would have realized that upon them rested the responsibility of cultivating this long-neglected portion of the vineyard.

God is calling upon His people to give Him of the means that He has entrusted to them, in order that institutions may be established in the destitute fields that are ripe for the harvest. He calls upon those who have money in the banks to put it into circulation. By giving of our substance to sustain God's work, we show in a practical manner that we love Him supremely and our neighbor as ourselves.

Let schools and sanitariums now be established in many places in the Southern States. Let centers of influence be made in many of the Southern cities by the opening of food stores and vegetarian restaurants. Let there also be facilities for the manufacture of simple, inexpensive health foods. But let not selfish, worldly policy be brought into the work, for God forbids this. Let unselfish men take hold of this work in the fear of God and with love for their fellow men.

The light given me is that in the Southern field, as elsewhere, the manufacture of health foods should be conducted, not as a speculation for personal gain, but as a business that God has devised whereby a door of hope may be opened for the people. In the South special consideration should be shown to the poor, who have been terribly neglected. Men of ability and economy are to be chosen to take up the food work; for, in order to make it a success, the greatest wisdom and economy must be exercised. God desires His people to do acceptable service in the preparation of healthful food, not only for their own families, which are their first responsibility, but for the help of the poor everywhere. They are to show Christlike liberality, realizing that they are representing God, and that all they have is His endowment.

Brethren, take hold of this work. Give no place to discouragement. Do not criticize those who are trying to do something in right lines, but go to work yourselves.

In connection with the health food business, various industries may be established that will be a help to the cause in the Southern field. All that men as missionaries for God can do for this field should now be done; for if ever a field needed medical missionary work, it is the South. During the time that has passed into eternity, many should have been in the South laboring together with God by doing personal work, and by giving of their means to sustain themselves and other workers in that field.

Small sanitariums should be established in many places. This will open doors for the entrance of Bible truth and will remove much of the prejudice that exists against those who look upon the colored people as having souls to be saved as well as the white people.

Had such lines of work been established for the colored people immediately after the proclamation of freedom, how different would be their condition today!

- ### In All Lands

The Lord is calling upon us to awake to a realization of our responsibilities. God has given to every man his work. Each one may live a life of usefulness. Let us learn all that we can and then be a blessing to others by imparting a knowledge of truth. Let everyone do according to his several ability, willingly helping to bear the burdens.

Everywhere there is a work to be done for all classes of society. We are to come close to the poor and the depraved, those who have fallen through intemperance. And, at the same time, we are not to forget the higher classes—the lawyers, ministers, senators, and judges, many of whom are slaves to intemperate habits. We are to leave no effort untried to show them that their souls are worth saving, that eternal life is worth striving for. To those in high positions we are to present the total abstinence pledge, asking them to give the money they would otherwise spend for the harmful indulgences of liquor and tobacco to the establishment of institutions where children and youth may be prepared to fill positions of usefulness in the world.

Great light has been shining upon us, but how little of this light we reflect to the world! Heavenly angels are waiting for human beings to co-operate with them in the practical carrying out of the principles of truth.

It is through the agency of our sanitariums and kindred enterprises that much of this work is to be done. These institutions are to be God's memorials, where His healing power can reach all classes, high and low, rich and poor. Every dollar invested in them for Christ's sake will bring blessings both to the giver and to suffering humanity.

Medical missionary work is the right hand of the gospel. It is necessary to the advancement of the cause of God. As through it men and women are led to see the importance of right habits of living, the saving power of the truth will be made known. Every city is to be entered by workers trained to do medical missionary work. As the right hand of the third angel's message, God's methods of treating disease will open doors for the entrance of present truth. Health literature must be circulated in many lands. Our physicians in Europe and other countries should awake to the necessity of having health works prepared by men who are on the ground and who can meet the people where they are with the most essential instruction.

The Lord will give to our sanitariums whose work is already established an opportunity to co-operate with Him in assisting newly established plants. Every new institution is to be regarded as a sister helper in the great work of proclaiming the third angel's message. God has given our sanitariums an opportunity to set in operation a work that will be as a stone instinct with life, growing as it is rolled by an invisible hand. Let this mystic stone be set in motion.

The Lord has instructed me to warn those who in the future establish sanitariums in new places, to begin their work in humility, consecrating their abilities to His service. The buildings erected are not to be large or expensive. Small local sanitariums are to be established in connection with our training schools. In these sanitariums young men and young women of ability and consecration are to be gathered—those who will conduct themselves in the love and fear of God, those who, when prepared for graduation, will not feel that they know all that they need to know, but will diligently study and carefully practice the lessons given by Christ. The righteousness of Christ will go before such ones, and the glory of God will be their rearward.

I have been given light that in many cities it is advisable for a restaurant to be connected with treatment rooms. The two can co-operate in upholding right principles. In connection with these it is sometimes advisable to have rooms that will serve as lodgings for the sick. These establishments will serve as feeders to the sanitariums located in the country and would better be conducted in rented buildings. We are not to erect in the cities large buildings in which to care for the sick, because God has plainly indicated that the sick can be better cared for outside of the cities. In many places it will be necessary to begin sanitarium work in the cities; but, as much as possible, this work should be transferred to the country as soon as suitable locations can be secured.

The light that has been given me is that, instead of devoting our energies to the upbuilding of a few mammoth medical institutions, we should establish many smaller ones. It is almost impossible to find talent to manage a large sanitarium as it should be managed. The workers are not all under the control of the Spirit of God as they should be, and a worldly spirit comes in.

The strength and joy of benefiting humanity lie not in expensive buildings. We must remember how many are suffering for want of necessary food and clothing. In erecting buildings we should not be influenced by a desire for appearance. We should do our duty, and leave the results with God who only can give success. Let any extra means that we may have be spent in providing proper health-restoring facilities. Let all our sanitariums be erected for health and happiness; let them be so located that the patients will have the blessing of the sunlight; let them be so arranged that every unnecessary step will be saved.

In this work it is best to make small beginnings in many places and allow God's providence to indicate how rapidly facilities should be increased. The small plants established will grow into larger institutions. There will be a distribution of responsibilities, and workers will thus gradually acquire greater mental and spiritual power. The establishment of these institutions will result in much good if all connected with them will suppress selfish ambition and keep ever in view the glory of God. Many of our people should be laboring in new fields, but let none seek notoriety. The minds of the laborers must be sanctified.

In all our work let us remember that the same Jesus who fed the multitude with five loaves and two small fishes is able today to give us the fruit of our labor. He who said to the fishers of Galilee, "Let down your nets for a draft," and who, as they obeyed, filled their nets till they broke, desires His people to see in this an evidence of what He will do for them today. The same God who gave the children of Israel manna from heaven still lives and reigns. He will guide His people and give skill and understanding in the work they are called to do. In answer to earnest prayer He will give wisdom to those who strive to do their duty conscientiously and intelligently. Under His blessing the work with which they are connected will grow to larger proportions, many will learn to be faithful burden bearers, and success will attend their efforts.

12. The Knowledge of Health Principles

We have come to a time when every member of the church should take hold of medical missionary work. The world is a lazar house filled with victims of both physical and spiritual disease. Everywhere people are perishing for lack of a knowledge of the truths that have been committed to us. The members of the church are in need of an awakening, that they may realize their responsibility to impart these truths. Those who have been enlightened by the truth are to be light bearers to the world. To hide our light at this time is to make a terrible mistake. The message to God's people today is: "Arise, shine; for thy light is come, and the glory of the Lord is risen upon thee."

On every hand we see those who have had much light and knowledge deliberately choosing evil in the place of good. Making no attempt to reform, they are growing worse and worse. But the people of God are not to walk in darkness. They are to walk in the light, for they are reformers.

Before the true reformer, the medical missionary work will open many doors. No one need wait until called to some distant field before beginning to help others. Wherever you are, you can begin at once. Opportunities are within the reach of everyone. Take up the work for which you are held responsible, the work that should be done in your home and in your neighborhood. Wait not for others to urge you to action. In the fear of God go forward without delay, bearing in mind your individual responsibility to Him who gave His life for you. Act as if you heard Christ calling upon you personally to do your utmost in His service. Look not to see who else is ready. If you are truly consecrated, God will, through your instrumentality, bring into the truth others whom He can use as channels to convey light to many that are groping in darkness.

All can do something. In an effort to excuse themselves, some say: "My home duties, my children, claim my time and my means." Parents, your children should be your helping hand, increasing your power and ability to work for the Master. Children are the younger members of the Lord's family. They should be led to consecrate themselves to God, whose they are by creation and by redemption. They should be taught that all their powers of body, mind, and soul are His. They should be trained to help in various lines of unselfish service. Do not allow your children to be hindrances. With you the children should share spiritual as well as physical burdens. By helping others they increase their own happiness and usefulness.

Let our people show that they have a living interest in medical missionary work. Let them prepare themselves for usefulness by studying the books that have been written for our instruction in these lines. These books deserve much more attention and appreciation than they have received. Much that is for the benefit of all to understand has been written for the special purpose of instruction in the principles of health. Those who study and practice these principles will be greatly blessed, both physically and spiritually. An understanding of the philosophy of health will be a safeguard against many of the evils that are continually increasing.

Many who desire to obtain knowledge in medical missionary lines have home duties that will sometimes prevent them from meeting with others for study. These may learn much in their own homes in regard to the expressed will of God concerning these lines of missionary work, thus increasing their ability to help others. Fathers and mothers, obtain all the help you can from the study of our books and publications. Read the Good Health, for it is full of valuable information. Take time to read to your children from the health books, as well as from the books treating more particularly on religious subjects. Teach them the importance of caring for the body, the house they live in. Form a home reading circle, in which every member of the family shall lay aside the busy cares of the day and unite in study. Fathers, mothers, brothers, sisters, take up this work heartily and see if the home church will not be greatly improved.

Especially will the youth who have been accustomed to reading novels and cheap storybooks receive benefit by joining in the evening family study. Young men and young women, read the literature that will give you true knowledge and that will be a help to the entire family. Say firmly: "I will not spend precious moments in reading that which will be of no profit to me and which only unfits me to be of service to others. I will devote my time and my thoughts to acquiring a fitness for God's service. I will close my eyes to frivolous and sinful things. My ears are the Lord's, and I will not listen to the subtle reasoning of the enemy. My voice shall not in any way be subject to a will that is not under the influence of the Spirit of God. My body is the temple of the Holy Spirit, and every power of my being shall be consecrated to worthy pursuits."

The Lord has appointed the youth to be His helping hand. If in every church they would consecrate themselves to Him, if they would practice self-denial in the home, relieving their careworn mother, the mother could find time to make neighborly visits, and, when opportunity offered, they could themselves give assistance by doing little errands of mercy and love. Books and papers treating on the subject of health and temperance could be placed in many homes. The circulation of this literature is an important matter; for thus precious knowledge can be imparted in regard to the treatment of disease, knowledge that would be a great blessing to those who cannot afford to pay for a physician's visits.

Parents should seek to interest their children in the study of physiology. There are but few among the youth who have any definite knowledge of the mysteries of life. The study of the wonderful human organism, the relation and dependence of its complicated parts, is one in which many parents take little interest. Although God says to them, "Beloved, I wish above all things that thou mayest prosper and be in health, even as thy soul prospereth," yet they do not understand the influence of the body upon the mind or of the mind upon the body. Needless trifles occupy their attention, and then they plead a lack of time as an excuse for not obtaining the information necessary to enable them properly to instruct their children.

If all would obtain a knowledge of this subject and would feel the importance of putting it to practical use, we should see a better condition of things. Parents, teach your children to reason from cause to effect. Show them that, if they violate the laws of health, they must pay the penalty by suffering. Show them that recklessness in regard to bodily health tends to recklessness in morals. Your children require patient, faithful care. It is not enough for you to feed and clothe them; you should seek also to develop their mental powers and to imbue their hearts with right principles.

But how often are beauty of character and loveliness of temper lost sight of in the eager desire for outward appearance! O parents, be not governed by the world's opinion; labor not to reach its standard. Decide for yourselves what is the great aim of life, and then bend every effort to reach that aim. You cannot with impunity neglect the proper training of your children. Their defective characters will publish your unfaithfulness.

The evils that you permit to pass uncorrected, the coarse, rough manners, the disrespect and disobedience, the habits of indolence and inattention, will bring dishonor to your names and bitterness into your lives. The destiny of your children rests to a great extent in your hands. If you fail in duty you may place them in the ranks of the enemy and make them his agents in ruining others; on the other hand, if you faithfully instruct them, if in your own lives you set before them a godly example, you may lead them to Christ, and they in turn will influence others, and thus many may be saved through your instrumentality.

Fathers and mothers, do you realize the importance of the responsibility resting upon you? Do you realize the necessity of guarding your children from careless, demoralizing habits? Allow your children to form only such associations as will have a right influence upon their characters. Do not allow them to be out in the evening unless you know where they are and what they are doing. Instruct them in the principles of moral purity. If you have neglected to teach them line upon line, precept upon precept, here a little and there a little, begin at once to do your duty. Take up your responsibilities and work for time and for eternity. Let not another day pass without confessing your neglect to your children. Tell them that you mean now to do your God-appointed work. Ask them to take hold with you in the reform. Make diligent efforts to redeem the past. No longer remain in the condition of the Laodicean church. In the name of the Lord I call upon every family to show its true colors. Reform the church in your own home.

As you faithfully do your duty in the home, the father as a priest of the household, the mother as a home missionary, you are multiplying agencies for doing good outside of the home. As you improve your own powers, you are becoming better fitted to labor in the church and in the neighborhood. By binding your children to yourselves and to God, fathers and mothers and children become laborers together with God.

The life of the true believer reveals an indwelling Saviour. The follower of Jesus is Christlike in spirit and in temper. Like Christ, he is meek and humble. His faith works by love and purifies the soul. His whole life is a testimony to the power of the grace of Christ. The pure doctrines of the gospel never degrade the receiver, never make him coarse, or rough, or uncourteous. The gospel refines, ennobles, and elevates, sanctifying the judgment and influencing the whole life.

God will not suffer one of His truehearted workers to be left alone to struggle against great odds and be overcome. He preserves as a precious jewel everyone whose life is hid with Christ in God. Of every such an one He says: "I ... will make thee as a signet: for I have chosen thee." Haggai 2:23.

13. The High Calling of Our Sanitarium Workers

The workers in our sanitariums have a high and holy calling. They need to awake to a realization of the sacredness of their work. The character of this work and the extent of its influence call for earnest effort and unreserved consecration.

In our sanitariums the sick and suffering are to be led to realize that they need spiritual help as well as physical restoration. They are to be given every advantage for the restoration of physical health; and they should be shown also what it means to be blessed with the light and life of Christ, what it means to be bound up with Him. They are to be led to see that the grace of Christ in the soul uplifts the whole being. And in no better way can they learn of Christ's life than by seeing it revealed in the lives of His followers.

The faithful worker keeps his eyes fixed on Christ. Remembering that his hope of eternal life is due to the cross of Christ, he is determined never to dishonor Him who gave His life for him. He takes a deep interest in suffering humanity. He prays and works, watching for souls as one that must give an account, knowing that the souls whom God brings in contact with truth and righteousness are worth saving.

Our sanitarium workers are engaged in a holy warfare. To the sick and the afflicted they are to present the truth as it is in Jesus; they are to present it in all its solemnity, yet with such simplicity and tenderness that souls will be drawn to the Saviour. Ever, in word and deed, they are to keep Him uplifted as the hope of eternal life. Not a harsh word is to be spoken, not a selfish act done. The workers are to treat all with kindness. Their words are to be gentle and loving. Those who show true modesty and Christian courtesy will win souls to Christ.

We should strive to restore to physical and spiritual health those who come to our sanitariums. Let us therefore make preparation to draw them for a season away from those surroundings that lead away from God, into a purer atmosphere. Out of doors, surrounded by the beautiful things that God has made, breathing the fresh, health-giving air, the sick can best be told of the new life in Christ. Here God's words can be taught. Here the sunshine of Christ's righteousness can shine into hearts darkened by sin. Patiently, sympathetically, lead the sick to see their need of the Saviour. Tell them that He gives power to the faint and that to those who have no might He increases strength.

We need to appreciate more fully the meaning of the words: "I sat down under His shadow with great delight." Song of Solomon 2:3. These words do not bring to our minds the picture of hasty transit, but of quiet rest. There are many professing Christians who are anxious and depressed, many who are so full of busy activity that they cannot find time to rest quietly in the promises of God, who act as if they could not afford to have peace and quietness. To all such Christ's invitation is: "Come unto Me, ... and I will give you rest." Matthew 11:28.

Let us turn from the dusty, heated thoroughfares of life to rest in the shadow of Christ's love. Here we gain strength for conflict. Here we learn how to lessen toil and worry, and how to speak and sing to the praise of God. Let the weary and the heavy-laden learn from Christ the lesson of quiet trust. They must sit under His shadow if they would be possessors of His peace and rest.

Those who engage in sanitarium work should have a treasure house full of rich experience because the truth is implanted in the heart and as a holy thing is tended and fed by the grace of God. Rooted and grounded in the truth, they should have a faith that works by love and purifies the soul. Constantly asking for blessings, they should keep the windows of the soul closed earthward against the malarious atmosphere of the world and opened heavenward to receive the bright beams of the Sun of Righteousness.

Who is preparing to take hold understandingly of medical missionary work? By this work the minds of those who come to our sanitariums for treatment are to be led to Christ and taught to unite their weakness with His strength. Every worker should be understandingly efficient. Then in a high, broad sense he can present the truth as it is in Jesus.

The workers in our sanitariums are continually exposed to temptation. They are brought in contact with unbelievers, and those who are not sound in the faith will be harmed by the contact. But those who are abiding in Christ will meet unbelievers as He met them, refusing to be drawn from their allegiance, but always ready to speak a word in season, always ready to sow the seeds of truth. They will watch unto prayer, firmly maintaining their integrity and daily showing the consistency of their religion. The influence of such workers is a blessing to many. By a well-ordered life they draw souls to the cross. A true Christian constantly acknowledges Christ. He is always cheerful, always ready to speak words of hope and comfort to the suffering.

"The fear of the Lord is the beginning of knowledge." Proverbs 1:7. One sentence of Scripture is of more value than ten thousand of man's ideas or arguments. Those who refuse to follow God's way will finally receive the sentence, "Depart from Me." But when we submit to God's way, the Lord Jesus guides our minds and fills our lips with assurance. We may be strong in the Lord and in the power of His might. Receiving Christ, we are clothed with power. An indwelling Saviour makes His power our property. The truth becomes our stock in trade. No unrighteousness is seen in the life. We are able to speak words in season to those who know not the truth. Christ's presence in the heart is a vitalizing power, strengthening the entire being.

I am instructed to say to our sanitarium workers that unbelief and self-sufficiency are the dangers against which they must constantly guard. They are to carry forward the warfare against evil with such earnestness and devotion that the sick will feel the uplifting influence of their unselfish efforts.

No taint of self-seeking is to mar our service. "Ye cannot serve God and mammon." Lift Him up, the Man of Calvary. Lift Him up by living faith in God, that your prayers may prevail. Do we realize how near Jesus will come to us? He is speaking to us individually. He will reveal Himself to everyone who is willing to be clothed with the robe of His righteousness. He declares: "I the Lord thy God will hold thy right hand." Let us place ourselves where He can hold us by the hand, where we can hear Him saying with assurance and authority: "I am He that liveth, and was dead; and, behold, I am alive for evermore."

14. A Message to Our Physicians

The Christian physician is to be to the sick a messenger of mercy, bringing to them a remedy for the sin-sick soul as well as for the diseased body. As he uses the simple remedies that God has provided for the relief of physical suffering, he is to speak of Christ's power to heal the maladies of the soul.

How necessary that the physician live in close communion with the Saviour! The sick and suffering with whom he deals need the help that Christ alone can give. They need prayers indited by His Spirit. The afflicted one leaves himself to the wisdom and mercy of the physician, whose skill and faithfulness may be his only hope. Let the physician, then, be a faithful steward of the grace of God, a guardian of the soul as well as of the body.

The physician who has received wisdom from above, who knows that Christ is his personal Saviour, because he has himself been led to the Refuge, knows how to deal with the trembling, guilty, sin-sick souls who turn to him for help. He can respond with assurance to the inquiry: "What must I do to be saved?" He can tell the story of the Redeemer's love. He can speak from experience of the power of repentance and faith. As he stands by the bedside of the sufferer, striving to speak words that will bring to him help and comfort, the Lord works with him and through him. As the mind of the afflicted one is fastened on the Mighty Healer, the peace of Christ fills his heart; and the spiritual health that comes to him is used as the helping hand of God in restoring the health of the body.

Precious are the opportunities that the physician has of awakening in the hearts of those with whom he is brought in contact a sense of their great need of Christ. He is to bring from the treasure house of the heart things new and old, speaking the words of comfort and instruction that are longed for. Constantly he is to sow the seeds of truth, not presenting doctrinal subjects, but speaking of the love of the sin-pardoning Saviour. Not only should he give instruction from the word of God, line upon line, precept upon precept; he is to moisten this instruction with his tears and make it strong with his prayers, that souls may be saved from death.

In their earnest, feverish anxiety to avert the peril of the body, physicians are in danger of forgetting the peril of the soul. Physicians, be on your guard, for at the judgment seat of Christ you must meet those at whose death-bed you now stand.

The solemnity of the physician's work, his constant contact with the sick and the dying, require that, so far as possible, he be removed from the secular duties that others can perform. No unnecessary burdens should be laid on him, that he may have time to become acquainted with the spiritual needs of his patients. His mind should be ever under the influence of the Holy Spirit, that he may be able to speak in season the words that will awaken faith and hope.

At the bedside of the dying no word of creed or controversy is to be spoken. The sufferer is to be pointed to the One who is willing to save all who come to Him in faith. Earnestly, tenderly, strive to help the soul that is hovering between life and death.

The physician should never lead his patients to fix their attention on him. He is to teach them to grasp with the hand of faith the outstretched hand of the Saviour. Then the mind will be illuminated with the light radiating from the Sun of Righteousness. What physicians attempt to do, Christ did in deed and in truth. They try to save life; He is life itself.

The physician's effort to lead the minds of his patients to healthy action must be free from all human enchantment. It must not grovel to humanity, but soar aloft to the spiritual, grasping the things of eternity.

The physician should not be made the object of unkind criticism. This places on him an unnecessary burden. His cares are heavy, and he needs the sympathy of those connected with him in the work. He is to be sustained by prayer. The realization that he is appreciated will give him hope and courage.

The intelligent Christian physician has a constantly increasing realization of the connection between sin and disease. He strives to see more and more clearly the relation between cause and effect. He sees that those who are taking the nurses' course should be given a thorough education in the principles of health reform, that they should be taught to be strictly temperate in all things, because carelessness in regard to the laws of health is inexcusable in those set apart to teach others how to live.

When a physician sees that a patient is suffering from an ailment caused by improper eating and drinking, yet neglects to tell him of this and to point out the need of reform, he is doing a fellow being an injury. Drunkards, maniacs, those who are given over to licentiousness—all appeal to the physician to declare clearly and distinctly that suffering is the result of sin. We have received great light on health reform. Why, then, are we not more decidedly in earnest in striving to counteract the causes that produce disease? Seeing the continual conflict with pain, laboring constantly to alleviate suffering, how can our physicians hold their peace? Can they refrain from lifting the voice in warning? Are they benevolent and merciful if they do not teach strict temperance as a remedy for disease?

Physicians, study the warning which Paul gave to the Romans: "I beseech you therefore, brethren, by the mercies of God, that ye present your bodies a living sacrifice, holy, acceptable unto God, which is your reasonable service. And be not conformed to this world: but be ye transformed by the renewing of your mind, that ye may prove what is that good, and acceptable, and perfect, will of God." Romans 12:1, 2.

The spiritual work of our sanitariums is not to be under the control of physicians. This work requires thought and tact and a broad knowledge of the Bible. Ministers possessing these qualifications should be connected with our sanitariums. They should uplift the standard of temperance from a

Christian point of view, showing that the body is the temple of the Holy Spirit and bringing to the minds of the people the responsibility resting upon them as God's purchased possession to make mind and body a holy temple, fit for the indwelling of the Holy Spirit. When temperance is presented as a part of the gospel, many will see their need of reform. They will see the evil of intoxicating liquors and that total abstinence is the only platform on which God's people can conscientiously stand. As this instruction is given, the people will become interested in other lines of Bible study.

15. The Value of Outdoor Life

The great medical institutions in our cities, called sanitariums, do but a small part of the good they might do were they located where the patients could have the advantages of outdoor life. I have been instructed that sanitariums are to be established in many places in the country and that the work of these institutions will greatly advance the cause of health and righteousness.

The things of nature are God's blessings, provided to give health to body, mind, and soul. They are given to the well to keep them well and to the sick to make them well. Connected with water treatment, they are more effective in restoring health than all the drug medication in the world.

In the country the sick find many things to call their attention away from themselves and their sufferings. Everywhere they can look upon and enjoy the beautiful things of nature—the flowers, the fields, the fruit trees laden with their rich treasure, the forest trees casting their grateful shade, and the hills and valleys with their varied verdure and many forms of life.

And not only are they entertained by these surroundings, but at the same time they learn most precious spiritual lessons. Surrounded by the wonderful works of God, their minds are lifted from the things that are seen to the things that are unseen. The beauty of nature leads them to think of the matchless charms of the earth made new, where there will be nothing to mar the loveliness, nothing to taint or destroy, nothing to cause disease or death.

Nature is God's physician. The pure air, the glad sunshine, the beautiful flowers and trees, the orchards and vineyards, and outdoor exercise amid these surroundings, are health-giving—the elixir of life. Outdoor life is the only medicine that many invalids need. Its influence is powerful to heal sickness caused by fashionable life, a life that weakens and destroys the physical, mental, and spiritual powers.

How grateful to weary invalids accustomed to city life, the glare of many lights, and the noise of the streets are the quiet and freedom of the country! How eagerly do they turn to the scenes of nature! How glad would they be for the advantages of a sanitarium in the country, where they could sit in the open air, rejoice in the sunshine, and breathe the fragrance of tree and flower! There are life-giving properties in the balsam of the pine, in the fragrance of the cedar and the fir. And there are other trees that are health-promoting. Let no such trees be ruthlessly cut down. Cherish them where they are abundant, and plant more where there are but few.

For the chronic invalid nothing so tends to restore health and happiness as living amid attractive country surroundings. Here the most helpless ones can be left sitting or lying in the sunshine or in the shade of the trees. They have only to lift their eyes and they see above them the beautiful foliage. They wonder that they have never before noticed how gracefully the boughs bend, forming a living canopy over them, giving them just the shade they need. A sweet sense of restfulness and refreshing comes over them as they listen to the murmuring breezes. The drooping spirits revive. The waning strength is recruited. Unconsciously the mind becomes peaceful, the fevered pulse more calm and regular. As the sick grow stronger, they will venture to take a few steps to gather some of the lovely flowers—precious messengers of God's love to His afflicted family here below.

Encourage the patients to be much in the open air. Devise plans to keep them out of doors, where, through nature, they can commune with God. Locate sanitariums on extensive tracts of land, where, in the cultivation of the soil, patients can have opportunity for healthful, outdoor exercise. Such exercise, combined with hygienic treatment, will work miracles in restoring and invigorating the diseased body and refreshing the worn and weary mind. Amid conditions so favorable the patients will not require so much care as if confined in a sanitarium in the city. Nor will they in the country be so much inclined to discontentment and repining. They will be ready to learn lessons in regard to the love of God, ready to acknowledge that He who cares so wonderfully for the birds and the flowers will care for the creatures formed in His own image. Thus opportunity is given physicians and helpers to reach souls, uplifting the God of nature before those who are seeking restoration to health.

In the night season I was given a view of a sanitarium in the country. The institution was not large, but it was complete. It was surrounded by beautiful trees and shrubbery, beyond which were orchards and groves. Connected with the place were gardens, in which the lady patients, when they chose, could cultivate flowers of every description, each patient selecting a special plot for which to care. Outdoor exercise in these gardens was prescribed as a part of the regular treatment.

Scene after scene passed before me. In one scene a number of suffering patients had just come to one of our country sanitariums. In another I saw the same company; but, oh, how transformed their appearance! Disease had gone, the skin was clear, the countenance joyful; body and mind seemed animated with new life.

I was also instructed that as those who have been sick are restored to health in our country sanitariums and return to their homes, they will be living object lessons, and many others will be favorably impressed by the transformation that has taken place in them. Many of the sick and suffering will turn from the cities to the country, refusing to conform to the habits, customs, and fashions of city life; they will seek to regain health in some one of our country sanitariums. Thus, though we are removed from the cities twenty or thirty miles, we shall be able to reach the people, and those who desire health will have opportunity to regain it under conditions most favorable.

God will work wonders for us if we will in faith co-operate with Him. Let us, then, pursue a sensible course, that our efforts may be blessed of heaven and crowned with success.

Why should not the young men and the young women who are seeking to obtain a knowledge of how to care for the sick have most liberally the advantage of nature's wonderful resources? Why should they not be most diligently taught to value and to use these resources?

In the location of sanitariums our physicians have missed the mark. They have not used the provisions of nature as they may. God desires that the places chosen for sanitarium work be beautiful, that the patients be surrounded with everything that delights the senses. May God help us to do our utmost to utilize the life-giving power of sunshine and fresh air. When we as a people closely follow the Lord's plan in our sanitarium work, nature's resources will be appreciated.

16. Out of the Cities

Those who have to do with the locating of our sanitariums should prayerfully study the character and aim of sanitarium work. They should ever bear in mind that they are working for the restoration of the image of God in man. In one hand they are to carry remedies for the relief of physical suffering, and in the other the gospel for the relief of sin-burdened souls. Thus they are to work as true medical missionaries. In many hearts they are to sow the seeds of truth.

No selfishness, no personal ambition, is to be allowed to enter into the work of selecting locations for our sanitariums. Christ came to this world to show us how to live and labor. Let us learn from Him not to choose for our sanitariums the places most agreeable to our taste, but those places best suited to our work.

Light has been given me that in medical missionary work we have lost great advantages by failing to realize the need of a change in our plans in regard to the location of sanitariums. It is the Lord's will that these institutions shall be established outside the city. They should be situated in the country, in the midst of surroundings as attractive as possible. In nature—the Lord's garden—the sick will always find something to divert their attention from themselves and lift their thoughts to God.

I have been instructed that the sick should be cared for away from the bustle of the cities, away from the noise of streetcars and the continual rattling of carts and carriages. People who come to our sanitariums from country homes will appreciate a quiet place; and in retirement patients will be more readily influenced by the Spirit of God.

The Garden of Eden, the home of our first parents, was exceedingly beautiful. Graceful shrubs and delicate flowers greeted the eye at every turn. In the garden were trees of every variety, many of them laden with fragrant and delicious fruit. On their branches the birds caroled their songs of praise. Adam and Eve, in their untainted purity, delighted in the sights and sounds of Eden. And today, although sin has cast its shadow over the earth, God desires His children to find delight in the works of His hands. To locate our sanitariums amidst the scenes of nature would be to follow God's plan; and the more closely this plan is followed, the more wonderfully will He work to restore suffering humanity. For our educational and medical institutions, places should be chosen where, away from the dark clouds of sin that hang over the great cities, the Sun of Righteousness can arise, "with healing in His wings." Malachi 4:2.

Let the leaders in our work instruct the people that sanitariums should be established in the midst of the most pleasant surroundings, in places not disturbed by the turmoil of the city, places where by wise instruction the thoughts of the patients can be bound up with the thoughts of God. Again and again I have described such places; but it seems that there has been no ear to hear. Recently in a most clear and convincing manner the advantage of establishing our institutions, especially our sanitariums and schools, outside the cities was presented to me.

Why are our physicians so eager to be located in the cities? The very atmosphere of the cities is polluted. In them, patients who have unnatural appetites to overcome cannot be properly guarded. To patients who are victims of strong drink, the saloons of a city are a continual temptation. To place our sanitariums where they are surrounded by ungodliness is to counterwork the efforts made to restore the patients to health.

In the future the condition of things in the cities will grow more and more objectionable, and the influence of city surroundings will be acknowledged as unfavorable to the accomplishment of the work that our sanitariums should do.

From the standpoint of health the smoke and dust of the cities are very objectionable. And the patients who for a large part of their time are shut up within four walls often feel that they are prisoners in their rooms. When they look out of a window they see nothing but houses, houses, houses. Those who are thus confined to their rooms are liable to brood over their suffering and sorrow. Sometimes an invalid is poisoned by his own breath.

Many other evils follow the establishment of great medical institutions in the large cities.

Why deprive patients of the health-restoring blessing to be found in outdoor life? I have been instructed that as the sick are encouraged to leave their rooms and spend time in the open air, cultivating flowers, or doing some other light, pleasant work, their minds will be called from self to something more health-giving. Exercise in the open air should be prescribed as a beneficial, life-giving necessity. The longer patients can be kept out of doors the less care will they require. The more cheerful their surroundings, the more hopeful will they be. Surround them with the beautiful things of nature; place them where they can see the flowers growing and hear the birds singing, and their hearts will break into song in harmony with the song of the birds. Shut them in rooms, and, be these rooms ever so elegantly furnished, they will grow fretful and gloomy. Give them the blessing of outdoor life; thus their souls will be uplifted. Relief will come to body and mind.

"Out of the cities" is my message. Our physicians ought to have been wide awake on this point long ago. I hope and pray and believe that they will now arouse to the importance of getting out into the country.

The time is near when the large cities will be visited by the judgments of God. In a little while these cities will be terribly shaken. No matter how large or how strong their buildings, no matter how many safeguards against fire may have been provided, let God touch these buildings, and in a few minutes or a few hours they are in ruins.

The ungodly cities of our world are to be swept away by the besom of destruction. In the calamities that are now befalling immense buildings and large portions of cities God is showing us what will come upon the whole earth. He has told us: "Now learn a parable of the fig tree; When his branch is yet tender, and putteth forth leaves, ye know that summer is nigh: so likewise ye, when ye shall see all these things, know that it [the coming of the Son of man] is near, even at the doors." Matthew 24:32, 33.

Brick and stone buildings are not the most desirable for a sanitarium, for they are generally cold and damp. It may be said that a brick building presents a much more attractive appearance, and that the building should be attractive. But we need roomy buildings; and if brick is too costly, we must build of wood. Economy must be our study. This is a necessity, because of the greatness of the work that must be done in many lines in God's moral vineyard.

It has been suggested that patients will not feel safe from fire in a wooden structure. But if we are in the country, and not in the cities where buildings are crowded together, a fire would originate from within, not from without; therefore brick would not be a safeguard. It should be presented to the patients that for health a wooden building is preferable to one of brick.

For years I have been given special light that we are not to center our work in the cities. The turmoil and confusion that fill these cities, the conditions brought about by the labor unions and the strikes, would prove a great hindrance to our work. Men are seeking to bring those engaged in the different trades under bondage to certain unions. This is not God's planning, but the planning of a power that we should in no wise acknowledge. God's word is fulfilling; the wicked are binding themselves up in bundles ready to be burned.

We are now to use all our entrusted capabilities in giving the last warning message to the world. In this work we are to preserve our individuality. We are not to unite with secret societies or with trade-unions. We are to stand free in God, looking constantly to Christ for instruction. All our movements are to be made with a realization of the importance of the work to be accomplished for God.

Light has been given me that the cities will be filled with confusion, violence, and crime, and that these things will increase till the end of this earth's history.

17. In the Country

In August, 1901, while attending the Los Angeles camp meeting, I was in the visions of the night in a council meeting. The question under consideration was the establishment of a sanitarium in Southern California. By some it was urged that this sanitarium should be built in the city of Los Angeles, and the objections to establishing it out of the city were pointed out. Others spoke of the advantages of a country location.

There was among us One who presented this matter very clearly and with the utmost simplicity. He told us that it would be a mistake to establish a sanitarium within the city limits. A sanitarium should have the advantage of plenty of land, so that the invalids can work in the open air. For nervous, gloomy, feeble patients, outdoor work is invaluable. Let them have flower beds to care for. In the use of rake and hoe and spade they will find relief for many of their maladies. Idleness is the cause of many diseases.

Life in the open air is good for body and mind. It is God's medicine for the restoration of health. Pure air, good water, sunshine, the beautiful surroundings of nature—these are His means for restoring the sick to health in natural ways. To the sick it is worth more than silver or gold to lie in the sunshine or in the shade of the trees.

In the country our sanitariums can be surrounded by flowers and trees, orchards and vineyards. Here it is easy for physicians and nurses to draw from the things of nature lessons teaching of God. Let them point the patients to Him whose hand has made the lofty trees, the springing grass, and the beautiful flowers, encouraging them to see in every opening bud and blossoming flower an expression of His love for His children.

It is the expressed will of God that our sanitariums shall be established as far from the cities as is consistent. So far as possible these institutions should be located in quiet, secluded places, where opportunity will be afforded for giving the patients instruction concerning the love of God and the Eden home of our first parents, which, through the sacrifice of Christ, is to be restored to man.

In the effort made to restore the sick to health, use is to be made of the beautiful things of the Lord's creation. Seeing the flowers, plucking the ripe fruit, listening to the happy songs of the birds, has a peculiarly exhilarating effect on the nervous system. From outdoor life men, women, and children gain a desire to be pure and guileless. By the influence of the quickening, reviving, life-giving properties of nature's great medicinal resources the functions of the body are strengthened, the intellect awakened, the imagination quickened, the spirits enlivened, and the mind prepared to appreciate the beauty of God's word.

Under these influences, combined with the influence of careful treatment and wholesome food, the sick find health. The feeble step recovers its elasticity. The eye regains its brightness. The hopeless become hopeful. The once despondent countenance wears an expression of cheerfulness. The complaining tones of the voice give place to tones of content. The words express the belief: "God is our refuge and strength, a very present help in trouble." Psalm 46:1. The clouded hope of the Christian is brightened. Faith returns.

The word is heard: "Yea, though I walk through the valley of the shadow of death, I will fear no evil: for Thou art with me; Thy rod and Thy staff they comfort me." "My soul doth magnify the Lord, and my spirit hath rejoiced in God my Saviour." "He giveth power to the faint; and to them that have no might He increaseth strength." Psalm 23:4; Luke 1:46, 47; Isaiah 40:29. The acknowledgment of God's goodness in providing these blessings invigorates the mind. God is very near and is pleased to see His gifts appreciated.

When the earth was created, it was holy and beautiful. God pronounced it very good. Every flower, every shrub, every tree, answered the purpose of its Creator. Everything upon which the eye rested was lovely and filled the mind with thoughts of the love of God. Through tempting man to sin, Satan hoped to counteract the tide of divine love flowing to the human race; but, instead of this, his work resulted in calling forth new and deeper manifestations of God's mercy and goodness.

It was not God's purpose that His people should be crowded into cities, huddled together in terraces and tenements. In the beginning He placed our first parents in a garden amidst the beautiful sights and attractive sounds of nature, and these sights and sounds He desires men to rejoice in today. The more nearly we come into harmony with God's original plan, the more favorable will be our position for the recovery and the preservation of health.

18. Not Among the Wealthy

It might seem to us that it would be best to select for our sanitariums places among the wealthy; that this would give character to our work and secure patronage for our institutions. But in this there is no light. "The Lord seeth not as man seeth." 1 Samuel 16:7. Man looks at the outward appearance; God looks at the heart. The fewer grand buildings there are

Section 2: Our Sanitarium Work

around our institutions, the less vexation we shall experience. Many of the wealthy property owners are irreligious and irreverent. Worldly thoughts fill their minds. Worldly amusements, merriment, and hilarity occupy their time. Extravagance in dress and luxurious living absorb their means. The heavenly messengers are not welcomed to their homes. They want God afar off. Humility is a difficult lesson for humanity to learn, and it is especially difficult for the rich and the self-indulgent. Those who do not regard themselves as accountable to God for all that they possess are tempted to exalt self, as if the riches comprehended by lands and bank stock made them independent of God. Full of pride and conceit, they place on themselves an estimate measured by their wealth.

There are many rich men who in God's sight are unfaithful stewards. In their acquirement and use of means He has seen robbery. They have neglected the great Proprietor of all and have not used the means entrusted to them to relieve the suffering and the oppressed. They have been laying up for themselves wrath against the day of wrath; for God will reward every man according as his work shall be. These men do not worship God; self is their idol. They put justice and mercy out of the mind, replacing them with avarice and strife. God says: "Shall I not visit them for these things?" Jeremiah 9:9.

God would not be pleased to have any of our institutions located in a community of this character, however great its apparent advantages. Selfish wealthy men have a molding influence upon other minds, and the enemy would work through them to hedge up our way. Evil associations are always detrimental to piety and devotion, and principles that are approved by God may be undermined by such associations. God would have none of us like Lot, who chose a home in a place where he and his family were brought into constant contact with evil. Lot went into Sodom rich; he left with nothing, led by an angel's hand, while messengers of wrath waited to pour forth the fiery blasts that were to consume the inhabitants of that highly favored city and blot out its entrancing beauty, making bleak and bare a place that God had once made very beautiful.

Our sanitariums should not be situated near the residences of rich men, where they will be looked upon as an innovation and an eyesore, and unfavorably commented upon, because they receive suffering humanity of all classes. Pure and undefiled religion makes those who are children of God one family, bound up with Christ in God. But the spirit of the world is proud, partial, exclusive, favoring only a few.

In erecting our buildings, we must keep away from the homes of the great men of the world, and let them seek the help they need by withdrawing from their associates into more retired places. We shall not please God by building our sanitariums among people extravagant in dress and living, who are attracted to those who can make a great display.

19. Consideration in Buildings

As the chosen people of God we cannot copy the habits, aims, practices, or fashions of the world. We are not left in darkness to pattern after worldly models and to depend on outward appearance for success. The Lord has told us whence comes our strength. "This is the word of the Lord unto Zerubbabel, saying, Not by might, nor by power, but by My Spirit, saith the Lord of hosts." Zechariah 4:6. As the Lord sees fit, He imparts to those who keep His way, power that enables them to exert a strong influence for good. On God they are dependent, and to Him they must give an account of the way in which they use the talents He has entrusted to them. They are to realize that they are God's stewards and are to seek to magnify His name.

Those whose affections are set on God will succeed. They will lose sight of self in Christ, and worldly attractions will have no power to allure them from their allegiance. They will realize that outward display does not give strength. It is not ostentation, outward show, that gives a correct representation of the work that we, as God's chosen people, are to do. Those who are connected with our sanitarium work should be adorned with the grace of Christ. This will give them the greatest influence for good.

The Lord is in earnest with us. His promises are given on condition that we faithfully do His will; therefore in the building of sanitariums He is to be made first and last and best in everything.

Let all who are connected with the service of God be guarded, lest by desire for display they lead others into indulgence and self-glorification. God does not want any of His servants to enter into unnecessary, expensive undertakings, which bring heavy burdens of debt upon the people, thus depriving them of means that would provide facilities for the work of the Lord. So long as those who claim to believe the truth for this time walk in the way of the Lord, to do justice and judgment, they may expect that the Lord will give them prosperity. But when they choose to wander from the narrow way, they bring ruin upon themselves and upon those who look to them for guidance.

Those who lead out in the establishment of medical institutions must set a right example. Even if the money is in sight, they should not use more than is absolutely needed. The Lord's work should be conducted with reference to the necessities of every part of His vineyard. We are all members of one family, children of one Father, and the Lord's revenue must be used with reference to the interests of His cause throughout the world. The Lord looks upon all parts of the field, and His vineyard is to be cultivated as a whole.

We must not absorb in a few places all the money in the treasury, but must labor to build up the work in many places. New territory is to be added to the Lord's kingdom. Other parts of His vineyard are to be furnished with facilities that will give character to the work. The Lord forbids us to use selfish schemes in His service. He forbids us to adopt plans that will rob our neighbor of facilities that would enable him to act his part in representing the truth. We are to love our neighbor as ourselves.

We must also remember that our work is to correspond with our faith. We believe that the Lord is soon to come, and should not our faith be represented in the buildings we erect? Shall we put a large outlay of money into a building that will soon be consumed in the great conflagration? Our money means souls, and it is to be used to bring a knowledge of the truth to those who, because of sin, are under the condemnation of God. Then let us bind about our ambitious plans; let us guard against extravagance or improvidence, lest the Lord's treasury become empty and the builders have not means to do their appointed work.

Much more money than was necessary has been expended on our older institutions. Those who have done this have supposed that this outlay would give character to the work. But this plea is no excuse for unnecessary expenditure.

God desires that the humble, meek, and lowly spirit of the Master, who is the Majesty of heaven, the King of glory, shall ever be revealed in our institutions. Christ's first advent is not studied as it should be. He came to be our example in all things. His life was one of strict self-denial. If we follow His example, we shall never expend means unnecessarily. Never are we to seek for outward show. Let our showing be such that the light of truth can shine through our good works, so that God will be glorified by the use of the very best methods to restore the sick and to relieve the suffering. Character is given to the work, not by investing means in large buildings, but by maintaining the true standard of religious principles, with noble Christlikeness of character.

The mistakes that have been made in the erection of buildings in the past should be salutary admonitions to us in the future. We are to observe where others have failed, and, instead of copying their mistakes, make improvements. In all our advance work we must regard the necessity of economy. There must be no needless expense. The Lord is soon to come, and our outlay in buildings is to be in harmony with our faith. Our means is to be used in providing cheerful rooms, healthful surroundings, and wholesome food.

Our ideas of building and furnishing our institutions are to be molded and fashioned by a true, practical knowledge of what it means to walk humbly with God. Never should it be thought necessary to give an appearance of wealth. Never should appearance be depended on as a means of success. This is a delusion. The desire to make an appearance that is not in every way appropriate to the work that God has given us to do, an appearance that could be kept up only by expending a large sum of money, is a merciless tyrant. It is like a canker that is ever eating into the vitals.

Men of common sense appreciate comfort above elegance and display. It is a mistake to suppose that, by keeping up an appearance, more patients, and therefore more means, would be gained. But even if this course would bring an increase of patronage, we could not consent to have our sanitariums furnished according to the luxurious ideas of the age. Christian influence is too valuable to be sacrificed in this way. All the surroundings, inside and outside our institutions, must be in harmony with the teachings of Christ and the expression of our faith. Our work in all its departments should be an illustration, not of display and extravagance, but of sanctified judgment.

It is not large, expensive buildings; it is not rich furniture; it is not tables loaded with delicacies, that will give our work influence and success. It is the faith that works by love and purifies the soul; it is the atmosphere of grace that surrounds the believer, the Holy Spirit working upon mind and heart, that makes him a savor of life unto life, and enables God to bless his work.

God can communicate with His people today and give them wisdom to do His will, even as He communicated with His people of old and gave them wisdom in building the tabernacle. In the construction of this building He gave a representation of His power and majesty; and His name is to be honored in the buildings that are erected for Him today. Faithfulness, stability, and fitness are to be seen in every part.

Those who have in hand the erecting of a sanitarium are to represent the truth by working in the spirit and love of God. As Noah in his day warned the world in the building of the ark, so, by the faithful work that is done today in erecting the Lord's institutions, sermons will be preached, and the hearts of some will be convicted and converted. Then let the workers feel the greatest anxiety for the constant help of Christ, that the institutions which are established may not be in vain.

While the work of building is going forward, let them remember that, as in the days of Noah and of Moses God arranged every detail of the ark and of the tabernacle, so in the building of His institutions today He Himself is watching the work done. Let them remember that the great Master Builder, by His word, by His Spirit, and by His providence, designs to direct His work. They should take time to ask counsel of Him.

The voice of prayer and the melody of holy song should ascend as sweet incense. All should realize their entire dependence upon God; they should remember that they are erecting an institution in which is to be carried forward a work of eternal consequence, and that, in doing this work, they are to be laborers together with God. "Looking unto Jesus" is ever to be our motto. And the assurance is: "I will instruct thee and teach thee in the way which thou shalt go: I will guide thee with Mine eye." Psalm 32:8.

20. Not for Pleasure Seekers

To Our Sanitarium Workers in Southern California—

I have a decided message for our people in Southern California. The Lord does not require them to provide facilities for the entertainment of tourists. The establishment of an institution for this purpose would be setting a wrong example before the Lord's people. The result would not justify the effort put forth.

Why do we establish sanitariums? That the sick who come to them for treatment may receive relief from physical suffering and may also receive spiritual help. Because of their condition of health they are susceptible to the sanctifying influence of the medical missionaries who labor for their restoration. Let us work wisely, for their best interests.

We are not building sanitariums for hotels. Receive into our sanitariums only those who desire to conform to right principles, those who will accept the foods that we can conscientiously place before them. Should we allow patients to have intoxicating liquor in their rooms, or should we serve them with meat, we could not give them the help they should receive in coming to our sanitariums. We must let it be known that from principle we exclude such articles from our sanitariums and our hygienic restaurants. Do we not desire to see our fellow beings freed from disease and infirmity, and in the enjoyment of health and strength? Then let us be as true to principle as the needle to the pole.

Those whose work it is to labor for the salvation of souls must keep themselves free from worldly policy plans. They must not, for the sake of obtaining the influence of someone who is wealthy, become entangled in plans dishonoring to their profession of faith. They must not sell their souls for financial advantage. They must do nothing that will retard the work of God and lower the standard of righteousness. We are God's servants, and we are to be workers together with Him, doing His work in His way, that all for whom we labor may see that our desire is to reach a higher standard of holiness. Those with whom we come in contact are to see that we not only talk of self-denial and sacrifice, but that we reveal it in our lives. Our example is to inspire those with whom we come in contact in our work, to become better acquainted with the things of God.

If we are to go to the expense of building sanitariums in order that we may work for the salvation of the sick and afflicted, we must plan our work in such a way that those we desire to help will receive the help they need. We are to do all in our power for the healing of the body; but we are to make the healing of the soul of far greater importance. Those who come to our sanitariums as patients are to be shown the way of salvation, that they may repent and hear the words: Thy sins are forgiven thee; go in peace, and sin no more.

Medical missionary work in Southern California is not to be carried forward by the establishment of one mammoth institution for the accommodation and entertainment of a promiscuous company of pleasure lovers, who would bring with them their intemperate ideas and practices. Such an institution would absorb the time and talent of workers who are needed elsewhere. Our capable men are to put forth their efforts in sanitariums established and conducted for the purpose of preparing minds for the reception of the gospel of Christ.

We are not to absorb the time and strength of men capable of carrying forward the Lord's work in the way He has outlined, in an enterprise for the accommodation and entertainment of pleasure seekers, whose greatest desire is to gratify self. To connect workers with such an enterprise would be perilous to their safety. Let us keep our young men and young women from all such dangerous influences. And should our brethren engage in such an enterprise, they would not advance the work of soul saving as they think they would.

Our sanitariums are to be established for one object, the advancement of present truth. And they are to be so conducted that a decided impression in favor of the truth will be made on the minds of those who come to them for treatment. The conduct of the workers, from the head manager to the worker occupying the humblest position, is to tell on the side of truth. The institution is to be pervaded by a spiritual atmosphere. We have a warning message to bear to the world, and our earnestness, our devotion to God's service, is to impress those who come to our sanitariums.

As soon as possible, sanitariums are to be established in different places in Southern California. Let a beginning be made in several places. If possible, let land be purchased on which buildings are already erected. Then, as the prosperity of the work demands, let appropriate enlargements be made.

We are living in the very close of this earth's history, and we are to move cautiously, understanding what the will of the Lord is and, imbued with His Spirit, doing work that will mean much to His cause, work that will proclaim the warning message to a world infatuated, deceived, perishing in sin.

In Southern California there are many properties for sale on which buildings suitable for sanitarium work are already erected. Some of these properties should be purchased and medical missionary work carried forward on sensible, rational lines. Several small sanitariums are to be established in Southern California for the benefit of the multitudes drawn there in the hope of finding health. Instruction has been given me that now is our opportunity to reach the invalids flocking to the health resorts of Southern California, and that a work may be done also in behalf of their attendants.

"Say not ye, there are yet four months, and then cometh harvest? behold, I say unto you, Lift up your eyes, and look on the fields; for they are white already to harvest." John 4:35.

For months I carried on my soul the burden of the medical missionary work in Southern California. Recently much light has been given me in regard to the manner in which God desires us to conduct sanitarium work. We are to encourage patients to spend much of their time out of doors. I have been instructed to tell our brethren to keep on the lookout for cheap, desirable properties in healthful places, suitable for sanitarium purposes.

Instead of investing in one medical institution all the means obtainable, we ought to establish smaller sanitariums in many places. Soon the reputation of the health resorts in Southern California will stand even higher than it stands at present. Now is our time to enter that field for the purpose of carrying forward medical missionary work.

21. Centralization

St. Helena, California
September 4, 1902
To the Leaders in Our Medical Work—

Dear Brethren: The Lord is working impartially for every part of His vineyard. It is men who disorganize His work. He does not give to His people the privilege of gathering in so much means to establish institutions in a few places, that nothing will be left for the establishment of similar institutions in other places.

Many plants are to be established in the cities of America, and especially in the Southern cities, where as yet little has been done. And in foreign lands many medical missionary enterprises are to be started and carried forward to success. The establishment of sanitariums is as essential in Europe and other foreign countries as in America.

The Lord desires His people to have a right understanding of the work to be done and, as faithful stewards, to move forward wisely in the investment of means. In the erection of buildings He desires them to count the cost to see whether they have enough with which to finish. He also desires them to remember that they should not selfishly gather all the means possible to invest in a few places, but that they should work with reference to the many other places where institutions must be established.

From the light given me, the managers of all our institutions, and especially of newly established sanitariums, are to be careful to economize in the expenditure of means, that they may be in a position to help similar institutions that are to be established in other parts of the world. Even if they have a large amount of money in the treasury, they should make every plan with reference to the needs of God's great missionary field.

It is not the Lord's will for His people to erect mammoth sanitariums anywhere. Many sanitariums are to be established. They are not to be large, but sufficiently complete to do a good and successful work.

Cautions have been given me in reference to the work of training nurses and medical missionary evangelists. We are not to centralize this work in any one place. In every sanitarium established, young men and young women should be trained to be medical missionaries. The Lord will open the way before them as they go forth to work for Him.

The evidences before us of the fulfillment of prophecy declare that the end of all things is at hand. Much important work is to be done out of and away from the places where in the past our work has been largely centered.

When we bring a stream of water into a garden to irrigate it, we do not provide for the watering of one place only, leaving the other parts dry and barren, to cry: "Give us water." And yet this represents the way in which the work has been carried forward in a few places, to the neglect of the great field. Shall the desolate places remain desolate? No. Let the stream flow through every place, carrying with it gladness and fertility.

Never are we to rely upon worldly recognition and rank. Never are we, in the establishment of institutions, to try to compete with worldly institutions in size or splendor. We shall gain the victory, not by erecting massive buildings, in rivalry with our enemies, but by cherishing a Christlike spirit—a spirit of meekness and lowliness. Better far the cross and disappointed hopes,

with eternal life at last, than to live with princes and forfeit heaven.

The Saviour of mankind was born of humble parentage, in a sin-cursed, wicked world. He was brought up in obscurity at Nazareth, a small town in Galilee. He began His work in poverty and without worldly rank. Thus God introduced the gospel, in a way altogether different from the way in which many in our day deem it wise to proclaim the same gospel.

At the very beginning of the gospel dispensation He taught His church to rely, not on worldly rank and splendor, but on the power of faith and obedience. The favor of God is of greater value than gold and silver. The power of His Spirit is of inestimable worth.

Thus saith the Lord: "Buildings will give character to My work only when those who erect them follow My instruction in regard to the establishment of institutions. Had those who have managed and sustained the work in the past always been controlled by pure, unselfish principles, there never would have been the selfish gathering of a large share of My means into one or two places. Institutions would have been established in many localities. The seeds of truth, sown in many more fields, would have sprung up and borne fruit to My glory.

Places that have been neglected are now to receive attention. My people are to do a sharp, quick work. Those who with purity of purpose fully consecrate themselves to Me, body, soul, and spirit, shall work in My way and in My name. Everyone shall stand in his lot, looking to Me, his Guide and Counselor.

I will instruct the ignorant, and anoint with heavenly eye salve the eyes of many who are now in spiritual darkness. I will raise up agents who will carry out My will to prepare a people to stand before Me in the time of the end. In many places that before this ought to have been provided with sanitariums and schools, I will establish My institutions, and these institutions will become educational centers for the training of workers."

The Lord will work upon human minds in unexpected quarters. Some who apparently are enemies of the truth will, in God's providence, invest their means to develop properties and erect buildings. In time these properties will be offered for sale at a price far below their cost. Our people will recognize the hand of Providence in these offers and will secure valuable property for use in educational work. They will plan and manage with humility, self-denial, and self-sacrifice. Thus men of means are unconsciously preparing auxiliaries that will enable the Lord's people to advance His work rapidly.

In various places, properties are to be purchased to be used for sanitarium purposes. Our people should be looking for opportunities to purchase properties away from the cities, on which are buildings already erected and orchards already in bearing. Land is a valuable possession. Connected with our sanitariums there should be lands, small portions of which can be used for the homes of the helpers and others who are receiving a training for medical missionary work.

I have been repeatedly shown that it is not wise to erect mammoth institutions. It is not by the largeness of an institution that the greatest work for souls is to be accomplished. A mammoth sanitarium requires many workers. And where so many are brought together, it is exceedingly difficult to maintain a high standard of spirituality. In a large institution it often happens that responsible places are filled by workers who are not spiritually minded, who do not exercise wisdom in dealing with those who, if wisely treated, would be awakened, convicted, and converted.

Not one quarter of the work has been done in opening the Scriptures to the sick that might have been done, and that would have been done in our sanitariums if the workers had themselves received thorough instruction in religious lines.

Where many workers are gathered together in one place, management of a much higher spiritual tone is required than has often been maintained in our large sanitariums.

We are on the verge of the eternal world. The judgments of God have already begun to fall upon the inhabitants of the land. God sends these judgments to bring men and women to their senses. He has a purpose in everything that He permits to take place in our world, and He desires us to be so spiritually minded that we shall be able to perceive His working in the events so unusual in the past, but now of almost daily occurrence.

We have before us a great work, the closing work of giving God's last warning message to a sinful world. But what have we done to give this message? Look, I beg of you, at the many, many places that have never yet been even entered. Look at our workers treading over and over the same ground, while around them is a neglected world, lying in wickedness and corruption —a world as yet unwarned. To me this is an awful picture. What appalling indifference we manifest to the needs of a perishing world!

22. The Sign of our Order

I have been instructed that our medical institutions are to stand as witnesses for God. They are established to relieve the sick and the afflicted, to awaken a spirit of inquiry, to disseminate light, and to advance reform. These institutions, rightly conducted, will be the means of bringing a knowledge of the reforms essential to prepare a people for the coming of the Lord, before many that otherwise it would be impossible for us to reach.

Many of the patrons of our medical institutions have high ideas in regard to the presence of God abiding in the institution they visit; and they are very susceptible to the spiritual influences that prevail. If all the physicians, nurses, and helpers are walking circumspectly before God, they have more than human power in dealing with these men and women. Every institution whose helpers are consecrated is pervaded by divine power; and the patrons not only obtain relief from bodily infirmities, but find a healing balm for their sin-sick souls.

Let the leaders among our people emphasize the necessity of a strong religious influence being maintained in our medical institutions. The Lord designs that these shall be places where He will be honored in word and in deed, places where His law will be magnified and the truths of the Bible made prominent. Medical missionaries are to do a great work for God. They are to be wide awake and vigilant, having on every piece of the Christian armor and fighting manfully. They are to be loyal to their Leader, obeying His commandments, including the one by which they reveal the sign of their order.

The observance of the Sabbath is the sign between God and His people. Let us not be ashamed to bear the sign that distinguishes us from the world. As I considered this matter in the night season recently, One of authority counseled us to study the instruction given the Israelites in regard to the Sabbath.

"Verily My Sabbaths ye shall keep," the Lord declared to them; "for it is a sign between Me and you throughout your generations; that ye may know that I am the Lord that doth sanctify you. Ye shall keep the Sabbath therefore; for it is holy unto you...Six days may work be done; but in the seventh is the Sabbath of rest, holy to the Lord: whosoever doeth any work in the Sabbath day, he shall surely be put to death. Wherefore the children of Israel shall keep the Sabbath, to observe the Sabbath throughout their generations, for a perpetual covenant. It is a sign between Me and the children of Israel forever." Exodus 31:13-17.

The Sabbath is ever the sign that distinguishes the obedient from the disobedient. With masterly power Satan has worked to make null and void the fourth commandment, that the sign of God may be lost sight of. The Christian world have trodden underfoot the Sabbath of the Lord and observe a sabbath instituted by the enemy. But God has a people who are loyal to Him. His work is to be carried forward in right lines. The people who bear His sign are to establish churches and institutions as memorials to Him. These memorials, however humble in appearance, will constantly bear witness against the false sabbath instituted by Satan, and in favor of the

Sabbath instituted by the Lord in Eden, when the morning stars sang together and all the sons of God shouted for joy.

A spirit of irreverence and carelessness in the observance of the Sabbath is liable to come into our sanitariums. Upon the men of responsibility in the medical missionary work rests the duty of giving instruction to physicians, nurses, and helpers in regard to the sanctity of God's holy day. Especially should every physician endeavor to set a right example. The nature of his duties naturally leads him to feel justified in doing on the Sabbath many things that he should refrain from doing. So far as possible he should so plan his work that he can lay aside his ordinary duties.

Often physicians and nurses are called upon during the Sabbath to minister to the sick, and sometimes it is impossible for them to take time for rest and for attending devotional services. The needs of suffering humanity are never to be neglected. The Saviour, by His example, has shown us that it is right to relieve suffering on the Sabbath. But unnecessary work, such as ordinary treatments and operations that can be postponed, should be deferred. Let the patients understand that physicians and helpers should have one day for rest. Let them understand that the workers fear God and desire to keep holy the day that He has set apart for His followers to observe as a sign between Him and them.

The educators and those being educated in our medical institutions should remember that to keep the Sabbath aright means much to them and to the patrons. In keeping the Sabbath, which God declares shall be kept holy, they give the sign of their order, showing plainly that they are on the Lord's side.

Now and ever we are to stand as a distinct and peculiar people, free from all worldly policy, unembarrassed by confederating with those who have not wisdom to discern God's claims so plainly set forth in His law. All our medical institutions are established as Seventh-day Adventist institutions to represent the various features of gospel medical missionary work and thus to prepare the way for the coming of the Lord. We are to show that we are seeking to work in harmony with heaven. We are to bear witness to all nations, kindreds, and tongues that we are a people who love and fear God, a people who keep holy His memorial of creation, the sign between Him and His obedient children that He sanctifies them. And we are plainly to show our faith in the soon coming of our Lord in the clouds of heaven.

As a people we have been greatly humiliated by the course that some of our brethren in responsible positions have taken in departing from the old landmarks. There are those who, in order to carry out their plans, have by their words denied their faith. This shows how little dependence can be placed on human wisdom and judgment. Now, as never before, we need to see the danger of being led unguardedly away from loyalty to God's commands. We need to realize that God has given us a decided message of warning for the world, even as He gave Noah a message of warning for the antediluvians. Let our people beware of belittling the importance of the Sabbath in order to link up with unbelievers. Let them beware of departing from the principles of our faith, making it appear that it is not wrong to conform to the world. Let them be afraid of heeding the counsel of any man, whatever his position may be, who works counter to that which God has wrought in order to keep His people separate from the world.

The Lord is testing His people to see who will be loyal to the principles of His truth. Our work is to proclaim to the world the first, second, and third angels' messages. In the discharge of our duties we are neither to despise nor to fear our enemies. To bind ourselves up by contracts with those not of our faith is not in the order of God. We are to treat with kindness and courtesy those who refuse to be loyal to God, but we are never, never to unite with them in counsel regarding the vital interests of His work.

Putting our trust in God, we are to move steadily forward, doing His work with unselfishness, in humble dependence upon Him, committing to His providence ourselves and all that concerns our present and future, holding the beginning of our confidence firm unto the end, remembering that we receive the blessings of heaven, not because of our worthiness, but because of Christ's worthiness and our acceptance, through faith in Him, of God's abounding grace.

I pray that my brethren may realize that the third angel's message means much to us and that the observance of the true Sabbath is to be the sign that distinguishes those who serve God from those who serve Him not. Let those who have become sleepy and indifferent awake. We are called to be holy, and we should carefully avoid giving the impression that it is of little consequence whether or not we retain the peculiar features of our faith. Upon us rests the solemn obligation of taking a more decided stand for truth and righteousness than we have taken in the past. The line of demarcation between those who keep the commandments of God and those who do not is to be revealed with unmistakable clearness. We are conscientiously to honor God, diligently using every means of keeping in covenant relation with Him, that we may receive His blessings, the blessings so essential for the people who are to be so severely tried. To give the impression that our faith, our religion, is not a dominating power in our lives is greatly to dishonor God. Thus we turn from His commandments, which are our life, denying that He is our God and that we are His people.

We are to invite everyone—the high and the low, the rich and the poor, all sects and classes—to share the benefits of our medical institutions. We receive into our institutions people of all denominations. But as for ourselves we are strictly denominational; we are sacredly denominated by God and are under His theocracy. But we are not unwisely to press upon anyone the peculiar points of our faith.

In order that men might not forget the true God, Jehovah gave them a memorial of His love and power —the Sabbath. He says: "Verily My Sabbaths ye shall keep: for it is a sign between Me and you." Exodus 31:13.

Concerning Israel, the Lord declared: "The people shall dwell alone, and shall not be reckoned among the nations." Numbers 23:9. To us as well as to ancient Israel these words apply. God's people are to stand alone. The observance of the seventh-day Sabbath is to be a sign between them and God, showing that they are to be a peculiar people, separate from the world in habit and practice. Through them God will work to gather from all nationalities a people for Himself.

— Section 3 —

Health Foods

"Eat ... for strength and not for drunkenness!" Ecclesiastes 10:17

23. Medical Missionary Work in the Cities

San Francisco, California, December 12, 1900.

There is work to be done in California, a work that has been strangely neglected. Let this work be delayed no longer. As doors open for the presentation of truth, let us be ready to enter. Some work has been done in the large city of San Francisco, but as we study the field we see plainly that only a beginning has been made. As soon as possible, well-organized efforts should be put forth in different sections of this city and also in Oakland. The wickedness of San Francisco is not realized. Our work in this city must broaden and deepen. God sees in it many souls to be saved.

In San Francisco a hygienic restaurant has been opened, also a food store and treatment rooms. These are doing a good work, but their influence should be greatly extended. Other restaurants similar to the one on Market Street should be opened in San Francisco and in Oakland. Concerning the effort that is now being made in these lines we can say: Amen and amen. And soon other lines of work that will be a blessing to the people will be established. Medical missionary evangelistic work should be carried forward in a most prudent and thorough manner. The solemn, sacred work of saving souls is to advance in a way that is modest and yet ever elevated.

Where are the working forces? Men and women who are thoroughly converted, men and women of discernment and keen foresight, should act as directors. Good judgment must be exercised in employing persons to do this special work—persons who love God and who walk before Him in all humility, persons who will be effective agencies in God's hand for the accomplishment of the object He has in view—the uplifting and saving of human beings.

Medical missionary evangelists will be able to do excellent pioneer work. The work of the minister should blend fully with that of the medical missionary evangelist. The Christian physician should regard his work as exalted as that of the ministry. He bears a double responsibility, for in him are combined the qualifications of both physician and gospel minister. His is a grand, a sacred, and a very necessary work.

The physician and the minister should realize that they are engaged in the same work. They should labor in perfect harmony. They should counsel together. By their unity they will bear witness that God has sent His only-begotten Son into the world to save all who will believe in Him as their personal Saviour.

Physicians whose professional abilities are above those of the ordinary doctor should engage in the service of God in the large cities. They should seek to reach the higher classes. Something is being done in this line in San Francisco, but much more should be done. Let there be no misconception of the nature and the importance of these enterprises. San Francisco is a large field and an important portion of the Lord's vineyard.

Medical missionaries who labor in evangelistic lines are doing a work of as high an order as are their ministerial fellow workers. The efforts put forth by these workers are not to be limited to the poorer classes. The higher classes have been strangely neglected. In the higher walks of life will be found many who will respond to the truth because it is consistent, because it bears the stamp of the high character of the gospel. Not a few of the men of ability thus won to the cause will enter energetically into the Lord's work.

The Lord calls upon those who are in positions of trust, those to whom He has entrusted His precious gifts, to use their talents of intellect and means in His service. Our workers should present before these men a plain statement of our plan of labor, telling them what we need in order to help the poor and needy and to establish this work on a firm basis. Some of these will be impressed by the Holy Spirit to invest the Lord's means in a way that will advance His cause. They will fulfill His purpose by helping to create centers of influence in the large cities. Interested workers will be led to offer themselves for various lines of missionary effort. Hygienic restaurants will be established. But with what carefulness should this work be done!

Every hygienic restaurant should be a school. The workers connected with it should be constantly studying and experimenting, that they may make improvement in the preparation of healthful foods. In the cities this work of instruction may be carried forward on a much larger scale than in smaller places. But in every place where there is a church, instruction should be given in regard to the preparation of simple, healthful foods for the use of those who wish to live in accordance with the principles of health reform. And the church members should impart to the people of their neighborhood the light they receive on this subject.

The students in our schools should be taught how to cook. Let tact and skill be brought into this branch of education. With all deceivableness of unrighteousness, Satan is working to turn the feet of the youth into paths of temptation that lead to ruin. We must strengthen and help them to withstand the temptations that are to be met on every side regarding the indulgence of appetite. To teach them the science of healthful living is to do missionary work for the Master.

Cooking schools are to be established in many places. This work may begin in a humble way, but as intelligent cooks do their best to enlighten others, the Lord will give them skill and understanding. The word of the Lord is: "Forbid them not, for I will reveal Myself to them as their Instructor." He will work with those who carry out His plans, teaching the people how to bring about reformation in their diet by the preparation of healthful, inexpensive foods. Thus the poor will be encouraged to adopt the principles of health reform; they will be helped to become industrious and self-reliant.

It has been presented to me that men and women of capability were being taught of God how to prepare wholesome, palatable foods in an acceptable manner. Many of these were young, and there were also those of mature age. I have been instructed to encourage the conducting of cooking schools in all places where medical missionary work is being done. Every inducement to lead the people to reform must be held out before them. Let as much light as possible shine upon them. Teach them to make every improvement that they can in the preparation of food, and encourage them to impart to others that which they learn.

Shall we not do all in our power to advance the work in all of our large cities? Thousands upon thousands who live near us need help in various ways. Let the ministers of the gospel remember that the Lord Jesus Christ said to His disciples: "Ye are the light of the world. A city that is set on a hill cannot be hid." "Ye are the salt of the earth: but if the salt have lost his savor, wherewith shall it be salted?" Matthew 5:14, 13.

The Lord Jesus will work miracles for His people. In the sixteenth of Mark we read: "So then after the Lord had spoken unto them, He was received up into heaven, and sat on the right hand of God. And they went forth, and preached everywhere, the Lord working with them, and confirming the word with signs following." Verses 19, 20. Here we are assured that the Lord was qualifying His chosen servants to take up medical missionary work after His ascension.

From the record of the Lord's miracles in providing wine at the wedding feast and in feeding the multitude, we may learn a lesson of the highest importance. The health food business is one of the Lord's own instrumentalities to supply a necessity. The heavenly Provider of all foods will not leave His people in ignorance in regard to the preparation of the best foods for all times and occasions.

24. The Restaurant Work

We must do more than we have done to reach the people of our cities. We are not to erect large buildings in the cities, but over and over again the light has been given me that we should establish in all our cities small plants which shall be centers of influence.

The Lord has a message for our cities, and this message we are to proclaim in our camp meetings and by other public efforts and also through our publications. In addition to this, hygienic restaurants are to be established in the cities, and by them the message of temperance is to be proclaimed. Arrangements should be made to hold meetings in connection with our restaurants. Whenever possible, let a room be provided where the patrons can be invited to lectures on the science of health and Christian temperance, where they can receive instruction on the preparation of wholesome food and on other important subjects. In these meetings there should be prayer and singing and talks, not only on health and temperance topics, but also on other appropriate Bible subjects. As the people are taught how to preserve physical health, many opportunities will be found to sow the seeds of the gospel of the kingdom.

The subjects should be presented in such a way as to impress the people favorably. There should be in the meetings nothing of a theatrical nature. The singing should not be done by a few only. All present should be encouraged to join in the song service. There are those who have a special gift of song, and there are times when a special message is borne by one singing alone or by several uniting in song. But the singing is seldom to be done by a few. The ability to sing is a talent of influence, which God desires all to cultivate and use to His name's glory.

Those who come to our restaurants should be supplied with reading matter. Their attention should be called to our literature on temperance and dietetic reform, and leaflets treating on the lessons of Christ should also be given them. The burden of supplying this reading matter should be shared by all our people. All who come should be given something to read. It may be that many will leave the tract unread, but some among those in whose hands you place it may be searching for light. They will read and study what you give them, and then pass it on to others.

The workers in our restaurants should live in such close connection with God that they will recognize the promptings of His Spirit to talk personally about spiritual things to such and such a one who comes to the restaurant. When self is crucified and Christ is formed within, the hope of glory, we shall reveal, in thought, word, and deed, the reality of our belief in the truth. The Lord will be with us, and through us the Holy Spirit will work to reach those who are out of Christ.

The Lord has instructed me that this is the work to be done by those conducting our restaurants. The pressure and rush of business must not lead to a neglect of the work of soul saving. It is well to minister to the physical wants of our fellow men, but if ways are not found to let the light of the gospel shine forth to those who come day by day for their meals, how is God glorified by our works?

When the restaurant work was started, it was expected that it would be the means of reaching many with the message of present truth. Has it done this?

To the workers in our restaurants the question was asked by One in authority: "To how many have you spoken regarding their salvation? How many have heard from your lips earnest appeals to accept Christ as a personal Saviour? How many have been led by your words to turn from sin to the service of the living God?"

As in our restaurants people are supplied with temporal food, let not the workers forget that they themselves and those whom they serve need to be constantly supplied with the bread of heaven. Let them watch constantly for opportunities to speak of the truth to those who know it not.

- ### Care of the Helpers

The managers of our restaurants are to work for the salvation of the employees. They must not overwork, because by so doing they will place themselves where they have neither strength nor inclination to help the workers spiritually. They are to devote their best powers to instructing their employees in spiritual lines, explaining the Scriptures to them and praying with them and for them. They are to guard the religious interests of the helpers as carefully as parents are to guard the religious interests of their children.

Patiently and tenderly they are to watch over them, doing all in their power to help them in the perfection of Christian characters. Their words are to be like apples of gold in pictures of silver; their actions are to be free from every trace of selfishness and harshness. They are to stand as minutemen, watching for souls as they that must give an account. They are to strive to keep their helpers standing on vantage ground, where their courage will constantly grow stronger and their faith in God constantly increase.

Unless our restaurants are conducted in this way, it will be necessary to warn our people against sending their children to them as workers. Many of those who patronize our restaurants do not bring with them the angels of God; they do not desire the companionship of these holy beings. They bring with them a worldly influence, and to withstand this influence the workers need to be closely connected with God. The managers of our restaurants must do more to save the young people in their employ. They must put forth greater efforts to keep them alive spiritually, so that their young minds will not be swayed by the worldly spirit with which they are constantly brought in contact. The girls and the young women in our restaurants need a shepherd. Every one of them needs to be sheltered by home influences.

There is danger that the youth, entering our institutions as believers, and desiring to help in the cause of God, will become weary and disheartened, losing their zeal and courage, and growing cold and indifferent. We cannot crowd these youth into small, dark rooms and deprive them of the privileges of home life and then expect them to have a wholesome religious experience.

It is important that wise plans be laid for the care of the helpers in all our institutions and especially for those employed in our restaurants. Good helpers should be secured, and every advantage should be provided that will aid them to grow in grace and in the knowledge of Christ. They are not to be left to the mercy of haphazard circumstances, with no regular time for prayer and no time at all for Bible study. When left thus, they become heedless and careless, indifferent to eternal realities.

With every restaurant there should be connected a man and his wife who can act as guardians of the helpers, a man and woman who love the Saviour and the souls for whom He died, and who keep the way of the Lord.

The young women should be under the care of a wise, judicious matron, a woman who is thoroughly converted, who will carefully guard the workers, especially the younger ones.

The workers are to feel that they have a home. They are God's helping hand, and they are to be treated as carefully and tenderly as Christ declared that the little child whom He set in the midst of His disciples was to be treated. "Whoso shall offend one of these little ones which believe in Me," He said, "it were better for him that a millstone were hanged about his neck, and that he were drowned in the depth of the sea." "Take heed that ye despise not one of these little ones; for I say unto you, That in heaven their angels do always behold the face of My Father which is in heaven." Matthew 18:6, 10. The care that should be given to these employees is one of the reasons in favor of having in a large city several small restaurants instead of one large one. But this is not the only reason why it will be best to establish several small restaurants in different parts of our large cities. The smaller restaurants will recommend the principles of health reform just as well as the larger establishment and will be much more easily managed. We are not commissioned to feed the world, but we are instructed to educate the people. In the smaller restaurants there will not be so much work to do, and the helpers will have more time to devote to the study of the word, more time to learn how to do their work well, and more time to answer the inquiries of the patrons who are desirous of learning about the principles of health reform.

If we fulfill the purpose of God in this work, the righteousness of Christ will go before us, and the glory of the Lord will be our rearward. But if there is no ingathering of souls, if the helpers themselves are not spiritually benefited, if they are not glorifying God in word and deed, why should we open and maintain such establishments? If we cannot conduct our restaurants to God's glory, if we cannot exert through them a strong religious influence, it would be better for us to close them up and use the talents of our youth in other lines of work. But our restaurants can be so conducted that they will be the means of saving souls. Let us seek the Lord earnestly for humility of heart, that He may teach us how to walk in the light of His counsel, how to understand His word, how to accept it, and how to put it into practice.

There is danger that our restaurants will be conducted in such a way that our helpers will work very hard day after day and week after week, and yet not be able to point to any good accomplished. This matter needs careful consideration. We have no right to bind our young people up in a work that yields no fruit to the glory of God.

There is danger that the restaurant work, though regarded as a wonderfully successful way of doing good, will be so conducted that it will promote merely the physical well-being of those whom it serves. A work may apparently bear the features of supreme excellence, but it is not good in God's sight unless it is performed with an earnest desire to do His will and fulfill His purpose. If God is not recognized as the author and end of our actions, they are weighed in the balances of the sanctuary and found wanting.

- **Closing our Restaurants on the Sabbath**

The question has been asked: "Should our restaurants be opened on the Sabbath?" My answer is: No, no! The observance of the Sabbath is our witness to God, the mark, or sign, between Him and us that we are His people. Never is this mark to be obliterated.

Were the workers in our restaurants to provide meals on the Sabbath the same as they do through the week for the mass of people who would come, where would be their day of rest? What opportunity would they have to recruit their physical and spiritual strength?

Not long since, special light was given me on this subject. I was shown that efforts would be made to break down our standard of Sabbath observance, that men would plead for the opening of our restaurants on the Sabbath; but that this must never be done.

A scene passed before me. I was in our restaurant in San Francisco. It was Friday. Several of the workers were busily engaged in putting up packages of such foods as could be easily carried by the people to their homes, and a number were waiting to receive these packages. I asked the meaning of this, and the workers told me that some among their patrons were troubled because, on account of the closing of the restaurant, they could not on the Sabbath obtain food of the same kind as that which they used during the week.

Realizing the value of the wholesome foods obtained at the restaurant, they protested against being denied them on the seventh day and pleaded with those in charge of the restaurant to keep it open every day in the week, pointing out what they would suffer if this were not done. "What you see today," said the workers, "is our answer to this demand for the health foods upon the Sabbath. These people take on Friday food that lasts over the Sabbath, and in this way we avoid condemnation for refusing to open the restaurant on the Sabbath."

The line of demarcation between our people and the world must ever be kept unmistakably plain. Our platform is the law of God, in which we are enjoined to observe the Sabbath day; for, as is distinctly stated in the thirty-first chapter of Exodus, the observance of the Sabbath is a sign between God and His people. "Verily My Sabbaths ye shall keep," He declares; "for it is a sign between Me and you throughout your generations; that ye may know that I am the Lord that doth sanctify you. Ye shall keep the Sabbath therefore; for it is holy unto you...It is a sign between Me and the children of Israel forever: for in six days the Lord made heaven and earth, and on the seventh day He rested, and was refreshed."

We are to heed a "Thus saith the Lord," even though by our obedience we cause great inconvenience to those who have no respect for the Sabbath. On one hand we have man's supposed necessities; on the other, God's commands. Which have the greatest weight with us?

In our sanitariums the family of patients, with the physicians, nurses, and helpers, must be fed upon the Sabbath, as any other family, with as little labor as possible. But our restaurants should not be opened on the Sabbath. Let the workers be assured that they will have this day for the worship of God. The closed doors on the Sabbath stamp the restaurant as a memorial for God, a memorial which declares that the seventh day is the Sabbath and that on it no unnecessary work is to be done.

I have been instructed that one of the principal reasons why hygienic restaurants and treatment rooms should be established in the centers of large cities is that by this means the attention of leading men will be called to the third angel's message. Noticing that these restaurants are conducted in a way altogether different from the way in which ordinary restaurants are conducted, men of intelligence will begin to inquire into the reasons for the difference in business methods, and will investigate the principles that lead us to serve superior food. Thus they will be led to a knowledge of the message for this time.

When thinking men find that our restaurants are closed on the Sabbath, they will make inquiries in regard to the principles that lead us to close our doors on Saturday. In answering their questions, we shall have opportunity to acquaint them with the reasons for our faith. We can give them copies of our periodicals and tracts, so that they may be able to understand the difference between "him that serveth God and him that serveth Him not."

Not all our people are as particular as they should be in regard to Sabbath observance. May God help them to reform. It becomes the head of every family to plant his feet firmly on the platform of obedience.

25. Healthful Foods

Cooranbong, N. S. W., March 10, 1900.

During the past night many things have been opened before me. The manufacture and sale of health foods will require careful and prayerful consideration.

There are many minds in many places to whom the Lord will surely give knowledge of how to prepare foods that are healthful and palatable, if He sees that they will use this knowledge righteously. Animals are becoming more and more diseased, and it will not be long until animal food will be discarded by many besides Seventh-day Adventists. Foods that are healthful and life-sustaining are to be prepared, so that men and women will not need to eat meat.

The Lord will teach many in all parts of the world to combine fruits, grains, and vegetables into foods that will sustain life and will not bring disease. Those who have never seen the recipes for making the health foods now on the market will work intelligently, experimenting with the food productions of the earth, and will be given light regarding the use of these productions. The Lord will show them what to do. He who gives skill and understanding to His people in one part of the world will give skill and understanding to His people in other parts of the world.

It is His design that the food treasures of each country shall be so prepared that they can be used in the countries for which they are suited. As God gave manna from heaven to sustain the children of Israel, so He will now give His people in different places skill and wisdom to use the productions of these countries in preparing foods to take the place of meat. These foods should be made in the different countries, for to transport them from one country to another makes them so expensive that the poor cannot afford them. It will never pay to depend upon America for the supply of health foods for other countries. Great difficulty will be found in handling the imported goods without financial loss.

All who handle the health foods are to work unselfishly for the benefit of their fellow men. Unless men allow the Lord to guide their minds, untold difficulties will arise as different ones engage in this work. When the Lord gives one skill and understanding, let that one remember that this wisdom was not given for his benefit only, but that with it he might help others.

No man is to think that he is the possessor of all knowledge regarding the preparation of health foods, or that he has the sole right to use the Lord's treasures of earth and tree in this work. No man is to feel free to use according to his own pleasure the knowledge God has given him on this subject. "Freely ye have received, freely give." Matthew 10:8.

It is our wisdom to prepare simple, inexpensive, healthful foods. Many of our people are poor, and healthful foods are to be provided that can be supplied at prices that the poor can afford to pay. It is the Lord's design that the poorest people in every place shall be supplied with inexpensive, healthful foods. In many places industries for the manufacture of these foods are to be established. That which is a blessing to the work in one place will be a blessing in another place where money is very much harder to obtain.

God is working in behalf of His people. He does not desire them to be without resources. He is bringing them back to the diet originally given to man. Their diet is to consist of the foods made from the materials He has provided. The materials principally used in these foods will be fruits and grains and nuts, but various roots will also be used.

The profits on these foods are to come principally from the world, rather than from the Lord's people. God's people have to sustain His work; they have to enter new fields and establish churches. On them rest the burdens of many missionary enterprises. No unnecessary burdens are to be placed upon them. To His people God is a present help in every time of need.

Great care should be exercised by those who prepare recipes for our health journals. Some of the specially prepared foods now being made can be improved, and our plans regarding their use will have to be modified. Some have used the nut preparations too freely. Many have written to me: "I cannot use the nut foods; what shall I use in the place of meat?" One night I seemed to be standing before a company of people, telling them that nuts are used too freely in their preparation of foods; that the system cannot take care of them when used as in some of the recipes given; and that, if used more sparingly, the results would be more satisfactory.

The Lord desires those living in countries where fresh fruit can be obtained during a large part of the year, to awake to the blessing they have in this fruit. The more we depend upon the fresh fruit just as it is plucked from the tree, the greater will be the blessing.

Some, after adopting a vegetarian diet, return to the use of flesh meat. This is foolish indeed and reveals a lack of knowledge of how to provide proper food in the place of meat.

Cooking schools, conducted by wise instructors, are to be held in America and in other lands. Everything that we can do should be done to show the people the value of the reform diet.

26. Manufacture of Health Foods

St. Helena, California, February 16, 1901.

Last night I seemed to be speaking to our people, telling them that, as Seventh-day Adventists, we must cultivate love, patience, and true courtesy. Jesus will strengthen the leaders of His people if they will learn of Him. God's people must strive to reach the very highest standard of excellence. Especially should those who are medical missionaries manifest in spirit, word, and character that they are following Christ Jesus, the divine Model of medical missionary effort.

I have a most earnest desire that in every place the work shall be carried forward in accordance with His commands. I see trouble ahead as high as mountains for our people in the way in which some things are now being done, and especially in regard to the health food business. As we advance we shall have to meet very difficult problems of human invention, which will bring much perplexity. Scheming tends to dishonesty.

With great skill, and with painstaking effort, Dr. Kellogg and his associates have prepared a special line of health foods. Their chief motive has been to benefit humanity, and God's blessing has rested upon their efforts. If they follow in the counsel of God, if they walk after the example of Christ, they will continue to advance; for God will give skill and understanding to those who seek Him unselfishly. In many respects improvements can be made in the health foods sent out from our factories. The Lord will teach His servants how to make food preparations that are more simple and less expensive. There are many whom He will teach in this line if they will walk in His counsel, and in harmony with their brethren.

• To Our Brethren in All Lands

The Lord has instructed me to say that He has not confined to a few persons all the light there is to be received in regard to the best preparations of health foods. He will give to many minds in different places tact and skill that will enable them to prepare health foods suitable for the countries in which they live.

God is the author of all wisdom, all intelligence, all talent. He will magnify His name by giving to many minds wisdom in the preparation of health foods. And when He does this, the making of these new foods is not to be looked upon as an infringement of the rights of those who are already manufacturing health foods, although in some respects the foods made by the different ones may be similar. God will take ordinary men and will give them skill and understanding in the use of the fruit of the earth. He deals impartially with His workers. Not one is forgotten by Him. He will impress businessmen who are Sabbathkeepers to establish industries that will provide employment for His people. He will teach His servants to prepare less expensive health foods which can be bought by the poor.

In all our plans we should remember that the health food work is the property of God and that it is not to be made a financial speculation for personal gain. It is God's gift to His people, and the profits are to be used for the good of suffering humanity everywhere.

Especially in the Southern States of North America many things will be devised and many facilities provided, that the poor and needy can sustain themselves by the health food industries. Under teachers who are laboring for the salvation of their souls, they will be taught how to cultivate and prepare for food those things that grow most readily in their locality.

• An Evil Work

Some of our brethren have done a work that has wrought great injury to the cause. The knowledge of methods for the manufacture of health foods, which God gave to His people as a means of helping to sustain His cause, these men have disclosed to worldly businessmen, who are using it for personal gain. They have sold the Lord's goods for personal profit. Those who have thus disclosed the secrets in their possession in regard to the preparation of health foods have abused a God-given trust. As they see the result of this betrayal of trust, some will sorely regret that they did not keep their own counsel and wait for the Lord to lead His servants and to work out His own plans. Some who obtain these secrets will scheme to hedge up the way of our sanitarium food work, and by misrepresentation will delude to their injury those who patronize them.

The health food business should not be borrowed or stolen from those who, by its management, are endeavoring to build up and advance the cause. Dr. Kellogg, with the help of others, has, at a large outlay of means, studied out the processes for the preparation of certain special foods, and has provided expensive facilities for their manufacture. This work has taken a great deal of precious time, for many experiments have had to be made. And it is right that those who have thus labored and invested their means should be allowed to reap the fruit of their labor.

As the Lord's steward, Dr. Kellogg should be allowed to control a reasonable income from the special products that he, by the blessing of God, has been enabled to produce, that he may have means wherewith to make appropriations for the advancement of the work of God as occasion may demand. Let no one having learned the secrets of their composition take up the preparation of these special foods and sell them for personal profit. Let no one give the impression that they are working in harmony with those who in the first place prepared these foods for sale, when they are not. No one has a right to engage in the manufacture of these foods in any selfish way. Let us all come near the Lord and with humble hearts seek to glorify Him in every act.

I have a warning for those who have a knowledge of the methods of manufacturing the special health foods produced in our factories. They are not to use their knowledge for selfish purposes or in a way that will misrepresent the cause. Neither are they to make this knowledge public. Let the churches take hold of this and show these brethren that such a course is a betrayal of trust and that it will bring reproach on the cause.

Let not those who have been and are employed in the work of making the health foods first prepared by Dr. Kellogg, or by any other pioneer in this work, disclose to others the secrets of the manufacture of the special foods; for thus they defraud the cause of that which should be used for its advancement. I beseech you, my brethren, to make straight paths for your feet, lest the lame be turned out of the way. Do not place information in the hands of those who, from lack of conscientious regard for health reform, may place impure articles on the market as health foods.

Stand on the side of righteousness in all your transactions; then you will not appear to disadvantage before God or man. Do not enter into any dishonest practices. Those who take up the manufacture of sanitarium health foods for personal profit are taking a liberty to which they have no right. Thus great confusion is caused. Some are now manufacturing and selling goods that profess to be health foods, but that contain unwholesome ingredients. Again, the foods are often of so inferior a quality that much harm is done to the cause by their sale, those who buy them supposing that all health foods are similar.

No one has any right to take advantage of the business arrangements that have been made in regard to sanitarium health foods. Those who handle the foods devised by Dr. Kellogg at large expense should first come to an understanding with him, or others who are working in harmony with him, and learn the best methods of handling these foods. He who enters selfishly into this work, at the same time giving his customers the impression that the profits on the goods he sells are used to aid benevolent enterprises, while in reality they are used for personal interests, is under the displeasure of God. By and by his business will fail, and he will get things into such a tangle that his brethren will have to buy him out to save the cause from disgrace.

The Lord is greatly displeased when His service is dishonored by the selfishness of those engaged in it. He wills that every part of His work shall be in harmony with every other part, joint connecting with joint.

The Lord wants His people to stand far above selfish interests. He wants them to conquer the temptations they meet. He calls for the communion of saints. He desires His workers to stand under His supervision. He will plane and polish the material for His temple, preparing each piece to fit closely to the other, that the building may be perfect and entire, wanting nothing.

Heaven is to begin on this earth. When the Lord's people are filled with meekness and tenderness, they will realize that His banner over them is love, and His fruit will be sweet to their taste. They will make a heaven below in which to prepare for heaven above.

27. Educate the People

St. Helena, California, August 20, 1902.

Wherever the truth is proclaimed, instruction should be given in the preparation of healthful foods. God desires that in every place the people shall be taught to use wisely the products that can be easily obtained. Skillful teachers should show the people how to utilize to the very best advantage the products that they can raise or secure in their section of the country. Thus the poor, as well as those in better circumstances, can learn to live healthfully.

From the beginning of the health reform work, we have found it necessary to educate, educate, educate. God desires us to continue this work of educating the people. We are not to neglect it because of the effect we may fear it will have on the sales of the health foods prepared in our factories. That is not the most important matter. Our work is to show the people how they can obtain and prepare the most wholesome food, how they can co-operate with God in restoring His moral image in themselves.

Our workers should exercise their ingenuity in the preparation of healthful foods. None are to pry into Dr. Kellogg's secrets, but all should understand that the Lord is teaching many minds in many places to make healthful foods. There are many products which, if properly prepared and combined, can be made into foods that will be a blessing to those who cannot afford to purchase the more expensive, specially prepared health foods. He who in the building of the tabernacle gave skill and understanding in all manner of cunning work, will give skill and understanding to His people in the combining of natural food products, thus showing them how to secure a healthful diet.

Knowledge in regard to the preparation of healthful foods is God's property and has been communicated to man in order that he may communicate it to his fellow men. In saying this I do not refer to the special preparations that it has taken Dr. Kellogg and others long study and much expense to perfect. I refer especially to the simple preparations that all can make for themselves, instruction in regard to which should be given freely to those who desire to live healthfully, and especially to the poor.

It is the Lord's design that in every place men and women shall be encouraged to develop their talents by preparing healthful foods from the natural products of their own section of the country. If they look to God, exercising their skill and ingenuity under the guidance of His Spirit, they will learn how to prepare natural products into healthful foods. Thus they will be able to teach the poor how to provide themselves with foods that will take the place of flesh meat. Those thus helped can in turn instruct others. Such a work will yet be done with consecrated zeal and energy. If it had been done before, there would today be many more people in the truth and many more who could give instruction. Let us learn what our duty is, and then do it. We are not to be dependent and helpless, waiting for others to do the work that God has committed to us.

In the use of foods we should exercise good, sound common sense. When we find that a certain food does not agree with us, we need not write letters of inquiry to learn the cause of the disturbance. Change the diet; use less of some foods; try other preparations. Soon we shall know the effect that certain combinations have on us. As intelligent human beings let us individually study the principles and use our experience and judgment in deciding what foods are best for us.

The foods used should be suited to the occupation in which we are engaged and the climate in which we live. Some foods that are suitable in one country will not do in another.

Section 3: Health Foods

There are some who would be benefited more by abstinence from food for a day or two every week than by any amount of treatment or medical advice. To fast one day a week would be of incalculable benefit to them.

I have been instructed that the nut foods are often used unwisely, that too large a proportion of nuts is used, that some nuts are not as wholesome as others. Almonds are preferable to peanuts; but peanuts, in limited quantities, may be used in connection with grains to make nourishing and digestible food.

Olives may be so prepared as to be eaten with good results at every meal. The advantages sought by the use of butter may be obtained by the eating of properly prepared olives. The oil in the olives relieves constipation; and for consumptives, and for those who have inflamed, irritated stomachs, it is better than any drug. As a food it is better than any oil coming secondhand from animals.

It would be well for us to do less cooking and to eat more fruit in its natural state. Let us teach the people to eat freely of the fresh grapes, apples, peaches, pears, berries, and all other kinds of fruit that can be obtained. Let these be prepared for winter use by canning, using glass, as far as possible, instead of tin.

Concerning flesh meat, we should educate the people to let it alone. Its use is contrary to the best development of the physical, mental, and moral powers. And we should bear a clear testimony against the use of tea and coffee. It is also well to discard rich desserts. Milk, eggs, and butter should not be classed with flesh meat. In some cases the use of eggs is beneficial. The time has not come to say that the use of milk and eggs should be wholly discarded. There are poor families whose diet consists largely of bread and milk. They have little fruit and cannot afford to purchase the nut foods. In teaching health reform, as in all other gospel work, we are to meet the people where they are. Until we can teach them how to prepare health reform foods that are palatable, nourishing, and yet inexpensive, we are not at liberty to present the most advanced propositions regarding health reform diet.

Let the diet reform be progressive. Let the people be taught how to prepare food without the use of milk or butter. Tell them that the time will soon come when there will be no safety in using eggs, milk, cream, or butter, because disease in animals is increasing in proportion to the increase of wickedness among men. The time is near when, because of the iniquity of the fallen race, the whole animal creation will groan under the diseases that curse our earth.

God will give His people ability and tact to prepare wholesome food without these things. Let our people discard all unwholesome recipes. Let them learn how to live healthfully, teaching to others what they have learned. Let them impart this knowledge as they would Bible instruction. Let them teach the people to preserve the health and increase the strength by avoiding the large amount of cooking that has filled the world with chronic invalids. By precept and example make it plain that the food which God gave Adam in his sinless state is the best for man's use as he seeks to regain that sinless state.

Those who teach the principles of health reform should be intelligent in regard to disease and its causes, understanding that every action of the human agent should be in perfect harmony with the laws of life. The light God has given on health reform is for our salvation and the salvation of the world. Men and women should be informed in regard to the human habitation, fitted up by our Creator as His dwelling place, and over which He desires us to be faithful stewards. "For ye are the temple of the living God; as God hath said, I will dwell in them, and walk in them; and I will be their God, and they shall be My people." 2 Corinthians 6:16.

Hold up the principles of health reform, and let the Lord lead the honest in heart. Present the principles of temperance in their most attractive form. Circulate the books that give instruction in regard to healthful living.

The people are in sad need of the light shining from the pages of our health books and journals. God desires to use these books and journals as mediums through which flashes of light shall arrest the attention of the people and cause them to heed the warning of the message of the third angel. Our health journals are instrumentalities in the field to do a special work in disseminating the light that the inhabitants of the world must have in this day of God's preparation. They wield an untold influence in the interests of health and temperance and social purity reform, and will accomplish great good in presenting these subjects in a proper manner and in their true light to the people.

The Lord has been sending us line upon line, and if we reject these principles we are not rejecting the messenger who teaches them, but the One who has given us the principles.

Reform, continual reform, must be kept before the people, and by our example we must enforce our teaching. True religion and the laws of health go hand in hand. It is impossible to work for the salvation of men and women without presenting to them the need of breaking away from sinful gratifications, which destroy the health, debase the soul, and prevent divine truth from impressing the mind. Men and women must be taught to take a careful view of every habit and every practice, and at once put away those things that cause an unhealthy condition of the body and thus cast a dark shadow over the mind.

God desires His light bearers ever to keep a high standard before them. By precept and example they must hold their perfect standard high above Satan's false standard, which, if followed, will lead to misery, degradation, disease, and death for both body and soul. Let those who have obtained a knowledge of how to eat and drink and dress so as to preserve health impart this knowledge to others. Let the poor have the gospel of health preached unto them from a practical point of view, that they may know how to care properly for the body, which is the temple of the Holy Spirit.

Section 4

The Publishing Work

"Lift up a standard for the people...Say ye to the daughter of Zion, Behold, thy salvation cometh." Isaiah 62:10, 11

28. God's Purpose in Our Publishing Houses

- **Witnesses for Truth**

"Ye are My witnesses, saith the Lord," "to proclaim liberty to the captives, and the opening of the prison to them that are bound; to proclaim the acceptable year of the Lord, and the day of vengeance of our God."

Our publishing work was established by the direction of God and under His special supervision. It was designed to accomplish a specific purpose. Seventh-day Adventists have been chosen by God as a peculiar people, separate from the world. By the great cleaver of truth He has cut them out from the quarry of the world and brought them into connection with Himself. He has made them His representatives and has called them to be ambassadors for Him in the last work of salvation. The greatest wealth of truth ever entrusted to mortals, the most solemn and fearful warnings ever sent by God to man, have been committed to them to be given to the world; and in the accomplishment of this work our publishing houses are among the most effective agencies.

These institutions are to stand as witnesses for God, teachers of righteousness to the people. From them truth is to go forth as a lamp that burneth. Like a great light in a lighthouse on a dangerous coast, they are constantly to send forth beams of light into the darkness of the world, to warn men of the dangers that threaten them with destruction.

Section 4: The Publishing Work

The publications sent forth from our printing houses are to prepare a people to meet God. Throughout the world they are to do the same work that was done by John the Baptist for the Jewish nation. By startling messages of warning, God's prophet awakened men from worldly dreaming. Through him God called backsliding Israel to repentance. By his presentation of truth he exposed popular delusions. In contrast with the false theories of his time, truth in his teaching stood forth as an eternal certainty. "Repent ye: for the kingdom of heaven is at hand," was John's message. Matthew 3:2. This same message, through the publications from our printing houses, is to be given to the world today.

The prophecy that John's mission fulfilled outlines our work: "Prepare ye the way of the Lord, make His paths straight." Verse 3. As John prepared the way for the first, so we are to prepare the way for the second, advent of the Saviour. Our publishing institutions are to exalt the claims of God's downtrodden law. Standing before the world as reformers, they are to show that the law of God is the foundation of all enduring reform. In clear, distinct lines they are to present the necessity of obedience to all His commandments. Constrained by the love of Christ, they are to co-operate with Him in building up the old waste places, raising up the foundations of many generations. They are to stand as repairers of the breach, restorers of paths to dwell in. Through their testimony the Sabbath of the fourth commandment is to stand as a witness, a constant reminder of God, to attract notice and arouse investigation that shall direct the minds of men to their Creator.

Let it never be forgotten that these institutions are to co-operate with the ministry of the delegates of heaven.

They are among the agencies represented by the angel flying "in the midst of heaven, having the everlasting gospel to preach unto them that dwell on the earth, and to every nation, and kindred, and tongue, and people, saying with a loud voice, Fear God, and give glory to Him; for the hour of His judgment is come." Revelation 14:6, 7.

From them is to go forth the terrible denunciation: "Babylon is fallen, is fallen, that great city, because she made all nations drink of the wine of the wrath of her fornication." Verse 8.

They are represented by the third angel that followed, "saying with a loud voice, If any man worship the beast and his image, and receive his mark in his forehead, or in his hand, the same shall drink of the wine of the wrath of God." Verses 9, 10.

And in a large degree through our publishing houses is to be accomplished the work of that other angel who comes down from heaven with great power and who lightens the earth with his glory.

Solemn is the responsibility that rests upon our houses of publication. Those who conduct these institutions, those who edit the periodicals and prepare the books, standing as they do in the light of God's purpose, and called to give warning to the world, are held by God accountable for the souls of their fellow men. To them, as well as to the ministers of the word, applies the message given by God to His prophet of old: "Son of man, I have set thee a watchman unto the house of Israel; therefore thou shalt hear the word at My mouth, and warn them from Me. When I say unto the wicked, O wicked man, thou shalt surely die; if thou dost not speak to warn the wicked from his way, that wicked man shall die in his iniquity; but his blood will I require at thine hand." Ezekiel 33:7, 8.

Never did this message apply with greater force than it applies today. More and more the world is setting at nought the claims of God. Men have become bold in transgression. The wickedness of the inhabitants of the world has almost filled up the measure of their iniquity. This earth has almost reached the place where God will permit the destroyer to work his will upon it. The substitution of the laws of men for the law of God, the exaltation, by merely human authority, of Sunday in place of the Bible Sabbath, is the last act in the drama. When this substitution becomes universal, God will reveal Himself. He will arise in His majesty to shake terribly the earth. He will come out of His place to punish the inhabitants of the world for their iniquity, and the earth shall disclose her blood and shall no more cover her slain.

The great conflict that Satan created in the heavenly courts is soon, very soon, to be forever decided. Soon all the inhabitants of the earth will have taken sides, either for or against the government of heaven. Now, as never before, Satan is exercising his deceiving power to mislead and to destroy every unguarded soul. We are called upon to arouse the people to prepare for the great issues before them. We must give warning to those who are standing on the very brink of ruin. God's people are to put forth every power in combating Satan's falsehoods and pulling down his strongholds. To every human being in the wide world who will give heed, we are to make plain the principles at stake in the great controversy—principles upon which hangs the eternal destiny of the soul. To the people far and near we are to bring home the question: "Are you following the great apostate in disobedience to God's law, or are you following the Son of God, who declared, 'I have kept My Father's commandments'?"

This is the work before us; for this our publishing institutions were established; it is this work that God expects at their hands.

• A Demonstration of Christian Principles

We are not only to publish the theory of the truth, but to present a practical illustration of it in character and life. Our publishing institutions are to stand before the world as an embodiment of Christian principles. In these institutions, if God's purpose for them is fulfilled, Christ Himself stands at the head of the working forces. Holy angels supervise the work in every department. And all that is done in every line is to bear the impress of heaven, to show forth the excellence of the character of God.

God has ordained that His work shall be presented to the world in distinct, holy lines. He desires His people to show by their lives the advantage of Christianity over worldliness. By His grace every provision has been made for us in all our transaction of business to demonstrate the superiority of heaven's principles over the principles of the world. We are to show that we are working upon a higher plane than that of worldlings. In all things we are to manifest purity of character, to show that the truth received and obeyed makes the receivers sons and daughters of God, children of the heavenly King, and that as such they are honest in their dealings, faithful, true, and upright in the small as well as the great things of life.

In all our work, even in mechanical lines, God desires that the perfection of His character shall appear. The exactness, skill, tact, wisdom, and perfection which He required in the building of the earthly tabernacle, He desires to have brought into everything that shall be done in His service. Every transaction entered into by His servants is to be as pure and as precious in His sight as were the gold and frankincense and myrrh which in sincere, uncorrupted faith the Wise Men from the East brought to the infant Saviour.

Thus in their business life Christ's followers are to be light bearers to the world. God does not ask them to make an effort to shine. He approves of no self-satisfied attempt to display superior goodness. He desires that their souls shall be imbued with the principles of heaven, and then, as they come in contact with the world, they will reveal the light that is in them. Their honesty, uprightness, and steadfast fidelity in every act of life will be a means of illumination.

The kingdom of God comes not with outward show. It comes through the gentleness of the inspiration of His word, through the inward working of His Spirit, the fellowship of the soul with Him who is its life. The greatest manifestation of its power is seen in human nature brought to the perfection of the character of Christ.

An appearance of wealth or position, expensive architecture or furnishings, are not essential to the advancement of the work of God; neither are achievements that win applause from men and administer to vanity. Worldly display, however imposing, is of no value with God.

While it is our duty to seek for perfection in outward things, it should ever be kept in mind that this aim is not to be made supreme. It must be held subordinate to higher interests. Above the seen and transitory, God values the unseen and eternal. The former is of worth only as it expresses the latter. The choicest productions of art possess no beauty that can compare with the beauty of character which is the fruit of the Holy Spirit's working in the soul.

When God gave His Son to the world, He endowed human beings with imperishable riches, riches compared with which the treasured wealth of men since the world began is nothingness. Christ came to the earth and stood before the children of men with the hoarded love of eternity, and this is the treasure that, through our connection with Him, we are to receive, to reveal, and to impart.

Our institutions will give character to the work of God just according to the consecrated devotion of the workers—by revealing the power of the grace of Christ to transform the life. We are to be distinguished from the world because God has placed His seal upon us, because He manifests in us His own character of love. Our Redeemer covers us with His righteousness.

In choosing men and women for His service, God does not ask whether they possess learning or eloquence or worldly wealth. He asks: "Do they walk in such humility that I can teach them My way? Can I put My words into their lips? Will they represent Me?"

God can use every person just in proportion as He can put His Spirit into the soul-temple. The work that He will accept is the work that reflects His image. His followers are to bear, as their credentials to the world, the ineffaceable characteristics of His immortal principles.

- **Missionary Agencies**

Our publishing houses are God's appointed centers, and through them is to be accomplished a work the magnitude of which is yet unrealized. There are lines of effort and influence as yet by them almost untouched in which God is calling for their co-operation.

As the message of truth advances into new fields, it is God's purpose that the work of establishing new centers shall be constantly going forward. Throughout the world His people are to raise memorials of His Sabbath, the sign between Him and them that He is the One who sanctifies them. At various points in missionary lands publishing houses must be established. To give character to the work, to be centers of effort and influence, to attract the attention of the people, to develop the talents and capabilities of the believers, to unify the new churches, and to second the efforts of the workers, giving them facilities for more ready communication with the churches and more rapid dissemination of the message —all these and many other considerations plead for the establishment of publishing centers in missionary fields.

In this work it is the privilege, yea, the duty, of our established institutions to participate. These institutions were founded in self-sacrifice. They have been built up by the self-denying gifts of God's people and the unselfish labor of His servants. God designs that they shall manifest the same spirit of self-sacrifice and do the same work in aiding the establishment of new centers in other fields.

For institutions as for individuals the same law holds true: They are not to become self-centered. As an institution becomes established and gains strength and influence, it is not to be constantly reaching out to secure greater facilities for itself. Of every institution, as of every individual, it is true that we receive to impart. God gives that we may give. Just as soon as an institution has gained a standing place for itself, it should reach out to aid other instrumentalities of God that are in greater need.

This is in accordance with the principles of both the law and the gospel—the principles exemplified in the life of Christ. The greatest evidence of the sincerity of our professed adherence to God's law and our profession of allegiance to our Redeemer is unselfish, self-sacrificing love for our fellow men.

It is the glory of the gospel that it is founded upon the principle of restoring in the fallen race the divine image by a constant manifestation of beneficence. God will honor that principle wherever manifest.

Those who follow Christ's example of self-denial for the truth's sake make a great impression on the world. Their example is convincing and contagious. Men see that there is among God's professed people that faith which works by love and purifies the soul from selfishness. In the lives of those who obey God's commandments, worldlings see convincing evidence that the law of God is a law of love to God and man.

God's work is ever to be a sign of His benevolence, and just as that sign is manifest in the working of our institutions, it will win the confidence of the people and bring in resources for the advancement of His kingdom. The Lord will withdraw His blessing where selfish interests are indulged in any phase of the work; but He will put His people in possession of good throughout the whole world, if they will use it for the uplifting of humanity. The experience of apostolic days will come to us when we wholeheartedly accept God's principle of benevolence—consent in all things to obey the leadings of His Holy Spirit.

- **Training Schools for Workers**

Our institutions should be missionary agencies in the highest sense, and true missionary work always begins with those nearest. In every institution there is missionary work to be done. From the manager to the humblest worker, all should feel a responsibility for the unconverted among their own number. They should put forth earnest effort to bring them to Christ. As the result of

such effort many will be won and will become faithful and true in service to God.

As our publishing houses take upon themselves a burden for missionary fields, they will see the necessity of providing for a broader and more thorough education of workers. They will realize the value of their facilities for this work and will see the need of qualifying the workers, not merely to build up the work within their own borders, but to give efficient help to institutions in new fields.

God designs that our publishing houses shall be successful educating schools, both in business and in spiritual lines. Managers and workers are ever to keep in mind that God requires perfection in all things connected with His service. Let all who enter our institutions to receive instruction understand this. Let opportunity be given for all to acquire the greatest possible efficiency. Let them become acquainted with different lines of work so that, if called to other fields, they will have an all-round training and thus be qualified to bear varied responsibilities.

Apprentices should be so trained that, after the necessary time spent in the institution, they can go forth prepared to take up intelligently the different lines of printing work, giving momentum to the cause of God by the best use of their energies and capable of imparting to others the knowledge they have received.

All the workers should be impressed with the fact that they are not only to be educated in business lines, but to become qualified to bear spiritual responsibilities. Let every worker be impressed with the importance of a personal connection with Christ, a personal experience of His power to save. Let the workers be educated as were the youth in the schools of the prophets.

Let their minds be molded by God through His appointed agencies. All should receive a training in Bible lines, should be rooted and grounded in the principles of truth, that they may keep the way of the Lord to do justice and judgment.

Let every effort be made to arouse and encourage the missionary spirit. Let the workers be impressed with a sense of the high privilege proffered them in this last work of salvation, to be used by God as His helping hand. Let each be taught to work for others, by practical labor for souls just where he is. Let all learn to look to the word of God for instruction in every line of missionary effort. Then, as the word of the Lord is communicated to them, it will supply their minds with suggestions for working the fields in such a way as to bring to God the best returns from all parts of His vineyard.

- **God's Purpose Fulfilled**

Christ desires by the fullness of His power so to strengthen His people that through them the whole world shall be encircled with an atmosphere of grace. When His people shall make a wholehearted surrender of themselves to God, this purpose will be accomplished. The word of the Lord to those connected with His institutions is: "Be ye clean, that bear the vessels of the Lord." Isaiah 52:11. In all our institutions let self-seeking give place to unselfish love and labor for souls nigh and afar off. Then the holy oil will be emptied from the two olive branches into the golden pipes, which will empty themselves into the vessels prepared to receive it. Then the lives of Christ's workers will indeed be an exposition of the truths of His word.

The love and fear of God, the sense of His goodness, His holiness, will circulate through every institution. An atmosphere of love and peace will pervade every department. Every word spoken, every work performed, will have an influence that corresponds to the influence of heaven. Christ will abide in humanity, and humanity will abide in Christ. In all the work will appear, not the character of finite man, but the character of the infinite God. The divine influence imparted by holy angels will impress the minds brought in contact with the workers; from these workers a fragrant influence will go forth.

When called to enter new fields, workers thus trained will go forth as representatives of the Saviour, fitted for usefulness in His service, capable of imparting to others, by precept and example, a knowledge of the truth for this time. The goodly fabric of character wrought out through divine power will receive light and glory from heaven, and will stand before the world as a witness pointing to the throne of the living God.

Then the work will move forward with solidity and redoubled strength. To the workers in every line will be imparted a new efficiency. The publications sent forth as God's messengers will bear the signet of the Eternal. Rays of light from the sanctuary above will attend the precious truths they bear. As never before, they will have power to awaken in souls a conviction of sin, to create a hungering and thirsting after righteousness, to beget a lively solicitude for the things that will never pass away. Men will learn of the reconciliation for iniquity and of the everlasting righteousness which the Messiah has brought in through His sacrifice. Many will be brought to share the glorious liberty of the sons of God, and will stand with God's people to welcome the soon coming, in power and glory, of our Lord and Saviour.

29. Our Denominational Literature

The power and efficiency of our work depend largely on the character of the literature that comes from our presses. Therefore great care should be exercised in the choice and preparation of the matter that is to go to the world. The greatest caution and discrimination are needed. Our energies should be devoted to the publication of literature of the purest quality and the most elevating character. Our periodicals must go forth laden with truth that has a vital, spiritual interest for the people.

God has placed in our hands a banner upon which is inscribed: "Here is the patience of the saints: here are they that keep the commandments of God, and the faith of Jesus." Revelation 14:12. This is a distinct, separating message, a message that is to give no uncertain sound. It is to lead the people away from the broken cisterns that contain no water, to the unfailing Fountain of the water of life.

• The Object of Our Publications

Our publications have a most sacred work to do in making clear, simple, and plain the spiritual basis of our faith. Everywhere the people are taking sides; all are ranging themselves either under the banner of truth and righteousness or under the banner of the apostate powers that are contending for the supremacy. At this time God's message to the world is to be given with such prominence and power that the people will be brought face to face, mind to mind, heart to heart, with truth. They must be brought to see its superiority over the multitudinous errors that are pushing their way into notice, to supplant, if possible, the word of God for this solemn time.

The great object of our publications is to exalt God, to call men's attention to the living truths of His word. God calls upon us to lift up, not our own standard, not the standard of this world, but His standard of truth.

It is only as we do this that His prospering hand can be with us. Consider God's dealings with His people in the past. Notice how, while they carried His banner, He exalted them before their enemies. But when in self-exaltation they departed from their allegiance, when they exalted a power and a principle that were opposed to Him, they were left to bring upon themselves disaster and defeat.

Consider the experience of Daniel. When called to stand before King Nebuchadnezzar, Daniel did not hesitate to acknowledge the source of his wisdom. Did that faithful recognition of God detract from Daniel's influence in the king's court? By no means; it was the secret of his power; it secured for him favor in the eyes of the ruler of Babylon. In God's name Daniel made known to the king the heaven-sent messages of instruction, warning, and rebuke, and he was not repulsed. Let God's workers of today read the firm, bold testimony of Daniel and follow his example.

Never does man show greater folly than when he seeks to secure acceptance and recognition in the world by sacrificing in any degree the allegiance and honor due to God. When we place ourselves where God cannot co-operate with us, our strength will be found weakness. All that is ever done toward restoring the image of God in man is done because God is the efficiency of the worker. It is His power alone that can restore the body, energize the mind, or renew the soul. In our publishing work, as in every other line of effort or Christian living, will be demonstrated the truth of Christ's words: "Without Me ye can do nothing." John 15:5.

God has given to men immortal principles, to which every human power will one day bow. He calls upon us to give to the world, by precept and by example, a demonstration of these principles. To those who honor Him by a faithful adherence to His word, the result will be glorious. It means much to stand by principles that will live through the eternal ages.

- ## Personal Experience Needed by Workers

The editors of our periodicals, the teachers in our schools, the presidents of our conferences, all need to drink of the pure streams of the river of the water of life. All need to understand more fully the words spoken by our Lord to the Samaritan woman: "If thou knewest the gift of God, and who it is that saith to thee, Give Me to drink; thou wouldest have asked of Him, and He would have given thee living water...Whosoever drinketh of the water that I shall give him shall never thirst; but the water that I shall give him shall be in him a well of water springing up into everlasting life." John 4:10-14.

The Lord's work needs to be distinguished from the common affairs of life. He says: "I will turn My hand upon thee, and purely purge away thy dross, and take away all thy tin: and I will restore thy judges as at the first, and thy counselors as at the beginning: afterward thou shalt be called, The city of righteousness, the faithful city. Zion shall be redeemed with judgment, and her converts with righteousness." Isaiah 1:25-27. These words are full of importance. They have a lesson for all who occupy the editorial chair.

The words of Moses possess deep meaning. "Nadab and Abihu, the sons of Aaron, took either of them his censer, and put fire therein, and put incense thereon, and offered strange fire before the Lord, which He commanded them not. And there went out fire from the Lord, and devoured them, and they died before the Lord. Then Moses said unto Aaron, This is it that the Lord spake, saying, I will be sanctified in them that come nigh Me, and before all the people I will be glorified." Leviticus 10:1-3.

This has a lesson for all who are handling the matter that goes forth from our publishing institutions. Sacred things are not to be mingled with the common. The papers that have so wide a circulation should contain more precious instruction than appears in the ordinary publications of the day. "What is the chaff to the wheat?" Jeremiah 23:28. We want pure wheat, thoroughly winnowed.

"The Lord spake thus to me with a strong hand, and instructed me that I should not walk in the way of this people, saying, Say ye not, A confederacy, to all them to whom this people shall say, A confederacy; neither fear ye their fear, nor be afraid. Sanctify the Lord of hosts Himself; and let Him be your fear, and let Him be your dread...Bind up the testimony, seal the law among My disciples...To the law and to the testimony: if they speak not according to this word, it is because there is no light in them." Isaiah 8:11-20.

I call the attention of all our workers to the sixth chapter of Isaiah. Read the experience of God's prophet when he saw "the Lord sitting upon a throne, high and lifted up, and His train filled the temple...Then said I, Woe is me! for I am undone; because I am a man of unclean lips, and I dwell in the midst of a people of unclean lips: for mine eyes have seen the King, the Lord of hosts. Then flew one of the seraphims unto me, having a live coal in his hand, which he had taken with the tongs from off the altar: and he laid it upon my mouth, and said, Lo, this hath touched thy lips; and thine iniquity is taken away, and thy sin purged. Also I heard the voice of the Lord, saying, Whom shall I send, and who will go for us? Then said I, Here am I; send me." Isaiah 6:1-8.

This is the experience needed by those who labor in all our institutions. There is danger that they will fail of maintaining a vital connection with God, of being sanctified through the truth. It is thus that they lose a sense of the power of the truth, lose the ability to discriminate between the sacred and the common.

My brethren in responsible positions, may the Lord not only anoint your eyes that they may see, but pour into your hearts the holy oil that from the two olive branches flows through the golden pipes into the golden bowl which feeds the lamps of the sanctuary. May He "give unto you the Spirit of wisdom and revelation in the knowledge of Him: the eyes of your understanding being enlightened; that ye may know what is the hope of His calling, ... and what is the exceeding greatness of His power to usward who believe." Ephesians 1:17-19.

As faithful householders, give meat in due season to the household of God. Present truth to the people. Work as if in full view of the whole universe of heaven. We have no time to lose—not a moment. Important issues must soon be met, and we need to be hidden in the cleft of the rock, that we may see Jesus and be quickened by His Holy Spirit.

• Matter for Publication

Let our periodicals be devoted to the publication of living, earnest matter. Let every article be full of practical, elevating, ennobling thoughts, thoughts that will give to the reader help and light and strength. Family religion, family holiness, is now to be honored as never before. If ever a people needed to walk before God as did Enoch, Seventh-day Adventists need to do so now, showing their sincerity by pure words, clean words, words full of sympathy, tenderness, and love.

There are times when words of reproof and rebuke are called for. Those who are out of the right way must be aroused to see their peril. A message must be given that shall startle them from the lethargy which enchains their senses. Moral renovation must take place, else souls will perish in their sins. Let the message of truth, like a sharp, two-edged sword, cut its way to the heart. Make appeals that will arouse the careless and bring foolish, wandering minds back to God.

The attention of the people must be arrested. Our message is a savor of life unto life or of death unto death. The destinies of souls are balancing. Multitudes are in the valley of decision. A voice should be heard crying: "If the Lord be God, follow Him: but if Baal, then follow him." 1 Kings 18:21.

At the same time nothing savoring of a harsh, denunciatory spirit is, under any circumstances, to be indulged. Let our periodicals contain no sharp thrusts, no bitter criticisms or cutting sarcasm. Satan has almost succeeded in expelling from the world the truth of God, and he is delighted when its professed advocates show that they are not under the influence of truth which subdues and sanctifies the soul.

Let the writers for our periodicals dwell as little as possible upon the objections or arguments of opponents. In all our work we are to meet falsehood with truth. Put truth against all personal hints, references, or insults. Deal only in the currency of heaven. Make use only of that which bears God's image and superscription. Press in truth, new and convincing, to undermine and cut away error.

God wants us to be always calm and forbearing. Whatever course others may pursue, we are to represent Christ, doing as He would do under similar circumstances. Our Saviour's power lay not in a strong array of sharp words. It was His gentleness, His unselfish, unassuming spirit, that made Him a conqueror of hearts. The secret of our success lies in revealing the same spirit.

- **Unity**

Those who speak to the people through our periodicals should preserve unity among themselves. Nothing that savors of dissension should be found in our publications. Satan is always seeking to cause dissension, for well he knows that by this means he can most effectually counteract the work of God. We should not give place to his devices. Christ's prayer for His disciples was:

"That they all may be one; as Thou, Father, art in Me, and I in Thee, that they also may be one in Us: that the world may believe that Thou hast sent Me." John 17:21. All true laborers for God will work in harmony with this prayer. In their efforts to advance the work all will manifest that oneness of sentiment and practice which reveals that they are God's witnesses, that they love one another. To a world that is broken up by discord and strife, their love and unity will testify to their connection with heaven. It is the convincing evidence of the divine character of their mission.

- **Items of Experience**

The editors of our papers need the co-operation of our laborers in the field and of our people far and near. In our papers should be found communications from the workers in all parts of the world—articles giving living experiences. We do not need romance; but in the daily life there are real experiences that, if told in short articles and in simple words, would be more fascinating than romance, while at the same time they would be an invaluable aid to Christian experience and to practical missionary work. We want truth, solid truth, from consecrated men, women, and youth.

You who love God, whose minds are stored with precious items of experience, and with the living realities of eternal life, kindle the flame of love and light in the hearts of God's people. Help them to deal with the problems of life.

The articles that go to thousands of readers should show purity, elevation, and sanctification of body, soul, and spirit on the part of the writers. The pen should be used, under the control of the Holy Spirit, as a means of sowing seed unto eternal life. Let the space in our papers be occupied with matter of real worth. Crowd in subjects weighty with eternal interests. God calls us into the mount to talk with Him, and when by faith we behold Him who is invisible, our words will be indeed a savor of life unto life.

- ## The Message for this Time

Let all have more to teach, to write, and to publish in regard to those things that are now to be fulfilled and that concern the eternal welfare of souls. Give meat in due season to the old and the young, to saints and to sinners. Let everything that can be said to awaken the church from its slumbers be brought forward without delay. Let no time be lost in dwelling on those things that are not essential, and that have no bearing upon the present necessities of the people. Read the first three verses of the Revelation, and see what work is enjoined upon those who claim to believe the word of God:

"The Revelation of Jesus Christ, which God gave unto Him, to show unto His servants things which must shortly come to pass; and He sent and signified it by His angel unto His servant John: who bare record of the word of God, and of the testimony of Jesus Christ, and of all things that he saw. Blessed is he that readeth, and they that hear the words of this prophecy, and keep those things which are written therein: for the time is at hand." Revelation 1:1-3.

• Publication of Books

Let more time be given to the publication and circulation of books containing present truth. Call attention to books dwelling on practical faith and godliness and to those that treat on the prophetic word. The people are to be educated to read the sure word of prophecy in the light of the living oracles. They need to know that the signs of the times are fulfilling.

It is God alone who can give success either in preparing or in circulating our publications. If in faith we maintain His principles, He will co-operate with us in placing the books in the hands of those whom they will benefit. The Holy Spirit is to be prayed for, trusted in, believed in. Humble, fervent prayer will do more to promote the circulation of our books than will all the expensive ornamentation in the world.

God has great and grand resources for man to lay hold of, and in the most simple manner will be developed the working of the divine agencies. The divine Teacher says: "My Spirit alone is competent to teach and to convict of sin. Externals make only a temporary impression upon the mind. I will enforce truth on the conscience, and men shall be My witnesses, throughout the world asserting My claims on man's time, his money, his intellect. All these I purchased on the cross of Calvary. Use My entrusted talents to proclaim the truth in its simplicity. Let the gospel be sent to all parts of the world, awakening burdened souls to inquire: 'What must I do to be saved?'"

• Prices

Our periodicals have been offered for a limited time on trial at a very low figure; but this has failed of accomplishing the object designed—to secure many permanent subscribers. These efforts are made at considerable expense, often at a loss, and with the best of motives; but if no reduction in price had been made, a greater number of permanent subscribers would have been obtained.

Plans have been made for lowering the prices of our books, without making a corresponding change in the cost of production. This is an error. The work should be kept on a paying basis. Let not the prices of books be lowered by special offers which may be termed inducements or bribes. God does not approve of these methods.

There is a demand for low-priced books, and this demand must be met. But the right plan is to lessen the cost of production.

In new fields, among ignorant or partially civilized peoples, there is great need of small books presenting the truth in simple language and abundantly illustrated. These books must be sold at a low price, and the illustrations must, of course, be inexpensive.

- **Translations**

A far greater effort should be made to extend the circulation of our literature in all parts of the world. The warning must be given in all lands and to all peoples. Our books are to be translated and published in many different languages. We should multiply publications on our faith in English, German, French, Danish-Norwegian, Swedish, Spanish, Italian, Portuguese, and many other tongues; and people of all nationalities should be enlightened and educated, that they, too, may join in the work.

Let our publishing houses do all in their power to diffuse to the world the light of heaven. In every way possible call the attention of the people of every nation and tongue to those things that will direct their minds to the Book of books.

Great care should be exercised in selecting the members of the book committee. The men who are to pass judgment on the books offered for publication should be few and well chosen. Only such as have an experimental knowledge of authorship are qualified to act in this capacity. Only those should be chosen whose hearts are under the control of the Spirit of God. They should be men of prayer, men who do not exalt self, but who love and fear God, and respect their brethren. Only such as, in distrust of self, are led by divine wisdom are competent to fill this important position.

30. Commercial Work

The Lord directed that publishing houses should be established for the promulgation of present truth and for the transaction of the various lines of business which this work embraces. At the same time they should keep in touch with the world, that the truth may be as a light set on a candlestick, to give light to all that are in the house. In God's providence, Daniel and his fellows were connected with the great men of Babylon, that these men might become acquainted with the religion of the Hebrews and know that God rules over all kingdoms.

Daniel in Babylon was placed in a most trying position; but while faithfully performing his duties as a statesman, he steadfastly refused to engage in any work that would militate against God. This course provoked discussion, and thus the Lord brought the faith of Daniel to the attention of the king of Babylon. God had light for Nebuchadnezzar, and through Daniel were presented to the king things foretold in the prophecies concerning Babylon and other kingdoms. By the interpretation of Nebuchadnezzar's dream, Jehovah was exalted as more powerful than earthly rulers. Thus, through the faithfulness of Daniel, God was honored. In like manner the Lord desires that our publishing houses shall witness for Him.

- **Opportunities in Commercial Work**

One of the means by which these institutions are brought in contact with the world is found in commercial work. A door is thus opened for the communication of the light of truth. The workmen may think themselves doing only worldly business, when they are engaged in the very work that will call out questions in regard to the faith and principles they hold. If they are of the right spirit they will be able to speak words in season. If the light of heavenly truth and love is in them, it cannot but shine out. The very manner in which they conduct business will make manifest the working of divine principles. Of our workers, the artisans, as of one of old, it may be said: "I have filled him with the Spirit of God, in wisdom, and in understanding, and in knowledge, and in all manner of workmanship." Exodus 31:3.

- **Not to Stand First**

In no case are the publishing institutions to be devoted chiefly to commercial work. When this work is given the first place, those connected with the publishing houses lose sight of the purpose for which they were established, and their work deteriorates.

There is danger that managers whose spiritual perception is perverted will enter into contracts to publish questionable matter merely for the sake of gain. As the result of taking in this work, the purpose for which the offices of publication were established is lost sight of, and the institutions are regarded very much as any other commercial enterprise would be. In this God is dishonored.

In some of our publishing houses the commercial work necessitates a constant increase of expensive machinery and other facilities. The outlay thus demanded is a heavy tax on the resources of the institution, and with a large amount of work there is required not only an increase of facilities, but a larger force of workers than can be properly disciplined.

It is claimed that the commercial work is a financial benefit to the office. But One of authority has made a correct estimate of the cost of this work at our leading publishing houses. He presented the true balance, showing that the loss exceeds the gain. He showed that this work causes the workers to be driven with a constant rush. In the atmosphere of hurry and bustle and worldliness, true piety and devotion wither.

It is not necessary that the commercial work should be entirely divorced from the publishing houses, for this would close the door against rays of light that should be given to the world. And connection with outside parties need be no more detrimental to the workers than was Daniel's work as a statesman a perversion of his faith and principles. But whenever it is found to interfere with the spirituality of the institution, let the outside work be excluded. Build up the work that represents the truth. Let this always come first, and the commercial work second. Our mission is to give to the world the message of warning and mercy.

- **Prices**

In the effort to secure outside patronage in order to relieve the publishing houses from financial embarrassment, prices have been set so low that the work brings no profit. Those who flatter themselves that there is a gain have not kept strict account of every outgo. Do not cut down prices in order to secure a job. Take only such work as will give a fair profit.

At the same time there should be in our business deal no shadow of selfishness or overreaching. Let no one take advantage of any man's ignorance or necessity by charging exorbitant prices for work done or for goods sold. There will be strong temptation to diverge from the straight path; there will be innumerable arguments in favor of conforming to custom and adopting practices that are really dishonest. Some urge that in dealing with sharpers one must conform to custom; that, should he maintain strict integrity, he could not carry on business and secure a livelihood.

Where is our faith in God? He owns us as His sons and daughters on condition that we come out from the world and be separate, and touch not the unclean thing. To His institutions as well as to individual Christians are addressed the words, "Seek ye first the kingdom of God, and His righteousness," and His promise is sure that all things needed for this life shall be added. Let it be written upon the conscience as with a pen of iron upon the rock, that real success, whether for this life or for the life to come, can be secured only by faithful adherence to the eternal principles of right.

- **Demoralizing Literature**

When our publishing houses do a large amount of commercial work, there is great danger that an objectionable class of literature will be brought in. Upon one occasion when these matters were brought to my attention, my Guide inquired of one occupying a responsible position in a publishing institution: "How much do you receive in payment for this work?" The figures were placed before Him. He said: "This is too small a sum. If you do business in this way, you meet with loss. But even should you receive a much larger sum, this class of literature could be published only at a great loss. The influence on the workers is demoralizing. All the messages that God shall send them, presenting the sacredness of the work, are neutralized by your action in consenting to print such matter."

The world is flooded with books that might better be consumed than circulated. Books upon Indian warfare and similar topics, published and circulated as a money- making scheme, might better never be read. There is satanic fascination in such books. The heartsickening relation of crimes and atrocities has a bewitching power upon many youth, exciting in them the desire to bring themselves into notice by the most wicked deeds. There are many works more strictly historical whose influence is little better. The enormities, the cruelties, the licentious practices, portrayed in these writings have acted as leaven in many minds, leading to the commission of similar acts. Books that delineate the satanic practices of human beings are giving publicity to evil works. The horrible details of crime and misery need not to be lived over, and none who believe the truth for this time should act a part in perpetuating their memory.

Love stories and frivolous, exciting tales constitute another class of books that is a curse to every reader. The author may attach a good moral and all through his work may weave religious sentiments, yet in most cases Satan is but clothed in angel robes the more effectually to deceive and allure. The mind is affected in a great degree by that upon which it feeds. The readers of frivolous, exciting tales become unfitted for the duties lying before them. They live an unreal life and have no desire to search the Scriptures, to feed upon the heavenly manna. The mind is enfeebled and loses its power to contemplate the great problems of duty and destiny.

I have been instructed that the youth are exposed to the greatest peril from improper reading. Satan is constantly leading both the young and those of mature age to be charmed with worthless stories. Could a large share of the books published be consumed, a plague would be stayed that is doing a fearful work in weakening the mind and corrupting the heart. None are so confirmed in right principles as to be secure from temptation. All this trashy reading should be resolutely discarded.

We have no permission from the Lord to engage either in the printing or in the sale of such publications; for they are the means of destroying many souls. I know of what I am writing, for this matter has been opened before me. Let not those who believe the message for this time engage in such work, thinking to make money. The Lord will put a blight upon the means thus obtained; He will scatter more than is gathered.

There is another class of literature, more defiling than the leprosy, more deadly than the plagues of Egypt, against which our publishing houses need unceasingly to guard. In accepting commercial work, let them beware lest matters presenting the very science of Satan be admitted into our institutions. Let not works setting forth the soul-destroying theories of hypnotism, spiritualism, Romanism, or other mysteries of iniquity find a place in our publishing houses.

Let nothing be handled by the employees that will sow one seed of doubt in regard to the authority or purity of the Scriptures. Upon no consideration let infidel sentiments be placed before the youth, whose minds so eagerly grasp anything new. At the very highest figures that might be paid, such work could be published only at infinite loss.

To allow matter of this character to pass through our institutions is to place in the hands of the employees and to present to the world the fruit of the forbidden tree of knowledge. It is to invite Satan to come in, with his bewitching science, to insinuate his principles in the very institutions that are set for the advancement of the sacred work of God. To publish matter of this character would be loading the guns of the enemy and placing them in their hands, to be used against the truth.

Think you that Jesus will stand in the publishing establishment to work through human minds by His ministering angels; think you that He will make the truth coming from the presses a power to warn the world, if Satan is allowed to pervert the minds of the workers right in the institution? Can God's blessing attend the publications coming from the press when from the same press are sent forth satanic heresy and delusion? "Doth a fountain send forth at the same place sweet water and bitter?" James 3:11.

The managers of our institutions need to realize that in accepting their position they become responsible for the mental food given to the workers while in the institution. They are responsible for the character of the matter that goes forth from our presses. They will be called to account for the influence exerted by the introduction of matter that would defile the institution, contaminate the workers, or mislead the world.

If such matter is allowed a place in our institutions, it will be found that the subtle power of Satan's sentiments is not easily cast out. If the tempter is allowed to sow his evil seed, it will germinate and bring forth fruit. There will be a harvest for his reaping in the very institutions established by the funds of God's people for the advancement of His work. It will result in sending forth to the world, in place of Christian workers, a company of educated infidels.

In these matters a responsibility rests not only upon the managers, but upon the employees. I have a word to say to the workers in every publishing house established among us: As you love and fear God, refuse to have anything to do with the knowledge against which God warned Adam. Let typesetters refuse to set a sentence of such matter. Let proofreaders refuse to read, pressmen to print, and binders to bind it. If asked to handle such matter, call for a meeting of the workers in the institution, that there may be an understanding as to what such things mean. Those in charge of the institution may urge that you are not responsible, that the managers must arrange these matters. But you are responsible—responsible for the use of your eyes, your hands, your mind. These are entrusted to you by God to be used for Him, not for the service of Satan.

When matters containing errors that counteract the work of God are printed in our houses of publication, God holds accountable not only those who allow Satan to lay a trap for souls, but those who in any way co-operate in the work of temptation.

My brethren in responsible positions, beware that you do not harness your workers to the car of superstition and heresy. Let not the institutions ordained by God to send out life-giving truth be made an agency for the dissemination of soul-destroying error.

Let our publishing houses, from the least to the greatest, refuse to print a line of such pernicious matter. Let it be understood by all with whom we have to do that from all our institutions literature containing the science of Satan is excluded.

We are brought into connection with the world, not that we may be leavened with the world's falsehood, but that as God's agencies we may leaven the world with His truth.

31. Publishing Houses in Mission Fields

There is much to be done in the way of establishing centers for our work in new fields. Missionary printing offices should be established in many places. In connection with our mission schools there should be facilities for printing and for training workers in this line. Where there are in training persons of various nationalities, speaking different languages, each should learn to print in his own tongue, also to translate into that tongue from the English. And while he is learning English, he should be teaching his language to such English-speaking students as may need to acquire it. Thus some of the foreign-born students might defray the expense of their education, and workers might be prepared to give valuable help in missionary enterprises.

In many cases the publishing work will have to be started on a small scale. It will have to contend with many difficulties and to be carried forward with few facilities. But none should be discouraged because of this. The world's way is to begin its work with pomp and show and boasting, but all will come to nought. God's way is to make the day of small things the beginning of the triumph of truth and righteousness. For this reason none need to be elated by a prosperous beginning or cast down by apparent feebleness. God is to His people riches and fullness and power as they look to the things that are not seen. To follow His direction is to choose the path of safety and true success. "This is the victory that overcometh the world, even our faith." 1 John 5:4.

Human power did not establish the work of God, neither can human power destroy it. To those who carry forward His work in face of difficulty and opposition, God will give the constant guidance and guardianship of His holy angels. His work on earth will never cease. The building of His spiritual temple will be carried forward until it shall stand complete, and the headstone shall be brought forth with shoutings: "Grace, grace unto it."

The Christian is to be a benefit to others. Thus he himself is benefited. "He that watereth shall be watered also himself." Proverbs 11:25. This is a law of the divine administration, a law by which God designs that the streams of beneficence shall be kept, like the waters of the great deep, in constant circulation, perpetually returning to their source. In the fulfilling of this law is the power of Christian missions.

I have been instructed that wherever by self-sacrifice and urgent efforts facilities for the establishment and advancement of the cause have been provided, and the Lord has prospered the work, those in that place should give of their means to help His servants who have been sent to new fields. Wherever the work has been established on a good foundation, the believers should feel themselves under obligation to help those in need, by transferring even at great sacrifice, a portion or all of the means which in former years was invested in behalf of the work in their locality. Thus the Lord designs that His work shall increase. This is the law of restitution in right lines.

32. Relation of Publishing Houses to One Another

Under the figure of the vine and its branches is illustrated the relation of Christ to His followers and the relation of His followers to one another. The branches are all related to one another, yet each has an individuality which is not merged in that of another. All have a common relation to the vine and depend upon it for their life, their growth, and their fruitfulness. They cannot sustain one another. Each for itself must be centered in the vine. And while the branches have a common likeness, they also present diversity. Their oneness consists in their common union with the vine, and through each, though not in just the same way, is manifested the life of the vine.

This figure has a lesson, not only for individual Christians, but for the institutions that are engaged in God's service. In their relation to one another each is to maintain its individuality. Union with one another comes through union with Christ. In Him each institution is united to every other, while at the same time its identity is not merged in that of another.

At times it has been urged that the interests of the cause would be furthered by a consolidation of our publishing houses, bringing them virtually under one management. But this, the Lord has shown, should not be. It is not His plan to centralize power in the hands of a few persons or to bring one institution under the control of another.

Our work has been presented to me as, in its beginning, a small, very small, rivulet. To the prophet Ezekiel was given the representation of waters issuing "from under the threshold of the house eastward, at the south side of the altar." Read Ezekiel 47. Especially mark verse 8: "Then said he unto me, These waters issue out toward the east country, and go down into the desert, and go into the sea: which being brought forth into the sea, the waters shall be healed."

So our work was presented to me as extending to the east and to the west, to the islands of the sea, and to all parts of the world. As the work extends, there will be great interests to be managed. The work is not to be centered in any one place. Human wisdom argues that it is more convenient to build up the interests where the work has already obtained character and influence, but mistakes have been made in this line. It is burden bearing that gives strength and development. And for the workers in different localities to be largely freed from responsibility means to place them where their characters will remain undeveloped and their powers will be repressed and weakened. The work is the Lord's, and it is not His will that the strength and efficiency shall be concentrated in any one place. Let each institution remain independent, working out God's plan under His direction.

• Consolidation

The policy of consolidation, wherever pursued, tends to the exaltation of the human in place of the divine. Those who bear responsibilities in the different institutions look to the central authority for guidance and support. As the sense of personal responsibility is weakened, they lose the highest and most precious of all human experiences, the constant dependence of the soul upon God. Not realizing their need, they fail of maintaining that constant watchfulness and prayer, that constant surrender to God, which alone can enable men to hear and to obey the teaching of His Holy Spirit. Man is placed where God should be. Those who are called to act in this world as heaven's ambassadors are content to seek wisdom from erring, finite men, when they might have the wisdom and strength of the unerring, infinite God.

The Lord does not design that the workers in His institutions shall look to or trust in man. He desires them to be centered in Him.

Never should our publishing houses be so related to one another that one shall have power to dictate as to the management of another. When so great power is placed in the hands of a few persons, Satan will make determined efforts to pervert the judgment, to insinuate wrong principles of action, to bring in a wrong policy; in so doing he can not only pervert one institution, but through this can gain control of others and give a wrong mold to the work in distant parts. Thus the influence for evil becomes widespread. Let each institution stand in its moral independence, carrying on its work in its own field. Let the workers in each feel that they are to do their work as in full view of God, His holy angels, and the unfallen worlds.

Should one institution adopt a wrong policy, let not another institution be corrupted. Let it stand true to the principles that were expressed in its establishment, carrying forward the work in harmony with these principles. Every institution should endeavor to work in harmony with every other just so far as this is consistent with truth and righteousness; but further than this none are to go toward consolidating.

- **Rivalry**

There should be no rivalry between our publishing houses. If this spirit is indulged, it will grow and strengthen, and will crowd out the missionary spirit. It will grieve the Spirit of God and will banish from the institution the ministering angels sent to be co-workers with those who cherish the grace of God.

Never should the managers of our institutions attempt, in the slightest degree, to take advantage of one another. Such efforts are most offensive to God. Sharp dealing, the effort to drive sharp bargains with one another, is a wrong that He will not tolerate. Every effort to exalt one institution at the expense of another is wrong. Every reflection or insinuation that tends to lessen the influence of an institution or its workers is contrary to the will of God. It is the spirit of Satan that prompts such effort. Once given place, it will work like leaven to corrupt the workers and to thwart God's purpose for His institution.

- **Co-operation**

Let every department of our work, every institution connected with our cause, be conducted on considerate, generous lines. Let every branch of the work, while maintaining its own distinctive character, seek to protect, strengthen, and build up every other branch. Men of varied abilities and characteristics are employed for carrying forward the various branches of the work. This has always been the Lord's plan. Each worker must give his own branch special effort; but it is the privilege of each to study and labor for the health and welfare of the whole body of which he is a member.

Not consolidation, not rivalry or criticism, but co-operation, is God's plan for His institutions, that "the whole body fitly joined together and compacted by that which every joint supplieth, according to the effectual working in the measure of every part," may make "increase of the body unto the edifying [building up] of itself in love." Ephesians 4:16.

33. The Canvasser

Through the failure of canvassers to meet their indebtedness, our tract societies have been involved in debt; they cannot meet their obligations to the publishing houses; thus these institutions become embarrassed, and their work is hindered. Some canvassers have thought themselves ill-treated when required to make prompt payment to the publishers for books received, but prompt remittal is the only successful way of conducting business.

The loose manner in which some canvassers have performed their work shows that they have important lessons to learn. Much haphazard work has been presented before me. By laxness in secular affairs some have formed habits of carelessness and slackness, and they have brought this deficiency into the Lord's work.

God calls for decided improvement in the various branches of the work. The business done in connection with His cause should be marked with greater precision and exactness. There must be firm, decided effort to bring about essential reforms.

"Cursed be he that doeth the work of the Lord negligently." Jeremiah 48:10, margin.

"If ye offer the blind for sacrifice, is it not evil? and if ye offer the lame and sick, is it not evil? offer it now unto thy governor; will he be pleased with thee, or accept thy person?" Malachi 1:8. "Cursed be the deceiver, which ... voweth, and sacrificeth unto the Lord a blemished thing: for I am a great King, saith the Lord of hosts, and My name is terrible." Verse 14, R.V.

34. The Author

God desires to bring men into direct relation with Himself. In all His dealings with human beings He recognizes the principle of personal responsibility. He seeks to encourage a sense of personal dependence and to impress the need of personal guidance. His gifts are committed to men as individuals. Every man has been made a steward of sacred trusts; each is to discharge his trust according to the direction of the Giver; and by each an account of his stewardship must be rendered to God.

In all this, God is seeking to bring the human into association with the divine, that through this connection man may become transformed into the divine likeness. Then the principle of love and goodness will be a part of his nature. Satan, seeking to thwart this purpose, constantly works to encourage dependence upon man, to make men the slaves of men. When he thus succeeds in turning minds away from God, he insinuates his own principles of selfishness, hatred, and strife.

In all our dealing with one another, God desires us carefully to guard the principle of personal responsibility to and dependence upon Him. It is a principle that should be especially kept in view by our publishing houses in their dealing with authors.

It has been urged by some that authors have no right to hold the stewardship of their own works; that they should give their works over to the control of the publishing house or of the conference; and that, beyond the expense involved in the production of the manuscript, they should claim no share of the profit; that this should be left with the conference or the publishing house, to be appropriated, as their judgment shall direct, to the various needs of the work. Thus the author's stewardship of his work would be wholly transferred from himself to others.

But not so does God regard the matter. The ability to write a book is, like every other talent, a gift from Him, for the improvement of which the possessor is accountable to God; and he is to invest the returns under His direction. Let it be borne in mind that it is not our own property which is entrusted to us for investment. If it were, we might claim discretionary power; we might shift our responsibility upon others, and leave our stewardship with them. But this cannot be, because the Lord has made us individually His stewards. We are responsible to invest this means ourselves. Our own hearts are to be sanctified; our hands are to have something to impart, as occasion demands, of the income that God entrusts to us.

It would be just as reasonable for the conference or the publishing house to assume control of the income which a brother receives from his houses or lands as to appropriate that which comes from the working of his brain.

Nor is there justice in the claim that, because a worker in the publishing house receives wages for his labor, his powers of body, mind, and soul belong wholly to the institution, and it has a right to all the productions of his pen. Outside the period of labor in the institution, the worker's time is under his own control, to use as he sees fit, so long as this use does not conflict with his duty to the institution. For that which he may produce in these hours, he is responsible to his own conscience and to God.

No greater dishonor can be shown to God than for one man to bring another man's talents under his absolute control. The evil is not obviated by the fact that the profits of the transaction are to be devoted to the cause of God. In such arrangements the man who allows his mind to be ruled by the mind of another is thus separated from God and exposed to temptation. In shifting the responsibility of his stewardship upon other men, and depending on their wisdom, he is placing man where God should be. Those who are seeking to bring about this shifting of responsibility are blinded as to the result of their action, but God has plainly set it before us. He says: "Cursed be the man that trusteth in man, and maketh flesh his arm." Jeremiah 17:5.

Let not authors be urged either to give away or to sell their right to the books they have written. Let them receive a just share of the profits of their work; then let them regard their means as a trust from God, to be administered according to the wisdom that He shall impart.

Those who possess the ability to write books should realize that they possess ability to invest the profits they receive. While it is right for them to place a portion in the treasury, to supply the general needs of the cause, they should feel it their duty to acquaint themselves with the necessities of the work, and with prayer to God for wisdom they should personally dispense their means where the need is greatest. Let them lead out in some line of benevolence. If their minds are under the direction of the Holy Spirit, they will have wisdom to perceive where means are needed, and in relieving this need they will be greatly blessed.

If the Lord's plan had been followed, a different state of things would now exist. So much means would not have been expended in a few localities, leaving so little for investment in the many, many places where the banner of truth has not yet been lifted.

Let our publishing houses beware lest in their dealing with God's workers, wrong principles be allowed to control. If connected with the institution there are men whose hearts are not under the direction of the Holy Spirit, they will be sure to sway the work into wrong lines. Some who profess to be Christians regard the business connected with the Lord's work as something wholly apart from religious service. They say: "Religion is religion, business is business. We are determined to make that which we handle a success, and we will grasp every possible advantage to promote this special line of work." Thus plans contrary to truth and righteousness are introduced with the plea that this or that must be done because it is a good work and for the advancement of the cause of God.

Men who through selfishness have become narrow and shortsighted feel it their privilege to crowd down the very ones whom God is using to diffuse the light He has given them. Through oppressive plans, workers who should stand free in God have been trammeled with restrictions by those who were only their fellow laborers. All this bears the stamp of the human, and not of the divine. It is the devising of men that leads to injustice and oppression. The cause of God is free from every taint of injustice. It seeks to gain no advantage by depriving the members of His family of their individuality or of their rights. The Lord does not sanction arbitrary authority, nor will He serve with the least selfishness or overreaching. To Him all such practices are abhorrent.

He declares: "I hate robbery for burnt offering." "Thou shalt not have in thine house divers measures, a great and a small. But thou shalt have a perfect and just weight, a perfect and just measure shalt thou have...All that do unrighteously, are an abomination unto the Lord thy God." Isaiah 61:8; Deuteronomy 25:14-16.

"He hath showed thee, O man, what is good; and what doth the Lord require of thee, but to do justly, and to love mercy, and to walk humbly with thy God?" Micah 6:8.

One of the very highest applications of these principles is found in the recognition of man's right to himself, to the control of his own mind, to the stewardship of his talents, the right to receive and to impart the fruit of his own labor. Strength and power will be in our institutions only as in all their connection with their fellow men they recognize these principles, —only as in their dealing they give heed to the instruction of the word of God.

Every power lent us by God, whether physical, mental, or spiritual, is to be sacredly cherished to do the work assigned us for our fellow men who are perishing in their ignorance. Every man is to stand at his post of duty untrammeled, each serving the Lord in humility, each responsible for his own work. "Whatsoever ye do, do it heartily, as to the Lord, and not unto men; knowing that of the Lord ye shall receive the reward of the inheritance: for ye serve the Lord Christ." He "will render to every man according to his deeds." Colossians 3:23, 24; Romans 2:6.

Satan's skill is exercised in devising plans and methods without number to accomplish his purposes. He works to restrict religious liberty and to bring into the religious world a species of slavery. Organizations, institutions, unless kept by the power of God, will work under Satan's dictation to bring men under the control of men; and fraud and guile will bear the semblance of zeal for truth and for the advancement of the kingdom of God. Whatever in our practice is not as open as the day belongs to the methods of the prince of evil.

Men fall into error by starting with false premises and then bringing everything to bear to prove the error true. In some cases the first principles have a measure of truth interwoven with the error; but it leads to no just action; and this is why men are misled. They desire to reign and become a power, and, in the effort to justify their principles, they adopt the methods of Satan.

If men resist the warnings the Lord sends them, they become even leaders in evil practices; such men assume to exercise the prerogatives of God—they presume to do that which God Himself will not do in seeking to control the minds of men. Thus they follow in the track of Romanism. They introduce their own methods and plans, and through their misconceptions of God they weaken the faith of others in the truth and bring in false principles that work like leaven to taint and corrupt institutions and churches.

Anything that lowers man's conception of righteousness and equity and impartial judgment, any device or precept that brings God's human agents under the control of human minds, impairs their faith in God, and separates the soul from Him.

God will not vindicate any device whereby man shall in the slightest degree rule or oppress his fellow man. As soon as a man begins to make an iron rule for other men, he dishonors God and imperils his own soul and the souls of his brethren.

35. The Church and the Publishing House

- ## Duty of the Church to the Publishing House

The members of a church within whose borders one of our publishing houses is situated are honored in having among them one of the Lord's special instrumentalities. They should appreciate this honor and should realize that it involves a most sacred responsibility. Their influence and example will go far in helping or hindering the institution in the accomplishment of its mission.

As we approach the last crisis, it is of vital moment that harmony and unity exist among the Lord's instrumentalities. The world is filled with storm and war and variance. Yet under one head—the papal power—the people will unite to oppose God in the person of His witnesses. This union is cemented by the great apostate. While he seeks to unite his agents in warring against the truth he will work to divide and scatter its advocates. Jealousy, evil surmising, evilspeaking, are instigated by him to produce discord and dissension. The members of Christ's church have the power to thwart the purpose of the adversary of souls. At such a time as this let them not be found at variance with one another or with any of the Lord's workers. Amidst the general discord let there be one place where harmony and unity exist because the Bible is made the guide of life. Let the people of God feel that a responsibility rests upon them to build up His instrumentalities.

Brethren and sisters, the Lord will be pleased if you will take hold heartily to sustain the publishing institution with your prayers and your means. Pray every morning and evening that it may receive God's richest blessing. Do not encourage criticism and complaining. Let no murmurs or complaints come from your lips; remember that angels hear these words. All must be led to see that these institutions are of God's appointment. Those who disparage them in order to serve their own interests must render an account to God. He designs that everything connected with His work shall be treated as sacred.

God wants us to do much more praying and much less talking. The threshold of heaven is flooded with the light of His glory, and He will let this light shine into the heart of everyone who will stand in right relation to Him.

Every institution will have to battle with difficulty. Trials are permitted in order to test the hearts of God's people. When adversity befalls one of the Lord's instrumentalities, it will be shown how much real faith we have in God and in His work. At such a time let none view matters in the worst light and give expression to doubt and unbelief. Do not criticize those who carry the burdens of responsibility. Let not the conversation in your homes be poisoned with criticism of the Lord's workers. Parents who indulge this criticizing spirit are not bringing before their children that which will make them wise unto salvation. Their words tend to unsettle the faith and confidence not only of the children, but of those older in years.

All have little enough of respect and reverence for sacred things. Satan will unite most zealously with the criticizer in fostering unbelief, envy, jealousy, and disrespect. Satan is always at work to imbue men with his spirit, to quench the love which should be sacredly cherished between brethren, to discourage confidence, to excite envy, evil surmisings, and the strife of tongues. Let us not be found acting as his co-workers. One heart open to his suggestions may sow many seeds of disaffection. Thus may be wrought a work whose results in the ruin of souls will never be fully manifest until the great day of final judgment.

Christ declares: "Whoso shall cause one of these little ones which believe on Me to stumble, it is profitable for him that a great millstone should be hanged about his neck, and that he should be sunk in the depth of the sea. Woe unto the world because of occasions of stumbling! for it must needs be that the occasions come; but woe to that man through whom the occasion cometh!" Matthew 18:6, 7, R.V.

A great responsibility is here placed upon the members of the church. Let them beware lest through inattention to the souls of those young in the faith, lest through sowing seeds of doubt and unbelief under the instigation of Satan, they be found guilty of the ruin of a soul. "Make straight paths for your feet, lest that which is lame be turned out of the way; but let it rather be healed. Follow peace with all men, and holiness, without which no man shall see the Lord: looking diligently lest any man fail of the grace of God; lest any root of bitterness springing up trouble you, and thereby many be defiled." Hebrews 12:13-15.

The power of Satanic agencies is great, and the Lord calls upon His people strengthen one another, "building up yourselves on your most holy faith."

Instead of co-operating with Satan, let everyone learn what it means to co-operate with God. In these depressing times He has a work to be done that demands the firm courage and faith which will enable us to sustain one another. All need to stand shoulder to shoulder and heart to heart as laborers together with God. What might not be accomplished in and through the grace of God if the members of the church would stand together, to sustain His workers, to help with their prayers and their influence when discouragement presses in on every side! Then is the time to work as faithful stewards.

Instead of criticism and censure, let our brethren and sisters have words of encouragement and confidence to speak in regard to the Lord's instrumentality. God calls upon them to encourage the hearts of those who carry the heavy burdens, for He is working with them. He calls upon His people to recognize the sustaining power in His instrumentality. Honor the Lord by endeavoring to the utmost of your ability to give it the influence that it should have.

As you have opportunity, speak to the workers; speak words that will be a strength and an inspiration. We are altogether too indifferent in regard to one another. Too often we forget that our fellow laborers are in need of strength and cheer. In times of special perplexity and burden, take care to assure them of your interest and sympathy. While you try to help them by your prayers, let them know that you do it. Send along the line God's message to His workers: "Be strong and of a good courage." Joshua 1:6.

The managers of our institutions have a most difficult task to maintain order and to discipline wisely the youth under their care. The members of the church can do much to stay up their hands. When the youth are unwilling to submit to the discipline of the institution, or in any matter of difference with their superiors are determined to have their own way, let not parents blindly sustain and sympathize with their children.

Better, far better might your children suffer, better lie in their graves, than be taught to treat lightly the principles that lie at the very foundation of loyalty to truth, to their fellow beings, and to God.

In cases of difficulty with the ones who have them in charge, go directly to those in authority and learn the truth. Bear in mind that the managers of the various departments understand much better than others can what regulations are essential. Manifest confidence in their judgment and respect for their authority. Teach your children to respect and honor the ones to whom God has shown respect and honor by placing them in positions of trust.

In no way can the members of the church more effectively second the efforts of the managers in our institutions than by giving in their own homes an example of right order and discipline. Let parents in their words and deportment give to their children an example of what they desire them to be. Let purity in speech and true Christian courtesy be constantly maintained. Let there be no encouragement to sin, no evil speaking or evil surmising. Teach the children and youth to respect themselves, to be true to principle, true to God. Teach them to respect and obey the law of God and the rules of the home. Then they will practice these principles in their lives and will carry them out in all their associations with others. They will love their neighbor as themselves; they will create a pure atmosphere and will exert an influence to encourage weak souls in the path that leads to holiness and heaven.

Children who receive such instruction will not be a burden, a cause of anxiety, in our institutions; they will be a support to those who bear responsibility. Under right instruction they will be prepared to fill places of trust, and by precept and example will constantly aid others to do right. They will put a just estimate upon their own endowments and will make the best use of their physical, mental, and spiritual powers. Such souls are fortified against temptation; they are not easily overcome. With the blessing of God such characters are light bearers; their influence tends to educate others for a business life which is a practical Christian life.

The members of the church, filled with Christ's love for souls, and awake to their privileges and opportunities, may exert upon the youth in our institutions an influence for good that is beyond estimate. Their example of faithfulness in the home, in business, and in the church, their manifestation of social kindness and Christian courtesy, combined with a genuine interest for the youth's spiritual well-being, will go far toward shaping the characters of these youths for the service of God and their fellow men, both in this life and in the life to come.

• Duty of the Publishing House to the Church

While the church has a responsibility to the publishing house, so also has the publishing house to the church. Each is to uphold the other. Those in positions of responsibility in the publishing houses should not allow themselves to be so pressed with work that they have no time for maintaining the spiritual interest. When this interest is kept alive in the publishing house, it will exert a powerful influence in the church; and when it is kept alive in the church, it will exert a powerful influence in the publishing house. God's blessing will rest on the work when it is so conducted that souls are won to Christ.

All the workers in the publishing house who profess the name of Christ should be workers in the church. It is essential to their own spiritual life that they improve every means of grace. They will obtain strength, not by standing as spectators, but by becoming workers.

Everyone should be enlisted in some line of regular, systematic labor in connection with the church. All should realize that as Christians this is their duty. By their baptismal vow they stand pledged to do all in their power to build up the church of Christ. Show them that love and loyalty to their Redeemer, loyalty to the standard of true manhood and womanhood, loyalty to the institution with which they are connected, demands this. They cannot be faithful servants of Christ, they cannot be men and women of real integrity, they cannot be acceptable workers in God's institution, while neglecting these duties.

The managers of the institution in its various departments should have a special care that the youth form right habits in these lines. When the meetings of the church are neglected or duties connected with its work are left undone, let the cause be ascertained. By kind, tactful effort endeavor to arouse the careless and to revive a waning interest.

None should allow their own work to excuse neglect of the Lord's sacred service. Much better might they lay aside the work which concerns themselves than neglect their duty to God.

To Brethren Entrusted With Responsibilities in the Publishing Houses:

I urge upon you the importance of attending our annual meetings, not merely the business meetings, but the meetings that will be for your spiritual enlightenment. You do not realize the necessity of having a close connection with heaven. Without this connection not one of you is safe; not one is qualified to do God's work acceptably.

In this work more than in any secular business, success is proportioned to the spirit of consecration and self-sacrifice with which the work is done. Those who bear responsibility as mangers in the work need to place themselves where they can be deeply impressed by the Spirit of God. You should have as much greater anxiety than do others to receive the baptism of the Holy Spirit and a knowledge of God and Christ, as your position of trust is more responsible than that of the common worker.

Natural and acquired endowments are all gifts of God and need to be constantly held under the control of His Spirit, of His divine, sanctifying power. You need to feel most deeply your lack of experience in this work and put forth earnest endeavor to acquire needed knowledge and wisdom, that you may use every faculty of body and mind in such a way as to glorify God.

"A new heart also will I give you." Christ must dwell in your hearts, as the blood is in the body, and circulate there as a vitalizing power. On this subject we cannot be too urgent. While truth must be our panoply, our convictions need to be strengthened by the living sympathies that characterized the life of Christ. If the truth, living truth, is not exemplified in the character, no man can stand. There is only one power that can either make us steadfast or keep us so—the grace of God, in truth. He who confides in aught else is already tottering, ready to fall.

The Lord desires you to rely on Him. Make the most of every opportunity to come to the light. If you remain apart from the holy influences that come from God, how can you discern spiritual things?

God calls upon us to make use of every opportunity for securing a preparation for His work. He expects you to put all your energies into its performance and to keep your hearts alive to its sacredness and its fearful responsibilities. God's eye is upon you. It is not safe for any one of you to bring into His presence a marred sacrifice, a sacrifice that costs neither study nor prayer. Such an offering He cannot accept.

I entreat you to awake and to seek God for yourselves. While Jesus of Nazareth is passing by, cry most earnestly unto Him, "Have mercy on me, O Lord, Thou Son of David," and you will receive sight. Through the grace of God you will receive that which will be more valuable to you than gold or silver or precious stones.

If there is ever one time above another when men need to preserve their connection with God, it is when they are called to bear special responsibility. It is not safe for us, when going into battle, to cast away our weapons. It is then that we need to be equipped with the whole armor of God. Every piece is essential.

Never entertain the thought that you can be Christians and yet withdraw within yourselves. Each one is a part of the great web of humanity, and the nature and quality of your experience will be largely determined by the experiences of those with whom you associate. Jesus says: "Where two or three are gathered together in My name, there am I in the midst." Matthew 18:20. Then let us not forsake the assembling of ourselves together, as the manner of some is; but exhort one another; and so much the more, as we see the day approaching.

Make the social meetings of the church as interesting as possible. Let everyone present feel that he has a duty to perform in the meeting. Cooperate with the heavenly angels, who are trying to make a right impression on every worker.

36. Sacredness of God's Instrumentalities

There are many who recognize no distinction between a common business enterprise, as a workshop, factory, or cornfield, and an institution established especially to advance the interests of the cause of God. But the same distinction exists that in ancient times God placed between the sacred and the common, the holy and the profane. This distinction He desires every worker in our institutions to discern and appreciate. Those who occupy a position in our publishing houses are highly honored. A sacred charge is upon them. They are called to be workers together with God. They should appreciate the opportunity of so close connection with the heavenly instrumentalities and should feel that they are highly privileged in being permitted to give to the Lord's institution their ability, their service, and their unwearying vigilance. They should have a vigorous purpose, a lofty aspiration, a zeal to make the publishing house just what God desires it to be—a light in the world, a faithful witness for Him, a memorial of the Sabbath of the fourth commandment.

"He hath made my mouth like a sharp sword; in the shadow of His hand hath He hid me, and made me a polished shaft; in His quiver hath He hid me; and said unto me, Thou art My servant, O Israel, in whom I will be glorified...It is a light thing that thou shouldest be My servant to raise up the tribes of Jacob, and to restore the preserved of Israel: I will also give thee for a light to the Gentiles, that thou mayest be My salvation unto the end of the earth."

Isaiah 49:2-6. This is the word of the Lord to all who are in any way connected with His appointed institutions. They are favored of God, for they are brought into channels where the light shines. They are in His special service, and they should not esteem this a light thing. Proportionate to their position of sacred trust should be their sense of responsibility and devotion. Cheap, common talk and trifling behavior should not be tolerated. A sense of the sacredness of the place should be encouraged and cultivated.

Over this, His appointed instrumentality, the Lord has a constant, watchful care. The machinery may be run by men who are skillful in its management; but how easy it would be to leave one little screw, one little part of the machinery, out of order, and how disastrous might be the result! Who has prevented casualties? The angels of God have supervision of the work. If the eyes of those who run the machinery could be opened, they would discern the heavenly guardianship. In every room in the publishing house where work is done, there is a witness taking note of the spirit in which it is performed, and marking the fidelity and unselfishness revealed.

If I have failed of presenting the light in which God regards His institutions,—as the centers through which He works in a special manner,—may He portray these things to your minds by His Holy Spirit, that you may understand the difference between common and sacred service.

Both the members of the church and the employees in the publishing house should feel that as workers together with God they have a part to act in guarding His institution. They should be faithful guardians of its interests in every line, seeking to shield it, not only from loss and disaster, but from all that could profane or contaminate. Never through act of theirs should its fair fame be tarnished, even by the breath of careless criticism or censure. God's institutions should be regarded by them as a holy trust, to be guarded as jealously as the ark was guarded by ancient Israel.

When the workers in the publishing house are educated to think of this great center as related to God and under His supervision; when they realize that it is a channel through which light from heaven is to be communicated to the world, they will regard it with great respect and reverence. They will cherish the best thoughts and the noblest feelings, that in their work they may have the co-operation of the heavenly intelligences. As the workers realize that they are in the presence of angels, whose eyes are too pure to behold iniquity, a strong restraint will be placed on thoughts, words, and actions. They will be given moral strength; for the Lord says: "Them that honor Me I will honor." 1 Samuel 2:30. Every worker will have a precious experience and will possess faith and power that will rise superior to circumstances. All will be able to say: "The Lord is in this place."

37. Dependence on God

The first lesson to be taught the workers in our institutions is the lesson of dependence upon God. Before they can attain success in any line, they must, each for himself, accept the truth contained in the words of Christ: "Without Me ye can do nothing."

Righteousness has its root in godliness. No human being is righteous any longer than he has faith in God and maintains a vital connection with Him. As a flower of the field has its root in the soil; as it must receive air, dew, showers, and sunshine, so must we receive from God that which ministers to the life of the soul. It is only through becoming partakers of His nature that we receive power to obey His commandments. No man, high or low, experienced or inexperienced, can steadily maintain before his fellowmen a pure, forceful life unless his life is hid with Christ in God. The greater the activity among men, the closer should be the communion of the heart with God.

The Lord has given instruction that the employees in the publishing houses are to be educated in religious lines. This work is of infinitely more consequence than financial gain. The spiritual health of the workers is to be the first consideration. Every morning take time to begin your work with prayer. Do not think this wasted time; it is time that will live through eternal ages. By this means success and spiritual victory will be brought in. The machinery will respond to the touch of the Master's hand. God's blessing is certainly worth asking for, and the work cannot be done aright unless the beginning is right. The hands of every worker must be strengthened, his heart must be purified, before the Lord can use him effectively.

If we would live a true Christian life, the conscience must be quickened by constant contact with the word of God. All the precious things which at infinite cost God has provided for us will do us no good; they cannot strengthen us and produce spiritual growth unless we appropriate them. We must eat the word of God— make it a part of ourselves.

Section 4: The Publishing Work

Let small companies assemble in the evening, at noon, or in the early morning to study the Bible. Let them have a season of prayer, that they may be strengthened, enlightened, and sanctified by the Holy Spirit. This work Christ wants to have done in the heart of every worker. If you yourselves will open the door to receive it, a great blessing will come to you. Angels of God will be in your assembly. You will feed upon the leaves of the tree of life. What testimonies you may bear of the loving acquaintance made with your fellow workers in these precious seasons when seeking the blessing of God. Let each tell his experience in simple words. This will bring more comfort and joy to the soul than all the pleasant instruments of music that could be brought into the churches. Christ will come into your hearts. It is by this means only that you can maintain your integrity.

Many seem to think the time lost that is devoted to seeking the Lord. But when He comes in to co-operate with human effort, and men and women co-operate with Him, a marked change will be seen in the work and in the results. Every heart that has been visited by the bright beams of the Sun of Righteousness will reveal the working of the Spirit of God in voice, mind, and character. The machinery will move as if oiled and guided by a masterly hand. There will be less friction when the spirit of the worker receives the oil from the two olive branches. The holy influences will be imparted to others in words of kindness, tenderness, love, and encouragement.

By God-fearing evangelists zealous efforts should be made in behalf of the apprentices, that they may be converted. They should be carefully instructed in regard to the truth. They should be encouraged to study the Bible daily and should have an instructor to read and study it with them.

The increasing knowledge of Christ that is gained by a study of the Scriptures, under the teaching of the Holy Spirit, enables the receiver to distinguish between right and wrong in all the affairs of life. If those connected with our publishing houses gain this knowledge and become rooted and grounded in the truth, they will keep the way of the Lord, to do justice and judgment.

Those who are handling sacred things in the publishing institutions and in every branch of God's work are to put forth the highest energies of their mental and moral powers. They are continually to study, not the will of man, but the will of God. His grace must be revealed in all their work.

We are to be "not slothful in business; fervent in spirit; serving the Lord." Romans 12:11. We are to be active in our work; but another element is to mingle with this energy—a living zeal in the service of God. Into our daily work we are to bring devotion, piety, godliness. If you carry on your business without this you make the greatest mistake of your lives; you commit robbery toward God while professing to serve Him.

38. Co-operation

In the establishment of institutions in new fields it is often necessary to place responsibilities upon persons not fully acquainted with the details of the work. These persons labor at great disadvantage, and, unless they and their fellow workers have an unselfish interest in the Lord's institution, there will result a condition of things that will hinder its prosperity.

Many feel that the line of work they are doing belongs solely to them and that no one else should make any suggestions in regard to it. These very ones may be ignorant as to the best methods of conducting the work; yet, if one ventures to offer them advice, they are offended and become more determined to follow their independent judgment. Again, some of the workers are not willing to help or instruct their fellow workmen. Others who are inexperienced do not wish their ignorance to be known. They make mistakes, at a cost of much time and material, because they are too proud to ask counsel.

The cause of the trouble it is not difficult to determine. The workers have been independent threads, when they should have regarded themselves as threads that must be woven together to help form the pattern.

These things grieve the Holy Spirit. God desires us to learn of one another. Unsanctified independence places us where He cannot work with us. With such a state of things Satan is well pleased.

There should be no secretiveness, no anxiety lest others gain a knowledge possessed by the few. Such a spirit gives rise to constant suspicion and restraint. Evil thinking and evil surmising are indulged, and brotherly love dies out of the heart.

Every line of God's work has a connection with every other line. Exclusiveness cannot exist in an institution where God presides; for He is the Lord of all tact, all ingenuity; He is the foundation of all correct methods. It is He who imparts knowledge concerning them, and no man is to look upon this knowledge as exclusively his own.

Each worker should feel an interest in every line of the work, and if God has given him foresight, capability, and knowledge that will help in any line, he should communicate that which he has received.

All the ability that can be connected with the institution, through disinterested effort, should be brought in to make it a success, a living, working agent for God. Consecrated workers who possess talents and influence are the ones whom the publishing houses need.

Every worker will be tested as to whether he is laboring for the advancement of the Lord's institution, or to serve his own interests. Those who have been converted will give daily evidence that they are not seeking to use for their personal benefit the advantages and knowledge they have gained. They realize that divine providence has given them these advantages, that, as the Lord's instrumentalities, they may serve His cause by doing superior work.

None should work from love of praise, or ambition for supremacy. The true worker will do his best because in so doing he can glorify God. He will try to improve all his faculties. He will perform his duties as unto God. His one desire will be that Christ may receive homage and perfect service.

Let the workers enlist all their energies in the effort to gain advantages for the Lord's work. In doing this they themselves will gain strength and efficiency.

39. Self-Control and Fidelity

We have no right to overtax either the mental or the physical powers so that we are easily excited and led to speak words which dishonor God. The Lord desires us to be always calm and forbearing. Whatever others may do, we are to represent Christ, doing as He would do under similar circumstances.

Every day one in a position of trust has decisions to make on which depend results of great importance. He has often to think rapidly, and this can be done successfully only by those who practice strict temperance. The mind strengthens under the correct treatment of the physical and the mental powers. If the strain is not too great, it acquires new vigor with every taxation.

None but a wholehearted Christian can be a true gentleman.

A neglect to conform in every particular to God's requirements means certain failure and loss to the wrongdoer. Failing to keep the way of the Lord, he robs his Maker of the service that is His due. This reacts upon himself; he fails of gaining that grace, that power, that force of character, which it is the privilege of each to receive who surrenders all to God. Living apart from Christ, he is exposed to temptation. He makes mistakes in his work for the Master. Untrue to principle in little things, he fails of doing God's will in things greater. He acts on the principles to which he has accustomed himself.

God cannot connect with those who live to please themselves, to make themselves first. Those who do this will in the end be last of all. The sin that is most nearly hopeless and incurable is pride of opinion, self-conceit. This stands in the way of all growth. When a man has defects of character, yet fails of realizing this; when he is so imbued with self-sufficiency that he cannot see his fault, how can he be cleansed? "They that be whole need not a physician, but they that are sick." Matthew 9:12. How can one improve when he thinks his ways perfect?

When one who is supposed to be led and taught by God turns out of the way, because of self-confidence, many follow his example. His false step may result in misleading thousands.

Consider the parable of the fig tree:

"A certain man had a fig tree planted in his vineyard; and he came and sought fruit thereon, and found none. Then said he unto the dresser of his vineyard, Behold, these three years I come seeking fruit on this fig tree, and find none: cut it down; why cumbereth it the ground? And he answering said unto him, Lord, let it alone this year also, till I shall dig about it, and dung it: and if it bear fruit, well: and if not, then after that thou shalt cut it down." Luke 13:6-9.

"Then after that." In these words there is a lesson for all who are connected with the work of God. A period of probation was granted to the tree that bore no fruit. And in like manner God bears long with His people. But of those who have had great advantages, and who are standing in positions of high and sacred trust, and yet bear no fruit, He says: "Cut it down; why cumbereth it the ground?"

Let those connected with the Lord's special instrumentalities remember that He will call for fruit from His vineyard. Proportionate to the blessings bestowed will be the returns required. Heavenly angels have visited and ministered in every place where God's institutions are established. Unfaithfulness in these institutions is a greater sin than it would be elsewhere, for it has a greater influence than it would elsewhere have. Unfaithfulness, injustice, dishonesty, conniving at wrong, obstruct the light which God designs shall shine forth from His instrumentalities.

The world is watching, ready to criticize with keenness and severity your words, your deportment, and your business transactions. Everyone who acts a part in connection with the work of God is watched, and is weighed by the scales of human discernment. Impressions, favorable or unfavorable to Bible religion, are constantly made on the minds of all with whom you have to do.

The world watches to see what fruit is borne by professed Christians. It has a right to look for self-denial and self-sacrifice from those who claim to believe advanced truth.

There have been, and will continue to be, among our workers those who do not feel their need of Jesus at every step. They think they cannot take time to pray and attend religious meetings. They have so much to do that they cannot find time to keep their souls in the love of God. When this is the case, Satan is on the ground to create vain imaginations.

Workers who are not diligent and faithful do incalculable harm. They set an example for others. In every institution there are some who are rendering wholehearted, cheerful service; but will not the leaven affect them? Shall the institution be left without some sincere examples of Christian fidelity? When men claiming to be representatives of Christ reveal that they are unconverted, their characters gross, selfish, impure, they should be separated from the work.

The workers need to realize the sacredness of the trust with which the Lord has honored them. Impulsive motives, fitful actions, must be put aside. Those who cannot distinguish between the sacred and the common are not safe stewards of high responsibilities. When tempted, they will betray their trust. Those who do not appreciate the privileges and opportunities of a connection with the work of God will not stand when the enemy presents his specious temptations. They are easily misled by selfish, ambitious projects. If, after the light has been presented to them, they still fail of distinguishing right from wrong, the sooner they are disconnected from the institution, the purer and more elevated will be the character of the work.

No one should be retained in any one of the Lord's institutions who in a crisis fails of realizing that His instrumentalities are sacred. If workers have no relish for the truth; if their connection with the institution makes them no better, brings to them no love for the truth, then, after sufficient trial, separate them from the work; for their irreligion and unbelief influence others. Through them evil angels work to mislead those who are brought in as apprentices. You should obtain for apprentices those who are promising youth, those who love God. But if you place them in connection with others who have no love for God, they are in constant danger from the irreligious influence. The halfhearted and worldly, those who are given to gossip, who dwell on the faults of others, while neglecting their own, should be separated from the work.

40. Danger from Improper Reading

As I see the danger that threatens the youth from improper reading I cannot forbear to present still further the warnings given me in regard to this great evil.

The harm that results to the workers from handling matter of an objectionable character is too little realized. Their attention is arrested and their interest aroused by the subject matter with which they are dealing. Sentences are imprinted in the memory. Thoughts are suggested. Almost unconsciously the reader is influenced by the spirit of the writer, and mind and character receive an impress for evil. There are some who have little faith and little power of self-control, and it is difficult for them to banish the thoughts suggested by such literature.

Before accepting the present truth, some had formed the habit of novel reading. Upon uniting with the church, they made an effort to overcome this habit. To place before this class reading similar to that which they have discarded is like offering intoxicants to the inebriate. Yielding to the temptation continually before them, they soon lose their relish for solid reading. They have no interest in Bible study. Their moral power becomes enfeebled. Sin appears less and less repulsive. There is manifest an increasing unfaithfulness, a growing distaste for life's practical duties. As the mind becomes perverted, it is ready to grasp any reading of a stimulating character. Thus the way is open for Satan to bring the soul fully under his domination.

Works that do not so decidedly mislead and corrupt are yet to be shunned if they impart a disrelish for the study of the Bible. This word is the true manna. Let all repress the desire for reading matter that is not food for the mind. You cannot possibly do the work of God with clear perception while the mind is occupied with this class of reading. Those who are in God's service should spend neither time nor money for light reading. What is the chaff to the wheat?

There is no time for engaging in trifling amusements, the gratification of selfish propensities. It is time that you were occupied with serious thoughts. And you cannot dwell upon the self-denying, self-sacrificing life of the world's Redeemer and find pleasure in joking and jesting and whiling away your time in foolishness. You are greatly in need of a practical experience in the Christian life. You need to train the mind for the work of God. The religious experience is to a great degree determined by the character of the books you read in your leisure moments.

If you love the Scriptures, and search them whenever there is opportunity, that you may come into possession of their rich treasures, then you may be assured that Jesus is drawing you to Himself.

"Beware lest any man spoil you through philosophy and vain deceit, after the tradition of men, after the rudiments of the world, and not after Christ. For in Him dwelleth all the fullness of the Godhead bodily. And ye are complete in Him." Colossians 2:8-10.

We cannot be complete in Christ and yet be ready to grasp those things that come from the so-called great men of the earth, and place their wisdom before the wisdom of the greatest Teacher the world has ever known. To seek knowledge from such sources is represented in the word as seeking to drink from broken cisterns that can hold no water.

Let the truth of God be the subject for contemplation and meditation. Read the Bible, and regard it as the voice of God speaking directly to you. Then will you find inspiration and that wisdom which is divine.

The gathering together of many books for study too often interposes between God and man a mass of knowledge that weakens the mind and makes it incapable of assimilating that which it has already received. The mind becomes dyspeptic. Wisdom is needed, that man may choose aright between these many authors and the word of life, that he may eat the flesh and drink the blood of the Son of God.

My brethren, discard the streams of the lowlands and come to the pure waters of Lebanon. Never can you walk in the light of God while you crowd the mind with a mass of matter which it cannot digest. It is time we resolved to have heaven's help and allow the mind to be impressed with the word of God. Let us close the door to so much reading. Let us pray more and eat the words of life. Unless there is a deeper work of grace in mind and heart, we can never see the face of God.

41. Avoid Debt

God does not want His work to be continually embarrassed with debt. When it seems desirable to add to the buildings or other facilities of an institution, beware of going beyond your means. Better to defer the improvements until Providence shall open the way for them to be made without contracting heavy debts and having to pay interest.

The publishing houses have been made places of deposit by our people and have thus been enabled to furnish means to support branches of the work in different fields and have aided in carrying other enterprises. This is well. None too much has been done in these lines. The Lord sees it all. But, from the light He has given me, every effort should be made to stand free from debt.

The publishing work was founded in self-denial and should be conducted upon strictly economical principles. The question of finance can be managed if, when there is a pressure for means, the workers will consent to a reduction in wages. This was the principle the Lord revealed to me to be brought into our institutions. When money is scarce, we should be willing to restrict our wants.

Let the proper estimate be placed upon the publications, and then let all in our publishing houses study to economize in every possible way even though considerable inconvenience is thus caused. Watch the little outgoes. Stop every leak. It is the little losses that tell heavily in the end. Gather up the fragments; let nothing be lost. Waste not the minutes in talking; wasted minutes mar the hours. Persevering diligence working in faith, will always be crowned with success.

Some think it beneath their dignity to look after small things. They think it the evidence of a narrow mind and a niggardly spirit. But small leaks have sunk many a ship. Nothing that would serve the purpose of any should be allowed to waste. A lack of economy will surely bring debt upon our institutions. Although much money may be received, it will be lost in the little wastes of every branch of the work. Economy is not stinginess.

Every man or woman employed in the publishing house should be a faithful sentinel, watching that nothing be wasted. All should guard against supposed wants that require an expenditure of means. Some men live better on four hundred dollars a year than others do on eight hundred. Just so it is with our institutions; some persons can manage them with far less capital than others can. God desires all the workers to practice economy, and especially to be faithful accountants.

Every worker in our institutions should receive fair compensation. If the workers receive suitable wages, they have the gratification of making donations to the cause. It is not right that some should receive a large amount and others, who are doing essential and faithful work, very little.

Yet there are cases where a difference must be made. There are men connected with the publishing houses who carry heavy responsibilities and whose work is of great value to the institution. In many other positions they would have far less care and, financially, much greater profit. All can see the injustice of paying such men no higher wages than are paid to mere mechanical workers.

If a woman is appointed by the Lord to do a certain work, her work should be estimated according to its value. Some may think it good policy to allow persons to devote their time and labor to the work without compensation. But God does not sanction such arrangements.

When self-denial is required because of a dearth of means, the burden is not to rest wholly upon a few persons. Let all unite in the sacrifice.

The Lord desires those entrusted with His goods to show kindness and liberality, not niggardliness. Let them not, in their deal, try to exact every cent possible. God looks with contempt on such methods.

Workers should receive compensation according to the hours they give in honest labor. The one who gives full time is to receive according to the time. If one enlists mind, soul, and strength in bearing the burdens, he is to be paid accordingly.

No man should be granted an exorbitant salary, even though he may possess special capabilities and qualifications. The work done for God and His cause is not to be placed on a mercenary basis. The workers in the publishing house have no more taxing labor, no greater expense, no more weighty responsibilities, than have the workers in other lines. Their labor is no more wearing than is that of the faithful minister. On the contrary, ministers, as a rule, make greater sacrifices than are made by the laborers in our institutions. Ministers go where they are sent; they are minutemen, ready to move at any moment, to meet any emergency. They are necessarily separated, to a great degree, from their families. The workers in the publishing houses, as a rule, have a permanent home and can live with their families. This is a great saving of expense and should be considered in its bearing on the relative compensation of laborers in the ministry and in the publishing houses.

Those who labor wholeheartedly in the Lord's vineyard, working to the utmost of their ability, are not the ones to set the highest estimate on their own services. Instead of swelling with pride and self-importance, and measuring with exactness every hour's work, they compare their efforts with the Saviour's work and account themselves unprofitable servants.

Brethren, do not study how little you may do in order to reach the very lowest standard; but arouse to grasp the fullness of Christ, that you may do much for Him.

The Lord wants men who see the work in its greatness and who understand the principles that have been interwoven with it from its rise. He will not have a worldly order of things come in to fashion the work in altogether different lines from those He has marked out for His people. The work must bear the character of its Originator.

In the sacrifice of Christ for fallen men, mercy and truth have met together, righteousness and peace have kissed each other. When these attributes are separated from the most wonderful and apparently successful work, there is nothing to it.

God has not singled out a few men for His favor and left others uncared for. He will not lift up one and cast down and oppress another. All who are truly converted will manifest the same spirit. They will treat their fellow men as they would treat Christ. No one will ignore the rights of another.

God's servants should have so great respect for the sacred work they are handling that they will not bring into it one vestige of selfishness.

42. Faith and Courage

The Lord directed Moses to recount to the children of Israel His dealings with them in their deliverance from Egypt and their wonderful preservation in the wilderness. He was to call to mind their unbelief and murmuring when brought into trial, and the Lord's great mercy and loving-kindness, which had never forsaken them. This would stimulate their faith and strengthen their courage. While they would be led to realize their own sin and weakness, they would realize also that God was their righteousness and strength.

It is just as essential that the people of God in this day should bear in mind how and when they have been tested, and where their faith has failed; where they have imperiled His cause by their unbelief and also by their self-confidence. God's mercy, His sustaining providence, His never-to-be-forgotten deliverances, are to be recounted, step by step. As God's people thus review the past, they should see that the Lord is ever repeating His dealings. They should understand the warnings given, and should beware not to repeat their mistakes. Renouncing all self-dependence, they are to trust in Him to save them from again dishonoring His name. In every victory that Satan gains, souls are imperiled. Some become the subjects of his temptations, never to recover themselves. Then let those who have made mistakes walk carefully, at every step praying: "Hold up my goings in Thy paths, that my footsteps slip not." Psalm 17:5.

God sends trials to prove who will stand faithful under temptation. He brings all into trying positions to see if they will trust in a power out of and above themselves. Everyone has undiscovered traits of character that must come to light through trial. God allows those who are self-sufficient to be sorely tempted, that they may understand their helplessness.

When trials come to us; when we can see before us, not an increase of prosperity, but a pressure necessitating sacrifice on the part of all, how shall we receive Satan's insinuation that we are to have a very hard time? If we listen to his suggestions, unbelief in God will spring up. At such a time we should remember that God has always had a care for His institutions. We should look at the work He has done, the reforms He has wrought. We should gather up the evidences of Heaven's blessings, the tokens for good, saying: Lord, we believe in Thee, in Thy servants, and in Thy work. We will trust in Thee. The publishing house is Thine own instrumentality, and we will not fail or be discouraged. Thou hast honored us by connecting us with Thy center. We will keep the way of the Lord, to do justice and judgment. We will act our part by being true to the work of God.

If we lack faith where we are when difficulties present themselves we would lack faith in any place.

Our greatest need is faith in God. When we look on the dark side we lose our hold on the Lord God of Israel. As the heart is opened to fears and conjectures, the path of progress is hedged up by unbelief. Let us never feel that God has forsaken His work.

There must be less talking unbelief, less imagining that this one and that one is hedging up the way. Go forward in faith; trust the Lord to prepare the way for His work. Then you will find rest in Christ. As you cultivate faith and place yourselves in right relation to God and by earnest prayer brace yourselves to do your duty you will be worked by the Holy Spirit. The many problems that are now mysterious you may solve for yourselves by continued trust in God. You need not be painfully indefinite because you are living under the guidance of the Holy Spirit. You may walk and work in confidence.

We must have less faith in what we can do and more faith in what the Lord can do for us, if we will have clean hands and pure hearts. You are not engaged in your own work; you are doing the work of God.

More love is needed, more frankness, less suspicion, less evil thinking. We need to be less ready to blame and accuse. It is this that is so offensive to God. The heart needs to be softened and subdued by love. The strengthless condition of our people results from the fact that their hearts are not right with God. Alienation from Him is the cause of the burdened condition of our institutions.

Do not worry. By looking at appearances, and complaining when difficulty and pressure come, you reveal a sickly, enfeebled faith. By your words and your works show that your faith is invincible. The Lord is rich in resources. He owns the world. Look to Him who has light, and power, and efficiency. He will bless everyone who is seeking to communicate light and love.

The Lord desires all to understand that their prosperity is hid with Him in Christ; that it is dependent on their humility and meekness, their wholehearted obedience and devotion. When they shall learn the lesson of the great Teacher, to die to self, to put no confidence in man, nor to make flesh their arm, then, as they call upon Him, the Lord will be to them a present help in every time of need. He will guide them in judgment. He will be at their right hand to give them counsel. He will say to them: "This is the way, walk ye in it."

Let the brethren in responsible positions talk faith and courage to the workers. Cast your net on the right side of the ship, the side of faith. As long as probation continues, show what can be done by a consecrated, living church.

We do not understand as we should the great conflict going on between invisible agencies, the controversy between loyal and disloyal angels. Over every man, good and evil angels strive. This is no make-believe conflict. It is not mimic battles in which we are engaged. We have to meet most powerful adversaries, and it rests with us to determine which shall win. We are to find our strength where the early disciples found theirs. "These all continued with one accord in prayer and supplication." "And suddenly there came a sound from heaven as of a rushing mighty wind, and it filled all the house where they were sitting." "And they were all filled with the Holy Ghost." Acts 1:14; 2:2, 4.

There is no excuse for defection or despondency, because all the promises of heavenly grace are for those who hunger and thirst after righteousness. The intensity of desire represented by hungering and thirsting is a pledge that the coveted supply will be given.

Just as soon as we realize our inability to do God's work and submit to be guided by His wisdom, the Lord can work with us. If we will empty the soul of self, He will supply all our necessities.

Place your mind and will where the Holy Spirit can reach for them, for He will not work through another man's mind and conscience to reach yours. With earnest prayer for wisdom, make the work of God your study. Take counsel of sanctified reason, surrendered wholly to God.

Look unto Jesus in simplicity and faith. Gaze upon Jesus until the spirit faints under the excess of light. We do not half pray. We do not half believe. "Ask, and it shall be given you." Luke 11:9. Pray, believe, strengthen one another. Pray as you never before prayed that the Lord will lay His hand upon you, that you may be able to comprehend the length and breadth and depth and height, and to know the love of Christ, which passeth knowledge, that you may be filled with all the fullness of God.

The fact that we are called upon to endure trial proves that the Lord Jesus sees in us something very precious, which He desires to develop. If He saw in us nothing whereby He might glorify His name He would not spend time in refining us. We do not take special pains in pruning brambles. Christ does not cast worthless stones into His furnace. It is valuable ore that He tests.

The blacksmith puts the iron and steel into the fire that he may know what manner of metal they are. The Lord allows His chosen ones to be placed in the furnace of affliction in order that He may see what temper they are of and whether He can mold and fashion them for His work.

43. Self-Sacrifice

The laws of Christ's kingdom are so simple, and yet so complete, that man-made additions will create confusion. And the more simple our plans for work in God's service, the more we shall accomplish. To adopt worldly policy in the work of God is to invite disaster and defeat. Simplicity and humility must characterize every effective effort for the advancement of His kingdom.

In order that the gospel may go to all nations, kindreds, tongues, and peoples, self-sacrifice must be maintained. Those in positions of trust are in all things to act as faithful stewards, conscientiously guarding the funds that have been created by the people. There must be care to prevent all needless outlay. In erecting buildings and providing facilities for the work, we should be careful not to make our preparation so elaborate as to consume money unnecessarily; for this means in every case inability to provide for the extension of the work in other fields, especially in foreign lands. Means are not to be drawn from the treasury to establish institutions in the home field, at a risk of crippling the advancement of truth in regions beyond.

God's money is to be used not only in your immediate vicinity, but in distant countries, in the islands of the sea. If His people do not engage in this work, God will surely remove the power that is not rightly appropriated.

Many among believers have scarcely food enough to eat, yet in their deep poverty they bring their tithes and offerings to the Lord's treasury. Many who know what it is to sustain the cause of God in hard and trying circumstances have invested means in the publishing houses.

They have willingly endured hardship and privation, and have watched and prayed for the success of the work. Their gifts and sacrifices express the fervent gratitude of their hearts to Him who has called them out of darkness into His marvelous light. Their prayers and their alms come up as a memorial before God. No incense more fragrant can ascend to heaven.

But the work of God in its wide extent is one, and the same principles should control in all its branches. It must bear the stamp of missionary work. Every department of the cause is related to all parts of the gospel field, and the spirit that controls one department will be felt throughout the entire field.

If a portion of the workers receive large wages, there are others, in different branches of the work, who also will call for high wages, and the spirit of self-sacrifice will become feeble. Other institutions will catch the same spirit, and the Lord's favor will be removed from them; for He can never sanction selfishness. Thus our aggressive work would come to an end. It is impossible to carry it forward except by constant sacrifice. From all parts of the world the calls are coming in for men and means to carry forward the work. Shall we be compelled to say: "You must wait; we have no money in the treasury"?

Some of the men of experience and piety, who led out in this work, who denied self and did not hesitate to sacrifice for its success, are now sleeping in the grave. They were God's appointed channels, His representative men, through whom the principles of spiritual life were communicated to the church. They had an experience of the highest value. They could not be bought or sold. Their purity and devotion and self-sacrifice, their living connection with God, were blessed to the upbuilding of the work. Our institutions were characterized by the spirit of self-sacrifice.

In the days when we were struggling with poverty, those who saw how wondrously God wrought for the cause felt that no greater honor could be bestowed upon them than to be bound up with the interests of the work by sacred links which connected them with God. Would they lay down the burden and make terms with the Lord from a money point of view? No, no. Should every timeserver forsake his post, they would never desert the work.

The believers who in the early history of the cause sacrificed for the upbuilding of the work were imbued with the same spirit. They felt that God demanded of all connected with His cause an unreserved consecration of body, soul, and spirit, of all their energies and capabilities, to make the work a success.

But in some respects the work has deteriorated. While it has grown in extent and facilities, it has waned in piety.

There is a lesson for us in the history of Solomon. The early life of this king of Israel was bright with promise. He chose the wisdom of God, and the glory of his reign excited the wonder of the world. He might have gone from strength to strength, from character to character, even approaching nearer the similitude of the character of God; but how sad his history; he was exalted to most sacred positions of trust, but he proved unfaithful. He grew into self-sufficiency, pride, self-exaltation.

The lust for political power and self-aggrandizement led him to form alliances with heathen nations. The silver of Tarshish and the gold of Ophir were procured at a terrible expense, even the sacrifice of integrity, the betrayal of sacred trusts. Association with idolaters corrupted his faith; one false step led to another; there was a breaking down of the barriers which God had erected for the safety of His people; his life was corrupted by polygamy; and at last he gave himself to the worship of false gods. A character that had been firm and pure and elevated became weak, marked with moral inefficiency.

Evil counselors were not wanting, who swayed that once noble, independent mind as they chose, because he did not make God his guide and counselor. His fine sensibilities became blunted; the conscientious, considerate spirit of his early reign was changed. Self-indulgence was his god; and, as the result, severe judgment and cruel tyranny marked his course. The extravagance practiced in selfish indulgence necessitated a grinding taxation upon the poor. From the wisest king that ever swayed a scepter, Solomon became a despot. As a king he had been the idol of the nation, and that which he said and did was copied. His example exerted an influence the result of which can be fully known only when the works of all shall come in review before God, and every man shall be judged according to the deeds done in the body.

Oh, how can God bear with the misdeeds of those who have had great light and advantages, and yet follow the course of their own choosing, to their eternal harm! Solomon, who at the dedication of the temple had solemnly charged the people, "Let your heart therefore be perfect with the Lord our God" (1 Kings 8:61), chose his own way, and in his heart separated from God. The mind that was once given to God and inspired of Him to write the most precious words of wisdom (the book of Proverbs),—truths which are immortalized,—that noble mind, through evil associations and yielding to temptation, became inefficient, weak in moral power, and Solomon dishonored himself, dishonored Israel, and dishonored God.

Looking upon this picture, we see what human beings become when they venture to separate from God. One false step prepares the way for another, and every step is taken more easily than the last. Thus souls are found following another leader than Christ.

All who occupy positions in our institutions will be tested. If they will make Christ their pattern, He will give them wisdom and knowledge and understanding; they will grow in grace and aptitude in Christ's way; their characters will be molded after His similitude. If they fail of keeping the way of the Lord, another spirit will control the mind and judgment, and they will plan without the Lord and will take their own course and leave the positions they have occupied. The light has been given them; if they depart from it, let no man present a bribe to induce them to remain. They will be a hindrance and a snare. The time has come when everything is to be shaken that can be shaken, that those things which cannot be shaken may remain. Every case is coming in review before God; He is measuring the temple and the worshipers therein.

— Section 5 —

In the Southern Field

"As a shepherd seeketh out his flock; ... so will I seek out My sheep, and will deliver them out of all places where they have been scattered." Ezekiel 34:12.

44. Needs of the Southern Field

The Lord expects far more of us than we have given Him in unselfish service for people of all classes in the Southern States of America. This field lies at our very doors, and in it there is a great work to be done for the Master. This work must be done now, while the angels continue to hold the four winds. There is no time to lose.

The Lord has long been waiting for human instrumentalities through whom to work. How much longer will He be obliged to wait for men and women to respond to the call: "Go work today in My vineyard"? Messengers of mercy are needed, not merely in a few places in the South, but throughout the whole field. Rich and poor are calling for the light.

Men and women should now be offering themselves to carry the truth into the highways and byways of this field. There are thousands who might give themselves to God for service. He would accept them and work through them, making them messengers of peace and hope.

The workers will meet with many who will harden their hearts against the conviction of God's Spirit; but they will meet also with many who are hungering for the bread of life, and who, receiving the message, will go forth to sow the seeds of truth.

When the Lord laid upon Moses the work of leading the children of Israel from Egypt, He gave him the assurance: "Certainly I will be with thee." "My presence shall go with thee, and I will give thee rest." Exodus 3:12; 33:14.

The same assurance is given to those who go forth to work for the Lord in the Southern field.

My brethren and sisters, commune with God, that you may be imbued with His Spirit, and then go forth to bestow on others the grace you have received. The example of the Saviour should inspire us to put forth earnest, self-sacrificing effort for the good of others. He came to this world as the unwearied servant of man's necessity. Love for the lost race was manifested in all that He said and did. He clothed His divinity with humanity, that He might stand among human beings as one of them, a sharer of their poverty and their griefs.

What a busy life He led! Day by day He might be seen entering the humble abodes of want and sorrow, speaking hope to the downcast and peace to the distressed. This is the work that He asks His people to do today. Humble, gracious, tenderhearted, pitiful, He went about doing good, lifting up the bowed-down and comforting the sorrowful. None who came to Him went away unhelped. To all He brought hope and gladness. Wherever He went he carried blessing.

We need to humble ourselves before God because so few of the members of His church are putting forth efforts that in any wise compare with the efforts that the Lord desires them to put forth. The opportunities that He has given us, the promises that He has made, the privileges that He has bestowed, should inspire us with far greater zeal and devotion. Every addition to the church should be one more agency for the carrying out of the plan of redemption. Every power of God's people should be devoted to bringing many sons and daughters to Him. In our service there is to be no indifference, no selfishness. Any departure from self-denial, any relaxation of earnest effort, means so much power given to the enemy.

- ## An Appeal for the Colored Race

The proclamation that freed the slaves in the Southern States opened doors through which Christian workers should have entered to tell the story of the love of God. In this field there were precious jewels that the Lord's workers should have searched for as for hidden treasure. But though the colored people have been freed from political slavery, many of them are still in the slavery of ignorance and sin. Many of them are terribly degraded. Is no message of warning to reach them? Had those to whom God has given great light and many opportunities done the work that He desires them to do, there would today be memorials all through the Southern field—churches, sanitariums, and schools. Men and women of all classes would have been called to the gospel feast.

The Lord is grieved by the woe in the Southern field. Christ has wept at the sight of this woe. Angels have hushed the music of their harps as they have looked upon a people unable, because of their past slavery, to help themselves. And yet those in whose hands God has placed the torch of truth, kindled from the divine altar, have not realized that to them is given the work of carrying the light to this sin-darkened field. There are those who have turned away from the work of rescuing the downtrodden and degraded, refusing to help the helpless. Let the servants of Christ begin at once to redeem their neglect, that the dark stain on their record may be wiped out.

The present condition of the Southern field is dishonoring to the Redeemer. But shall it lead us to believe that the commission which Christ gave to His disciples when He told them to preach the gospel to all nations, cannot be fulfilled? No, No! Christ has power for the fulfillment of His commission. He is fully able to do the work laid upon Him. In the wilderness, armed with the weapon, "It is written," He met and overcame the strongest temptations that the enemy could bring against Him. He proved the power of the word. It is God's people who have failed. That His word has not the power on hearts that it ought to have is shown by the present condition of the world. But it is because men have chosen to disobey, not because the word has less power.

- ## **A Call from the Colored Race**

The Lord has looked with sadness upon that most pitiful of all sights, the colored race in slavery. He desires us, in our work for them, to remember their providential deliverance from slavery, their common relationship to us by creation and by redemption, and their right to the blessings of freedom.

Some time ago I seemed to be, during the night season, in a meeting in which the work in the Southern field was being discussed. The questions were asked by a company of intelligent colored people: "Has God no message for the colored people of the South? Have they no souls to save? Does not the new covenant include them? If the Lord is soon to come, is it not time that something was done for the Southern field?"

"We do not," it was said, "question the need of missions in foreign lands. But we do question the right of those who claim to have present truth to pass by millions of human beings in their own country, many of whom are as ignorant as the heathen. Why is it that so little is done for the colored people of the South, many of whom are ignorant and destitute, and need to be taught that Christ is their Creator and Redeemer? How can they believe in Him of whom they have not heard? How can they hear without a preacher? And how can one preach except he be sent?"

"We lay this matter before those who profess to believe the truth for this time. What are you doing for the unenlightened colored race? Why have you not a deeper sense of the necessities of the Southern field? Does there not rest upon ministers of the gospel the responsibility of setting in operation plans whereby this people can be educated? Does not the commission of the Saviour teach this? Is it right for professing Christians to hold themselves aloof from this work, allowing a few to carry the burden? In all your plans for medical missionary work and foreign missionary work, has God given you no message for us?"

Then He who has authority arose, and called upon all to give heed to the instruction that the Lord has given in regard to the work in the South. He said: "Much more evangelistic work should be done in the South. There should be a hundred workers where now there is but one. Let the people of God awake. Think you that the Lord will bless those who have felt no burden for this work, and who permit the way of its advancement to be hedged up?"

As these words were spoken, deep feeling was manifested. Some offered themselves as missionaries, while others sat in silence, apparently taking no interest in the subject.

Then the words were spoken: "The South is a most unpromising field; but how changed would it be from what it is now if, after the colored people had been released from slavery, men and women had worked for them as Christians ought to work, teaching them how to care for themselves!"

The condition of the colored people in the South is no more disheartening than was the condition of the world when Christ left heaven to come to its aid. He saw humanity sunken in wretchedness and sinfulness. He knew that men and women were depraved and degraded, and that they cherished the most loathsome vices. Angels marveled that Christ should undertake what seemed to them a hopeless task. They marveled that God could tolerate a race so sinful. They could see no room for love. But "God so loved the world, that He gave His only-begotten Son, that whosoever believeth in Him should not perish, but have everlasting life." John 3:16.

Christ came to this earth with a message of mercy and forgiveness. He laid the foundation for a religion by which Jew and Gentile, black and white, free and bond, are linked together in one common brotherhood, recognized as equal in the sight of God. The Saviour has a boundless love for every human being. In each one He sees capacity for improvement. With divine energy and hope He greets those for whom He has given His life. In His strength they can live a life rich in good works, filled with the power of the Spirit.

• A Gospel for the Poor

The poverty of the people to whom we are sent is not to prevent us from working for them. Christ came to this earth to walk and work among the poor and suffering. They received the greatest share of His attention. And today, in the person of His children, He visits the poor and needy, relieving woe and alleviating suffering.

Take away suffering and need, and we should have no way of understanding the mercy and love of God, no way of knowing the compassionate, sympathetic heavenly Father. Never does the gospel put on an aspect of greater loveliness than when it is brought to the most needy and destitute regions. Then it is that its light shines forth with the clearest radiance and the greatest power. Truth from the word of God enters the hovel of the peasant; rays from the Sun of Righteousness light up the rude cottage of the poor, bringing gladness to the sick and suffering. Angels of God are there, and the simple faith shown makes the crust of bread and the cup of water a banquet. The sin-pardoning Saviour welcomes the poor and ignorant, and gives them to eat of the bread that comes down from heaven. They drink of the water of life. Those who have been loathed and abandoned are through faith and pardon raised to the dignity of sons and daughters of God. Lifted above the world, they sit in heavenly places in Christ. They may have no earthly treasure, but they have found the pearl of great price.

• What can be Done

How best to accomplish the work in this difficult field is the problem before us. Long years of neglect have made it far more difficult than it would otherwise have been. Obstructions have been accumulating.

Great progress might have been made in medical missionary work. Sanitariums might have been established. The principles of health reform might have been proclaimed. This work is now to be taken up. And into it not a vestige of selfishness is to be brought. It is to be done with an earnestness, perseverance, and devotion that will open doors through which the truth can enter, and that to stay.

In the South there is much that could be done by lay members of the church, persons of limited education. There are men, women, and children who need to be taught to read. These poor souls are starving for a knowledge of God.

Our people in the South are not to wait for eloquent preachers, talented men; they are to take up the work which the Lord places before them, and do their best. He will accept and work through humble, earnest men and women, even though they may not be eloquent or highly educated. My brethren and sisters, devise wise plans for labor, and go forward, trusting in the Lord. Do not indulge the feeling that you are capable and keen-sighted. Begin and continue in humility. Be a living exposition of the truth. Make the word of God the man of your counsel. Then the truth will go with power, and souls will be converted.

Let Sabbathkeeping families move to the South and live out the truth before those who know it not. These families can be a help to one another, but let them be careful to do nothing that will hedge up their way. Let them do Christian help work, feeding the hungry and clothing the naked. This will have a far stronger influence for good than the preaching of sermons. Deeds, as well as words, of sympathy are needed. Christ prefaced the giving of His message by deeds of love and benevolence. Let these workers go from house to house, helping where help is needed, and, as opportunity offers, telling the story of the cross. Christ is to be their text. They need not dwell upon doctrinal subjects; let them speak of the work and sacrifice of Christ. Let them hold up His righteousness, in their lives revealing His purity.

The true missionary must be armed with the mind of Christ. His heart must be filled with Christlike love; and he must be true and steadfast to principle.

In many places schools should be established, and those who are tender and sympathetic, who, like the Saviour, are touched by the sight of woe and suffering, should teach old and young. Let the word of God be taught in a way that will enable all to understand it. Let the pupils be encouraged to study the lessons of Christ. This will do more to enlarge the mind and strengthen the intellect than any other study. Nothing gives such vigor to the faculties as contact with the word of God.

The cotton field is not to be the only means whereby the colored people can gain a livelihood. They are to be taught how to till the soil, how to cultivate various crops, and how to plant and care for orchards. Painstaking effort is to be put forth to develop their capabilities. Thus will be awakened in them the thought that they are of value with God, because they are His property.

Among the colored people some will be found whose intellect has been too long darkened for them to be speedily fitted for usefulness. But they may be taught to know God. The bright beams of the Sun of Righteousness may shine into the darkened chambers of their minds. It is their privilege to have the life that measures with the life of God. Plant in their minds uplifting, ennobling thoughts. Live before them lives that will make plain the difference between vice and purity, darkness and light. Let them read in your lives what it means to be a Christian. The chain that has been let down from the throne of God is long enough to reach to the lowest depths. Christ is able to lift the most sinful out of the pit of degradation, and to place them where they will be acknowledged as children of God, heirs with Christ to an immortal inheritance.

Many are utterly discouraged. Because they have been despised and forsaken they have become stoical. They are looked upon as unable to comprehend or to receive the gospel of Christ. Yet by the miracle of divine grace they may be changed. Under the ministration of the Holy Spirit the stupidity that makes their uplifting appear so hopeless will pass away. The dull, clouded mind will awake. The slave of sin will be set free. Spiritual life will revive and strengthen. Vice will disappear, and ignorance will be overcome. Through the faith that works by love the heart will be purified and the mind enlightened.

There are others among the colored people who have quick perceptions and bright minds. Many of the colored race are rich in faith and trust. God sees among them precious jewels that will one day shine out brightly. The colored people deserve more from the hands of the white people than they have received. There are thousands who have minds capable of cultivation and uplifting. With proper labor, many who have been looked upon as hopeless will become educators of their race. Through the grace of God the race that the enemy has for generations oppressed may rise to the dignity of God-given manhood and womanhood.

The Lord desires the desert places of the South, where the outlook appears so forbidding, to become as the garden of God. Let our people arouse and redeem the past. The obligation to work for the colored people rests heavily upon us. Shall we not try to repair, as far as lies in our power, the injury that in the past has been done to these people? Shall not the number of missionaries to the South be multiplied? Shall we not hear of many volunteers who are ready to enter this field to bring souls out of darkness and ignorance into the marvelous light in which we rejoice? God will pour out His Spirit upon those who respond to His call. In the strength of Christ they may do a work that will fill heaven with rejoicing.

"Thus saith the Lord God; Behold, I, even I, will both search My sheep, and seek them out...So will I seek out My sheep, and will deliver them out of all places where they have been scattered in the cloudy and dark day...I will feed My flock, and I will cause them to lie down, saith the Lord God. I will seek that which was lost, and bring again that which was driven away, and will bind up that which was broken, and will strengthen that which was sick...And I will make with them a covenant of peace...And I will make them and the places round about My hill a blessing; and I will cause the shower to come down in his season; there shall be showers of blessing...Thus shall they know that I the Lord their God am with them...And ye My flock, the flock of My pasture, are men, and I am your God, saith the Lord God."

45. Centers of Influence

A good beginning has been made in the Southern field. In the forward march of events the Lord has wrought most wonderfully for the advancement of His work. Battles have been fought, victories won. Favorable impressions have been made; much prejudice has been removed.

In the night season I was taken by my Guide from place to place, from city to city, in the South. I saw the great work to be done—that which ought to have been done years ago. We seemed to be looking at many places. Our first interest was for the places where the work has already been established and for those where the way has opened for a beginning to be made. I saw where there are institutions for the advancement of the Lord's work. One of these places was Graysville, and another, Huntsville, where we have industrial schools. These schools are to receive encouragement and help, for the Lord led in their establishment. Each has advantages of its own.

From the light given me I know that the work at Hildebran, if properly managed, will be a great blessing to the surrounding country. I have been instructed that we must establish schools in just such districts, away from the cities and their temptations.

Eternity alone will reveal the work accomplished for the colored people by the small schools at Vicksburg, Yazoo City, and other points in the South. In this field we need many more such schools.

We must provide greater facilities for the education and training of the youth, both white and colored, in the South. Schools are to be established away from the cities, where the youth can learn to cultivate the soil and thus help to make themselves and the school self-supporting. In connection with these schools all the different lines of work, whether agricultural or mechanical, that the situation of the place will warrant are to be developed. Let means be gathered for the establishment of such schools. In them students may gain an education that, with God's blessing, will prepare them to win souls to Christ. If they unite with the Saviour they will grow in spirituality and will become valuable workers in His vineyard.

With our larger schools should be connected small sanitariums, that the students may have opportunity to gain a knowledge of medical missionary work. This line of work is to be brought into our schools as part of the regular instruction. Small sanitariums should be established in connection with the schools at Graysville and Huntsville.

• Nashville as a Center

As a people we should take a special interest in the work at Nashville. At the present time this city is a point of great importance in the Southern field. Our brethren selected Nashville as a center for work in the South because the Lord in His wisdom directed them there. It is a favorable place in which to make a beginning. Our workers will find it easier to labor in this city for the colored race than in many other cities of the South. In this city much interest is taken in the colored people by those not of our faith. In and near the city are large educational institutions for the colored people. The influence of these institutions has prepared the way for us to make this city a center for our work.

Into the institutions of learning at Nashville the truth is to find entrance. There are those in these institutions who are to be reached by the third angel's message. Everything that can be done to interest these teachers and students in the message of present truth should now be done, and it should be done in a wise and understanding manner. From the experienced teachers may be learned precious lessons regarding the best ways of helping the colored people.

The truth is also to be brought before those who have given of their means and influence for the benefit of the colored race. They have taken a noble stand for the uplifting of this people. They are to see a representation of our work that will be to them an object lesson. We are to do all we can to remove the prejudice that exists in their minds against our work. If the efforts we put forth are in accordance with God's will, many among them will be convicted and converted. The Lord causes light to shine on the pathway of those who are seeking for light.

Nashville is within easy access of Graysville and Huntsville. By the work in Nashville, the work at Graysville and Huntsville is to be confirmed and settled. Graysville and Huntsville are near enough to Nashville to strengthen the work there and to be strengthened by it.

It was in accordance with God's purpose that the publishing work was started at Nashville. In the Southern field there is need of a printing office for the publication of the truth for this time, and especially for printing reading matter suitable for the different classes of people in this field. And there is no city in the South better suited than Nashville for the carrying forward of publishing work. The establishing of such an institution is an advance movement. If rightly managed, this institution will give character to the work in the South and to many souls will be the means of imparting a knowledge of the truth. The Nashville publishing house will still need to be assisted for a time by gifts and offerings.

Sanitarium work also has been begun in Nashville. This must be wisely managed and given support. Medical missionary work is indeed the helping hand of the gospel ministry. It opens the way for the entrance of truth.

I am instructed to caution my brethren in the Southern field not to move hastily in establishing large enterprises and new centers just now, in a way that will divide their workers and their means, thus weakening their forces at this critical time in their work. Let them wait until some of the interests that have been started approach more nearly to perfection. Let them not rush into new enterprises before the institutions at Graysville and Huntsville are more firmly established and the interests centering in Nashville are strengthened.

As yet there are comparatively few places in the South that have been worked. There are many, many cities in which nothing has been done. Centers of influence may be established in many places by the opening up of health food stores, hygienic restaurants, and treatment rooms. Not all that needs to be done can be specified before a beginning is made. Let those in charge of the Southern work pray over the matter, and remember that God is guiding. Let no narrowness or selfishness be manifested. Plan to carry forward the work simply, sensibly, economically.

46. Instruction to Workers

Slowly but surely the wheel of Providence is turning. We know not how soon our Lord will say: "It is done." His coming is drawing nigh. Soon our opportunities for work will be forever past. Only a little while longer shall we be permitted to labor. My brethren, will you not strive with earnest effort to establish memorials for God throughout the Southern States? Churches should be raised up; houses of worship should be built; small schools and sanitariums should be established; and the publishing interests should be strengthened.

The lines of work to be established in different places in the South will need men and women of wisdom and prayer, men and women who will carry the work forward from stage to stage soundly, intelligently—toiling, praying, working economically, as laborers of God's appointment. The situation calls for personal, untiring, united effort.

One brick upon another, and the highest wall is made;
One flake upon another, and the deepest snow is laid.

Patient continuance in well-doing—this is to be our motto. We are to put forth persevering effort, advancing step by step until the race is run, the victory gained.

When the publishing work at Nashville was started, it was the avowed purpose of the workers to keep out of debt; but in their desperate effort to make brick without straw, our brethren were led to depart from this purpose, and, as the result, the work has become involved in difficulty. But God's workmen at Nashville are not, because of this, to become discouraged. The work must not cease. Let all now seek most earnestly to avoid the mistakes of the past. Let them guard themselves as with a fence of barbed wire against the inclination to go into debt. Let them say firmly: "Henceforth we will advance no faster than the Lord shall indicate and the means in hand shall allow, even though the good work has to wait for a while. In beginning in new places, we will labor in narrow quarters, rather than involve the Lord's cause in debt."

Let not those become disheartened who have labored so earnestly to bring the work in the Southern field to its present state of advancement. Let all do their best to place the work at Nashville on a solid basis. The Lord has in charge those who have striven valiantly to do that which so greatly needed to be done. In His pity and kindness and love, the Lord has mercy on them. He still accepts them as His co-workers. He knows all about every one of them. They have had to pass through the fire of affliction, as they have done the breaking-up pioneer work. God will be glorified in those who have been laborers together with Him in breaking up the ground in fields that have never before been worked.

Brethren, we have a great work before us in the Southern field, a work that as yet we have only begun. We must not continue to stand as we have stood for years, dreading this work. There are those who have done stern, hard labor, and the Lord recognizes and commends their self-sacrificing efforts. He has blessed them. They have received their reward by seeing those they helped placing their feet on the Rock of Ages and in turn helping others.

My brethren in the Southern field, I ask you, in the name of the Lord God of Israel, to quit you like men. The Lord is at the helm. He will give His servants grace and wisdom. It is God's purpose that men entrusted with responsibility should counsel and pray together in Christian unity. In unity there is a life, a power, that can be obtained in no other way. There will be a vast power in the church when the energies of the members are united under the control of the Spirit. Then will God be able to work mightily through His people for the conversion of sinners.

God lives and reigns. He will open the way for the neglected Southern field to be cultivated for Him. Let the workers there come up to the help of the Lord and with joy proclaim His truth. The Lord is soon coming. Talk it, pray it, believe it. Make it a part of the life. You will have to meet a doubting, objecting spirit, but this will give way before firm, consistent trust in God. When perplexities or hindrances present themselves, lift the soul to God in songs of thanksgiving. Gird on the Christian armor, and be sure that your feet are "shod with the preparation of the gospel of peace." Preach the truth with boldness and fervor. Remember that the Lord looks in compassion upon this field and that He knows its poverty and its need. The efforts you are making will not prove a failure.

Our churches in the South are to have a spiritual resurrection. A great and solemn work is before the members of every church. They are to come close to Christ in self-denial and self-sacrifice, their one aim being to give God's message of mercy to their fellow men. Let them labor guardedly and with humility, each having respect for the work of the others. Some can labor in one way and some in another, as the Lord may call and lead them.

But let none mourn that they cannot glorify God in the use of talents that He has not entrusted to their keeping. God holds us responsible only for the work that He has placed in our hands. One thing all can do: They can avoid making the work of others unnecessarily hard by criticizing their efforts, putting stones in front of the car their brethren are trying to push uphill. If any are unwilling to put their shoulder to the wheel, let them at least refrain from hindering those who are working. God calls for laborers who will refuse to discourage their fellow laborers.

As God's people labor earnestly, humbly, self-sacrificingly, they will gain the rich reward of which Job speaks: "When the ear heard me, then it blessed me; ... the blessing of him that was ready to perish came upon me: and I caused the widow's heart to sing for joy...I was a father to the poor: and the cause which I knew not I searched out." Job 29:11-16.

The blessing of good works will follow into the eternal world those who deny self for the sake of their Saviour. When the redeemed stand around the throne of God, those who have been saved from sin and degradation will come to those who labored for them, with the words of greeting: "I was without God and without hope in the world. I was perishing in corruption and sin. I was starving for physical and for spiritual food. You came to me in love and pity, and fed and clothed me. You pointed me to the Lamb of God, that taketh away the sin of the world."

My brethren in the South, be strong, yea, be strong. The hand of oppression and robbery shall not afflict you if you will exalt the holy principles of God's law. When the enemy comes in like a flood, the Spirit of the Lord will lift up a standard for you against him. You are engaged in an important work, and you are to take heed, to watch and pray, to make straight paths for your feet, lest the lame be turned out of the way. Work with an eye single to the glory of God, with a sense of your individual responsibility. Remember that the Lord alone can make your efforts successful.

The workers in the South must reach the highest spiritual attainments, in order that their work in this field may be a success. Private prayer, family prayer, prayer in public gatherings for the worship of God— all are essential. And we are to live our prayers. We are to co-operate with Christ in His work. Union with Christ and with one another is our only safety. Let us not make it possible for Satan to point to our churches, saying: "Behold how these people, standing under the banner of Christ, hate one another. We have nothing to fear from them while they spend more strength in fighting among themselves than in warfare with my forces."

We are to learn from past experience how to avoid failure. We pray to our heavenly Father, "Lead us not into temptation," and then, too often, we fail to guard our feet against leading us into temptation. We are to keep away from the temptations by which we are easily overcome. Our success is wrought out by ourselves through the grace of Christ. We are to roll out of the way the stone of stumbling that has caused us and others so much sadness.

In establishing the work in new places, economize in every possible way. Gather up the fragments; let nothing be lost. The work of soul saving must be carried on in the way that Christ has marked out. He declares: "If any man will come after Me, let him deny himself, and take up his cross, and follow Me." Matthew 16:24. Only by obeying this word can we be His disciples. We are nearing the end of this earth's history, and the different lines of God's work are to be carried forward with much more self-sacrifice than has yet been manifested.

We are in this world to help one another. In Christ's work there were no territorial lines, and those who attempt to make such lines in His work today might better pray: "Lord, give me a new heart." When they have the mind of Christ they will see the many parts of the Lord's vineyard that are still unworked. Never will they say: "Our means are needed to carry forward the interests we have in hand. It is of no use to call for means from us."

Day by day human beings are deciding a question of life or death, deciding whether they will have eternal life or eternal destruction. And yet many of those professing to serve the Lord are content to occupy their time and attention with matters of little importance. They are content to be at variance with one another. If they were consecrated to the service of the Master, they would not be contending like a family of unruly children. Everyone would be standing at his post of duty, working with heart and soul as a missionary of the cross of Christ. The Holy Spirit would abide in the hearts of the laborers, and works of righteousness would be wrought. The workers would carry with them into their service the prayers and sympathies of an awakened church. They would receive their orders from Christ, and would have no time for contention. Messages would come from lips touched by a live coal from the divine altar. Earnest, purified words would be spoken. Humble, heartbroken prayers of faith would ascend to heaven. While with one hand the workers would take hold of Christ, with the other they would grasp sinners and draw them to the Saviour.

"What man of you, having an hundred sheep, if he lose one of them, doth not leave the ninety and nine in the wilderness, and go after that which is lost, until he find it? And when he hath found it, he layeth it on his shoulders, rejoicing. And when he cometh home, he calleth together his friends and neighbors, saying unto them, Rejoice with me; for I have found my sheep which was lost. I say unto you, that likewise joy shall be in heaven over one sinner that repenteth, more than over ninety and nine just persons, which need no repentance."

"Either what woman having ten pieces of silver, if she lose one piece, doth not light a candle, and sweep the house, and seek diligently till she find it? And when she hath found it, she calleth her friends and her neighbors together, saying, Rejoice with me; for I have found the piece which I had lost. Likewise, I say unto you, there is joy in the presence of the angels of God over one sinner that repenteth." Luke 15:4-10.

47. Be of Good Courage

To those who are laboring in the South I would say: Be not discouraged by the present feebleness of the work. You have had to struggle against difficulties that have at times threatened to overcome you. But by God's help you have been enabled to move forward. If all in our ranks knew how difficult it was in years past to establish the work in places that have since become important centers, they would realize that it takes courage to face an unpromising situation and to declare, with hands uplifted to heaven: "We will not fail nor become discouraged." Those who have not broken the ground in new and difficult fields do not realize the difficulties of pioneer work. If they could understand God's working they would not only rejoice because of what has been done, but they would see cause for rejoicing in the future of the work.

My brethren, there is no reason for discouragement. The good seed is being sown. God will watch over it, causing it to spring up and bring forth an abundant harvest. Remember that many of the enterprises for soul saving have, at the beginning, been carried forward amidst great difficulty.

I am instructed to say to you: Move guardedly, doing always that which the Lord commands. Move forward courageously, assured that the Lord will be with those who love and serve Him. He will work in behalf of His covenant-keeping people. He will not suffer them to become a reproach. He will purify all who yield themselves to Him, and will make them a praise in the earth. Nothing else in this world is so dear to God as His church. He will work with mighty power through humble, faithful men. Christ is saying to you today: "I am with you, co-operating with your faithful, trusting efforts, and giving you precious victories. I will strengthen you as you sanctify yourselves to My service. I will give you success in your efforts to arouse souls dead in trespasses and sins."

Unswerving faith and unselfish love will overcome the difficulties that arise in the path of duty to hinder aggressive warfare. As those inspired by this faith go forward in the work of saving souls, they will run and not be weary, will walk and not faint.

I assure you that if you work in right lines, God will make your enemies to be at peace with you. He will uphold and strengthen you. Make a covenant with God that you will guard well your words. "If any man offend not in word, the same is a perfect man, and able also to bridle the whole body." James 3:2. Remember that a revengeful speech never makes one feel that he has gained a victory. Let Christ speak through you. Do not lose the blessing that comes from thinking no evil.

Remember that prayer is the source of your strength. A worker cannot gain success while he hurries through his prayers and rushes away to look after something that he fears may be neglected or forgotten. He gives only a few hurried thoughts to God; he does not take time to think, to pray, to wait upon the Lord for a renewal of physical and spiritual strength. He soon becomes weary. He does not feel the uplifting, inspiring influence of God's Spirit. He is not quickened by fresh life. His jaded frame and tired brain are not soothed by personal contact with Christ.

"Wait on the Lord: be of good courage, and He shall strengthen thine heart: wait, I say, on the Lord." "It is good that a man should both hope and quietly wait for the salvation of the Lord." Psalm 27:14; Lamentations 3:26. There are those who work all day and far into the night to do what seems to them must be done. The Lord looks pityingly upon these weary, heavy-laden burden bearers and says to them: "Come unto Me, ... and I will give you rest." Matthew 11:28.

God's workers will meet with turmoil, discomfort, and weariness. At times, uncertain and distracted, they are almost in despair. When this restless nervousness comes, let them remember Christ's invitation: "Come ye yourselves apart, ... and rest awhile." The Saviour "giveth power to the faint; and to them that have no might He increaseth strength." Isaiah 40:29.

Difficulties will arise that will try your faith and patience. Face them bravely. Look on the bright side. If the work is hindered, be sure that it is not your fault, and then go forward, rejoicing in the Lord. Heaven is full of joy. It resounds with the praises of Him who made so wonderful a sacrifice for the redemption of the human race. Should not the church on earth be full of praise? Should not Christians publish throughout the world the joy of serving Christ? Those who in heaven join with the angelic choir in their anthem of praise must learn on earth the song of heaven, the keynote of which is thanksgiving.

Never let your courage fail. Never talk unbelief because appearances are against you. As you work for the Master you will feel pressure for want of means, but the Lord will hear and answer your petitions for help. Let your language be: "The Lord God will help me; therefore shall I not be confounded: therefore have I set my face like a flint, and I know that I shall not be ashamed." Isaiah 50:7.

If you make a mistake, turn your defeat into victory.

The lessons that God sends will always, if well learned, bring help in due time. Put your trust in God. Pray much, and believe. Trusting, hoping, believing, holding fast the hand of Infinite Power, you will be more than conquerors.

True workers walk and work by faith. Sometimes they grow weary with watching the slow advance of the work when the battle wages strong between the powers of good and evil. But if they refuse to fail or be discouraged they will see the clouds breaking away and the promise of deliverance fulfilling. Through the mist with which Satan has surrounded them, they will see the shining of the bright beams of the Sun of Righteousness.

Work in faith, and leave results with God. Pray in faith, and the mystery of His providence will bring its answer. At times it may seem that you cannot succeed. But work and believe, putting into your efforts faith, hope, and courage. After doing what you can, wait for the Lord, declaring His faithfulness, and He will bring His word to pass. Wait, not in fretful anxiety, but in undaunted faith and unshaken trust.

"If God be for us, who can be against us? He that spared not His own Son, but delivered Him up for us all, how shall He not with Him also freely give us all things? ... Who shall separate us from the love of Christ? shall tribulation, or distress, or persecution, or famine, or nakedness, or peril, or sword? ... Nay, in all these things we are more than conquerors through Him that loved us. For I am persuaded, that neither death, nor life, nor angels, nor principalities, nor powers, nor things present, nor things to come, nor height, nor depth, nor any other creature, shall be able to separate us from the love of God, which is in Christ Jesus our Lord."

— Section 6 —

Counsels to Burden Bearers

"As every man hath received the gift, even so minister the same one to another, as good stewards of the manifold grace of God." 1 Peter 4:10

48. Ministers and Business Matters

I have been instructed in regard to the importance of our ministers' keeping free from responsibilities that should be largely borne by businessmen. In the night season I was in an assembly consisting of a number of our brethren who bear the burden of the work. They were deeply perplexed over financial affairs and were consulting as to how the work could be managed most successfully. Some thought that the number of workers might be limited and yet all the results essential be realized. One of the brethren occupying a position of responsibility was explaining his plans and stating what he desired to see accomplished. Several others presented matters for consideration. Then One of dignity and authority arose, and proceeded to state principles for our guidance.

To several ministers the Speaker said: "Your work is not the management of financial matters. It is not wise for you to undertake this. God has burdens for you to bear, but if you carry lines of work for which you are not adapted, your efforts in presenting the word will prove unsuccessful. This will bring upon you discouragement that will disqualify you for the very work you should do, a work requiring careful discrimination and sound, unselfish judgment."

Those who are employed to write and to speak the word should attend fewer committee meetings. They should entrust many minor matters to men of business ability and thus avoid being kept on a constant strain that robs the mind of its natural vigor. They should give far more attention to the preservation of physical health, for vigor of mind depends largely upon vigor of body. Proper periods of sleep and rest and an abundance of physical exercise are essential to health of body and mind. To rob nature of her hours for rest and recuperation by allowing one man to do the work of four, or of three, or even of two, will result in irreparable loss.

- ## Educate Men in Business Lines

Those who think that a man's fitness for a certain position qualifies him to fill several other positions are liable to make mistakes when planning for the advancement of the work. They are liable to place upon one the cares and burdens that should be divided among several.

Experience is of great value. The Lord desires to have men of intelligence connected with His work, men qualified for various positions of trust in our conferences and institutions. Especially are consecrated businessmen needed, men who will carry the principles of truth into every business transaction. Those placed in charge of financial affairs should not assume other burdens, burdens that they are incapable of bearing; nor is the business management to be entrusted to incompetent men. Those in charge of the work have erred sometimes in permitting the appointment of men devoid of tact and ability to manage important financial interests.

Men of promise in business lines should develop and perfect their talents by most thorough study and training. They should be encouraged to place themselves where, as students, they can rapidly gain a knowledge of right business principles and methods. Not one business man now connected with the cause needs to be a novice. If men in any line of work ought to improve their opportunities to become wise and efficient, it is those who are using their ability in the work of building up the kingdom of God in our world. In view of the fact that we are living so near the close of this earth's history, there should be greater thoroughness in labor, more vigilant waiting, watching, praying, and working. The human agent should strive to attain perfection, that he may be an ideal Christian, complete in Christ Jesus.

- **Right Principles Essential**

Those who labor in business lines should take every precaution against falling into error through wrong principles or methods. Their record may be like that of Daniel in the courts of Babylon. When all his business transactions were subjected to the closest scrutiny, not one faulty item could be found. The record of his business life, incomplete though it is, contains lessons worthy of study. It reveals the fact that a businessman is not necessarily a scheming, policy man. He may be a man instructed of God at every step. Daniel, while prime minister of the kingdom of Babylon, was a prophet of God, receiving the light of heavenly inspiration. His life is an illustration of what every Christian businessman may be.

God does not accept the most splendid service unless self is laid upon the altar, a living, consuming sacrifice. The root must be holy, else there can be no sound, healthy fruit, which alone is acceptable to God. The heart must be converted and consecrated. The motives must be right. The inner lamp must be supplied with the oil that flows from the messengers of heaven through the golden tubes into the golden bowl. The Lord's communication never comes to man in vain.

Truths, precious, vital truths, are bound up with man's eternal well-being both in this life and in the eternity that is opening before us. "Sanctify them through Thy truth: Thy word is truth." John 17:17. The word of God is to be practiced. It will live and endure forever. While worldly ambitions, worldly projects, and the greatest plans and purposes of men will perish like the grass, "they that be wise shall shine as the brightness of the firmament; and they that turn many to righteousness as the stars for ever and ever." Daniel 12:3.

At this time God's cause is in need of men and women who possess rare qualifications and good administrative powers; men and women who will make patient, thorough investigation of the needs of the work in various fields; those who have a large capacity for work; those who possess warm, kind hearts, cool heads, sound sense, and unbiased judgment; those who are sanctified by the Spirit of God and can fearlessly say, No, or Yea and Amen, to propositions; those who have strong convictions, clear understanding, and pure, sympathetic hearts; those who practice the words, "All ye are brethren;" those who strive to uplift and restore fallen humanity.

49. Take Time to Talk with God

Special instruction has been given me in regard to our ministers. It is not God's will that they should seek to be rich. They should not engage in worldly enterprises, for this disqualifies them for giving their best powers to spiritual things. But they are to receive wages enough to support themselves and their families. They are not to have so many burdens laid upon them that they cannot give proper attention to the church in their own family, for it is their special duty to train their children for the Lord.

It is a great mistake to keep a minister constantly at work in business lines, going from place to place, and sitting up late at night in attendance at board meetings and committee meetings. This brings upon him weariness and discouragement. Ministers should have time to rest to obtain from God's word the rich nourishment of the bread of life. They should have time to drink refreshing drafts of consolation from the stream of living water.

Let ministers and teachers remember that God holds them accountable to fill their office to the best of their ability, to bring into their work their very best powers. They are not to take up duties that conflict with the work that God has given them.

When ministers and teachers, pressed under the burden of financial responsibility, enter the pulpit or the schoolroom with wearied brain and overtaxed nerves, what else can be expected than that common fire will be used instead of the sacred fire of God's kindling? The strained, tattered efforts disappoint the listeners and hurt the speaker. He has had no time to seek the Lord, no time to ask in faith for the unction of the Holy Spirit.

That the efforts of God's workers may be successful, they must receive the grace and efficiency that He alone can give. "Ask, and ye shall receive" (John 16:24), is the promise. Then why not take time to ask, to open the mind to the impressions of the Holy Spirit, that the soul may be revived by a fresh supply of life? Christ Himself was much in prayer. Whenever He had opportunity, He went apart to be alone with God. As we bow before God in humble prayer, He places a live coal from His altar upon our lips, sanctifying them to the work of giving Bible truth to the people.

I am instructed to say to my fellow workers: If you would have the rich treasures of heaven, you must have secret communion with God. Unless you do this, your soul will be as destitute of the Holy Spirit as were the hills of Gilboa of dew and rain. When you hurry from one thing to another, when you have so much to do that you cannot take time to talk with God, how can you expect power in your work?

The reason so many of our ministers preach tame, lifeless discourses is that they allow a variety of things of a worldly nature to take their time and attention. Unless there is constant growth in grace, we shall be wanting in words suitable for the occasion. Commune with your own heart, and then commune with God. Unless you do this, your efforts will be fruitless, made thus by unsanctified hurry and confusion.

Ministers and teachers, let your work be fragrant with rich spiritual grace. Do not make it common by mixing it with common things. Move onward and upward. Cleanse yourselves from all filthiness of the flesh and of the spirit, perfecting holiness in the fear of the Lord.

We need to be converted daily. Our prayers should be more fervent; then they will be more effectual. Stronger and stronger should be our confidence that God's Spirit will be with us, making us pure and holy, as upright and fragrant as the cedar of Lebanon.

Gospel ministers are to keep their office free from all things secular or political, employing all their time and talents in lines of Christian effort.

To fasten a minister to one place by giving him the oversight of business matters connected with the work of the church is not conducive to his spirituality. To do this is not in accordance with the Bible plan as outlined in the sixth chapter of Acts. Study this plan, for it is approved of God. Follow the word.

He who holds forth the word of life is not to allow too many burdens to be placed upon him. He must take time to study the word and to examine self. If he closely searches his own heart, and gives himself to the Lord, he will better understand how to grasp the hidden things of God.

Instead of choosing the work most pleasing to us, and refusing to do something that our brethren think we should do, we are to inquire: "Lord, what wilt Thou have me to do?" Instead of marking out the way that natural inclination prompts us to follow, we are to pray: "Teach me Thy way, O Lord, and lead me in a plain path." Psalm 27:11.

Financial Details of City Work. Our ministers should learn to let business and financial matters alone. Over and over again I have been instructed that this is not the work of the ministry. They are not to be heavily burdened with the business details even of city work, but are to be in readiness to visit places where an interest in the message has been awakened, and especially to attend our camp meetings. When these meetings are in progress, our workers are not to think that they must remain in the cities to attend to business matters connected with various lines of city work; nor are they to hurry away from the camp meetings in order to do this kind of work.

Those in charge of our conferences should find businessmen to look after the financial details of city work. If such men cannot be found, let facilities be provided for training men to bear these burdens.

Consecrated Financiers. The Scandinavian institutions need not have been in the position in which they are, and they would not be in this position had our brethren in America, years ago, done what they should have done. A man of experience in business lines, with a practical knowledge of bookkeeping, should have been sent to Europe to superintend the keeping of the accounts in our institutions there. And if this work demanded more than one man, more than one should have been sent. Thus thousands and thousands of dollars would have been saved.

Such men should be employed in our work in America, men who are devoted to God, men who know what the principles of heaven are, men who have learned what it means to walk with God. If such men had superintended the financial affairs of our conferences and institutions, there would today be plenty of money in the treasury; and our institutions would now stand as God has declared they should stand, helping the work by self-denial and self-sacrifice.

50. The Work of the Ministry

Many fields ripe for the harvest have not yet been entered because of our lack of self-sacrificing helpers. These fields must be entered, and many laborers should go to them with the expectation of bearing their own expenses. But some of our ministers are little disposed to take upon them the burden of this work, little disposed to labor with the wholehearted benevolence that characterized the life of our Lord.

God is grieved as He sees the lack of self-denial and perseverance in His servants. Angels are amazed at the spectacle. Let workers for Christ study His life of self-sacrifice. He is our example. Can the ministers of today expect to be called on to endure less hardship than did the early Christians, the Waldenses, and reformers in every age in their efforts to carry the gospel to every land?

God has entrusted to His ministers the work of proclaiming His last message of mercy to the world. He is displeased with those who do not throw their whole energies into this all-important work. Unfaithfulness on the part of the appointed watchmen on the walls of Zion endangers the cause of truth and exposes it to the ridicule of the enemy. It is time for our ministers to understand the responsibility and sacredness of their mission. There is a woe upon them, if they fail of performing the work which they themselves acknowledge that God has placed in their hands.

Not a few ministers are neglecting the very work that they have been appointed to do. Why are those who are set apart for the work of the ministry placed on committees and boards? Why are they called upon to attend so many business meetings, many times at great distance from their fields of labor? Why are not business matters placed in the hands of businessmen? The ministers have not been set apart to do this work. The finances of the cause are to be properly managed by men of ability, but ministers are set apart for another line of work. Let the management of financial matters rest on others than those ordained to the ministry.

Ministers are not to be called hither and thither to attend board meetings for the purpose of deciding common business questions. Many of our ministers have done this work in the past, but it is not the work in which the

Lord wishes them to engage. Too many financial burdens have been placed on them. When they try to carry these burdens, they neglect to fulfill the gospel commission. God looks upon this as a dishonor to His name.

The Lord's great vineyard demands from His servants that which it has not yet received— earnest, persevering labor for souls. The ministry is becoming weak and enfeebled, and under its tame service the churches also are becoming weak. As the result of their labors the ministers have but little to show in the conversion of souls. The truth is not carried into the barren places of the earth. These things are depriving God of the glory that belongs to Him. He calls for workers who will be producers as well as consumers.

The world is to be warned. Ministers should work earnestly and devotedly, opening new fields and engaging in personal labor for souls, instead of hovering over the churches that already have great light and many advantages.

51. Committee Meetings

Let those who attend committee meetings remember that they are meeting with God, who has given them their work. Let them come together with reverence and consecration of heart. They meet to consider important matters connected with the Lord's cause. In every particular their actions are to show that they are desirous of understanding His will in regard to the plans to be laid for the advancement of His work. Let them not waste a moment in unimportant conversation; for the Lord's business should be conducted in a businesslike, perfect way. If some member of a committee is careless and irreverent, let him be reminded that he is in the presence of a Witness by whom all actions are weighed.

I have been instructed that committee meetings are not always pleasing to God. Some have come to these meetings with a cold, hard, critical, loveless spirit. Such may do great harm; for with them is the presence of the evil one, that keeps them on the wrong side. Not infrequently their unfeeling attitude toward measures under consideration brings in perplexity, delaying decisions that should be made. God's servants, in need of rest of mind, and sleep, have been greatly distressed and burdened over these matters. In the hope of reaching a decision, they continue their meetings far into the night. But life is too precious to be imperiled in this way. Let the Lord carry the burden. Wait for Him to adjust the difficulties. Give the weary brain a rest. Unreasonable hours are destructive to the physical, the mental, and the moral powers. If the brain were given proper periods of rest, the thoughts would be clear and sharp, and business would be expedited.

• The Relation of Diet to Board Meetings

Before our brethren assemble in council or board meetings, each one should present himself before God, carefully searching the heart and critically examining the motives. Pray that the Lord may reveal self to you so that you may not unwisely criticize or condemn propositions.

At bountiful tables men often eat much more than can be easily digested. The overburdened stomach cannot do its work properly. The result is a disagreeable feeling of dullness in the brain, and the mind does not act quickly. Disturbance is created by improper combinations of food; fermentation sets in; the blood is contaminated and the brain confused.

The habit of overeating, or of eating too many kinds of food at one meal, frequently causes dyspepsia. Serious injury is thus done to the delicate digestive organs. In vain the stomach protests and appeals to the brain to reason from cause to effect. The excessive amount of food eaten, or the improper combination, does its injurious work. In vain do disagreeable premonitions give warning. Suffering is the consequence. Disease takes the place of health.

Some may ask, What has this to do with board meetings? Very much. The effects of wrong eating are brought into council and board meetings. The brain is affected by the condition of the stomach. A disordered stomach is productive of a disordered, uncertain state of mind. A diseased stomach produces a diseased condition of the brain and often makes one obstinate in maintaining erroneous opinions. The supposed wisdom of such a one is foolishness with God.

I present this as the cause of the situation in many council and board meetings, where questions demanding careful study have been given but little consideration, and decisions of the greatest importance have been hurriedly made. Often when there should have been unanimity of sentiment in the affirmative, decided negatives have entirely changed the atmosphere pervading a meeting. These results have been presented to me again and again.

I present these matters now because I am instructed to say to my brethren in the ministry: By intemperance in eating you disqualify yourselves for seeing clearly the difference between sacred and common fire. And by this intemperance you also reveal your disregard for the warnings that the Lord has given you. His word to you is: "Who is among you that feareth the Lord, that obeyeth the voice of His servant, that walketh in darkness, and hath no light? let him trust in the name of the Lord, and stay upon his God. Behold, all ye that kindle a fire, that compass yourselves about with sparks: walk in the light of your fire, and in the sparks that ye have kindled. This shall ye have of Mine hand; ye shall lie down in sorrow." Isaiah 50:10, 11.

Shall we not draw near to the Lord, that He may save us from all intemperance in eating and drinking, from all unholy, lustful passion, all wickedness? Shall we not humble ourselves before God, putting away everything that corrupts the flesh and the spirit, that in His fear we may perfect holiness of character?

Let everyone who sits in council and committee meetings write in his heart the words: I am working for time and for eternity; and I am accountable to God for the motives that prompt me to action. Let this be his motto. Let the prayer of the psalmist be his prayer: "Set a watch, O Lord, before my mouth; keep the door of my lips. Incline not my heart to any evil thing." Psalm 141:3, 4.

In counseling for the advancement of the work, no one man is to be a controlling power, a voice for the whole. Proposed methods and plans are to be carefully considered so that all the brethren may weigh their relative merits and decide which should be followed. In studying the fields to which duty seems to call us it is well to take into account the difficulties that will be encountered in these fields.

So far as possible, committees should let the people understand their plans in order that the judgment of the church may sustain their efforts. Many of the church members are prudent and have other excellent qualities of mind. Their interest should be aroused in the progress of the cause. Many may be led to have a deeper insight into the work of God and to seek for wisdom from above to extend Christ's kingdom by saving souls perishing for the word of life. Men and women of noble minds will yet be added to the number of those of whom it is said: "Ye have not chosen Me, but I have chosen you, ... that ye should go and bring forth fruit." John 15:16.

52. Church Discipline

In dealing with erring church members, God's people are carefully to follow the instruction given by the Saviour in the eighteenth chapter of Matthew.

Human beings are Christ's property, purchased by Him at an infinite price, bound to Him by the love that He and His Father have manifested for them. How careful, then, we should be in our dealing with one another! Men have no right to surmise evil in regard to their fellow men. Church members have no right to follow their own impulses and inclinations in dealing with fellow members who have erred. They should not even express their prejudices regarding the erring, for thus they place in other minds the leaven of evil. Reports unfavorable to a brother or sister in the church are communicated from one to another of the church members. Mistakes are made and injustice is done because of an unwillingness on the part of someone to follow the directions given by the Lord Jesus.

"If thy brother shall trespass against thee," Christ declared, "go and tell him his fault between thee and him alone." Matthew 18:15. Do not tell others of the wrong. One person is told, then another, and still another; and continually the report grows, and the evil increases, till the whole church is made to suffer. Settle the matter "between thee and him alone." This is God's plan. "Go not forth hastily to strive, lest thou know not what to do in the end thereof, when thy neighbor hath put thee to shame. Debate thy cause with thy neighbor himself; and discover not a secret to another." Proverbs 25:8, 9. Do not suffer sin upon your brother; but do not expose him, and thus increase the difficulty, making the reproof seem like a revenge. Correct him in the way outlined in the word of God.

Do not suffer resentment to ripen into malice. Do not allow the wound to fester and break out in poisoned words, which taint the minds of those who hear. Do not allow bitter thoughts to continue to fill your mind and his. Go to your brother, and in humility and sincerity talk with him about the matter.

Whatever the character of the offense, this does not change the plan that God has made for the settlement of misunderstandings and personal injuries. Speaking alone and in the spirit of Christ to the one who is in fault will often remove the difficulty. Go to the erring one, with a heart filled with Christ's love and sympathy, and seek to adjust the matter. Reason with him calmly and quietly. Let no angry words escape your lips. Speak in a way that will appeal to his better judgment. Remember the words: "He which converteth the sinner from the error of his way shall save a soul from death, and shall hide a multitude of sins." James 5:20.

Take to your brother the remedy that will cure the disease of disaffection. Do your part to help him. For the sake of the peace and unity of the church, feel it a privilege as well as a duty to do this. If he will hear you, you have gained him as a friend.

All heaven is interested in the interview between the one who has been injured and the one who is in error. As the erring one accepts the reproof offered in the love of Christ, and acknowledges his wrong, asking forgiveness from God and from his brother, the sunshine of heaven fills his heart. The controversy is ended; friendship and confidence are restored. The oil of love removes the soreness caused by the wrong. The Spirit of God binds heart to heart, and there is music in heaven over the union brought about.

As those thus united in Christian fellowship offer prayer to God and pledge themselves to deal justly, to love mercy, and to walk humbly with God, great blessing comes to them. If they have wronged others they continue the work of repentance, confession, and restitution, fully set to do good to one another. This is the fulfilling of the law of Christ.

"But if he will not hear thee, then take with thee one or two more, that in the mouth of two or three witnesses every word may be established." Matthew 18:16. Take with you those who are spiritually minded, and talk with the one in error in regard to the wrong. He may yield to the united appeals of his brethren. As he sees their agreement in the matter, his mind may be enlightened.

"And if he shall neglect to hear them," what then shall be done? Shall a few persons in a board meeting take upon themselves the responsibility of disfellowshiping the erring one? "If he shall neglect to hear them, tell it unto the church." Verse 17. Let the church take action in regard to its members.

"But if he neglect to hear the church, let him be unto thee as an heathen man and a publican." Verse 17. If he will not heed the voice of the church, if he refuses all the efforts made to reclaim him, upon the church rests the responsibility of separating him from fellowship. His name should then be stricken from the books.

No church officer should advise, no committee should recommend, nor should any church vote, that the name of a wrongdoer shall be removed from the church books, until the instruction given by Christ has been faithfully followed. When this instruction has been followed, the church has cleared herself before God. The evil must then be made to appear as it is, and must be removed, that it may not become more and more widespread. The health and purity of the church must be preserved, that she may stand before God unsullied, clad in the robes of Christ's righteousness.

If the erring one repents and submits to Christ's discipline, he is to be given another trial. And even if he does not repent, even if he stands outside the church, God's servants still have a work to do for him. They are to seek earnestly to win him to repentance. And, however aggravated may have been his offense, if he yields to the striving of the Holy Spirit and, by confessing and forsaking his sin, gives evidence of repentance, he is to be forgiven and welcomed to the fold again. His brethren are to encourage him in the right way, treating him as they would wish to be treated were they in his place, considering themselves lest they also be tempted.

"Verily I say unto you," Christ continued, "whatsoever ye shall bind on earth shall be bound in heaven: and whatsoever ye shall loose on earth shall be loosed in heaven." Verse 18.

This statement holds its force in all ages. On the church has been conferred the power to act in Christ's stead. It is God's instrumentality for the preservation of order and discipline among His people. To it the Lord has delegated the power to settle all questions respecting its prosperity, purity, and order. Upon it rests the responsibility of excluding from its fellowship those who are unworthy, who by their un-Christlike conduct would bring dishonor on the truth. Whatever the church does that is in accordance with the directions given in God's word will be ratified in heaven.

Matters of grave import come up for settlement by the church. God's ministers, ordained by Him as guides of His people, after doing their part are to submit the whole matter to the church, that there may be unity in the decision made.

The Lord desires His followers to exercise great care in dealing with one another. They are to lift up, to restore, to heal. But there is to be in the church no neglect of proper discipline. The members are to regard themselves as pupils in a school, learning how to form characters worthy of their high calling. In the church here below, God's children are to be prepared for the great reunion in the church above. Those who here live in harmony with Christ may look forward to an endless life in the family of the redeemed.

God's love for the fallen race is a peculiar manifestation of love—a love born of mercy, for human beings are all undeserving. Mercy implies imperfection of the object toward which it is shown. It is because of sin that mercy was brought into active exercise.

It may be that much work needs to be done in your character building, that you are a rough stone, which must be squared and polished before it can fill a place in God's temple. You need not be surprised if with hammer and chisel God cuts away the sharp corners of your character until you are prepared to fill the place He has for you. No human being can accomplish this work. Only by God can it be done. And be assured that He will not strike one useless blow. His every blow is struck in love, for your eternal happiness. He knows your infirmities and works to restore, not to destroy.

53. "Consider One Another"

You will often meet with souls that are under the stress of temptation. You know not how severely Satan may be wrestling with them. Beware lest you discourage such souls and thus give the tempter an advantage.

Whenever you see or hear something that needs to be corrected, seek the Lord for wisdom and grace, that in trying to be faithful you may not be severe.

It is always humiliating to have one's errors pointed out. Do not make the experience more bitter by needless censure. Unkind criticism brings discouragement, making life sunless and unhappy.

My brethren, prevail by love rather than by severity. When one at fault becomes conscious of his error, be careful not to destroy his self-respect. Do not seek to bruise and wound, but rather to bind up and heal.

No human being possesses sensibilities so acute or a nature so refined as does our Saviour. And what patience He manifests toward us. Year after year He bears with our weakness and ignorance, with our ingratitude and waywardness. Notwithstanding all our wanderings, our hardness of heart, our neglect of His holy words, His hand is stretched out still. And He bids us: "Love one another; as I have loved you." John 13:34.

Brethren, regard yourselves as missionaries, not among heathen, but among your fellow workers. It requires a vast amount of time and labor to convince one soul in regard to the special truths for this time. And when souls are turned from sin to righteousness, there is joy in the presence of the angels. Think you that the ministering spirits who watch over these souls are pleased to see how indifferently they are treated by many who claim to be Christians? Man's preferences rule. Partiality is manifested. One is favored, while another is treated harshly.

The angels look with awe and amazement upon the mission of Christ to the world. They marvel at the love that moved Him to give Himself a sacrifice for the sins of men. But how lightly human beings regard the purchase of His blood!

We need not begin by trying to love one another. The love of Christ in the heart is what is needed. When self is submerged in Christ, true love springs forth spontaneously.

In patient forbearance we shall conquer. It is patience in service that brings rest to the soul. It is through humble, diligent, faithful toilers that the welfare of Israel is promoted. A word of love and encouragement will do more to subdue the hasty temper and willful disposition than all the faultfinding and censure that you can heap upon the erring one.

The Master's message must be declared in the Master's spirit. Our only safety is in keeping our thoughts and impulses under the control of the Great Teacher. Angels of God will give to every true worker a rich experience in doing this. The grace of humility will mold our words into expressions of Christlike tenderness.

54. To the Teachers in Our Schools

My Dear Brethren and Sisters: The Lord will work in behalf of all who will walk humbly with Him. He has placed you in a position of trust. Walk carefully before Him. God's hand is on the wheel. He will guide the ship past the rocks into the haven. He will take the weak things of this world to confound the things that are mighty.

I pray that you will make God your Counselor. You are not amenable to any man, but are under God's direction. Keep close to Him. Do not take worldly ideas as your criterion. Let there be no departure from the Lord's methods of working. Use not common fire, but the sacred fire of the Lord's kindling.

Be of good courage in your work. For many years I have kept before our people the need, in the education of the youth, of an equal taxation of the physical and mental powers. But for those who have never proved the value of the instruction given to combine manual training with the study of books, it is hard to understand and carry out the directions given.

Do your best to impart to your students the blessings God has given you. With a deep, earnest desire to help them, carry them over the ground of knowledge. Come close to them. Unless teachers have the love and gentleness of Christ abounding in their hearts, they will manifest too much of the spirit of a harsh, domineering master.

The Lord wishes you to learn how to use the gospel net. That you may be successful in your work, the meshes of your net must be close. The application of the Scriptures must be such that the meaning shall be easily discerned. Then make the most of drawing in the net. Come right to the point. However great a man's knowledge, it is of no avail unless he is able to communicate it to others. Let the pathos of your voice, its deep feeling, make an impression on hearts. Urge your students to surrender themselves to God. "Keep yourselves in the love of God, looking for the mercy of our Lord Jesus Christ unto eternal life. And of some have compassion, making a difference: and others save with fear, pulling them out of the fire; hating even the garment spotted by the flesh." Jude 21-23. As you follow Christ's example you will have the precious reward of seeing your students won to Him.

- **Aggressive Effort**

The Lord God of Israel is hungry for fruit. He calls upon His workers to branch out more than they are doing. He desires them to make the world their field of labor rather than to work only for our churches. The apostle Paul went from place to place, preaching the truth to those in the darkness of error. He labored for a year and six months at Corinth, and proved the divine character of his mission by raising up a flourishing church, composed of Jews and Gentiles. Christ never confined His labors to one place. The towns and cities of Palestine resounded with the truths that fell from His lips.

- **Christ's Greeting to the World**

The Sermon on the Mount is heaven's benediction to the world, a voice from the throne of God. It was given to mankind to be to them the law of duty and the light of heaven, their hope and consolation in despondency. Here the Prince of preachers, the Master Teacher, utters the words that the Father gave Him to speak.

The Beatitudes are Christ's greeting, not only to those who believe, but to the whole human family. He seems to have forgotten for a moment that He is in the world, not in heaven; and He uses the familiar salutation of the world of light. Blessings flow from His lips as the gushing forth of a long-sealed current of rich life.

Christ leaves us in no doubt as to the traits of character that He will always recognize and bless. From the ambitious favorites of the world He turns to those whom they disown, pronouncing all blessed who receive His light and life. To the poor in spirit, the meek, the lowly, the sorrowful, the despised, the persecuted, He opens His arms of refuge, saying: "Come unto Me, ... and I will give you rest." Matthew 11:28.

Christ can look on the misery of the world without a shade of sorrow for having created man. In the human heart He sees more than sin, more than misery. In His infinite wisdom and love He sees man's possibilities, the height to which he may attain. He knows that, even though human beings have abused their mercies and destroyed their God-given dignity, yet the Creator is to be glorified in their redemption.

The Sermon on the Mount is an example of how we are to teach. What pains Christ has taken to make mysteries no longer mysteries, but plain, simple truths! There is in His instruction nothing vague, nothing hard to understand.

"He opened His mouth, and taught them." Matthew 5:2. His words were spoken in no whispered tones, nor was His utterance harsh and disagreeable. He spoke with clearness and emphasis, with solemn, convincing force.

"And it came to pass, when Jesus had ended these sayings, the people were astonished at His doctrine: for He taught them as one having authority, and not as the scribes." Matthew 7:28, 29.

An earnest, prayerful study of the Sermon on the Mount will prepare us to proclaim the truth, to give to others the light we have received. We are first to take heed to ourselves, receiving with humble hearts the principles of truth and working them out in perfect obedience. This will bring joy and peace. Thus we eat the flesh and drink the blood of the Son of God, and we grow strong in His strength. Our lives are assimilated to His life. Our spirit, our inclinations, our habits, are conformed to the will of Him of whom God declared: "This is My beloved Son, in whom I am well pleased." Matthew 3:17.

Throughout all time the words that Christ spoke from the mount of Beatitudes will retain their power. Every sentence is a jewel from the treasure house of truth. The principles enunciated in this discourse are for all ages and for all classes of men. With divine energy Christ expressed His faith and hope as He pointed out class after class as blessed because of having formed righteous characters. Living the life of the Life-giver, through faith in Him, everyone can reach the standard held up in His words. Is not such an attainment worth lifelong, untiring effort?

- **The Outlook**

We are nearing the close of this earth's history. We have before us a great work, the closing work of giving the last warning message to a sinful world. There are men who will be taken from the plow, from the vineyard, from various other branches of work, and sent forth by the Lord to give this message to the world.

The world is out of joint. As we look at the picture, the outlook seems discouraging. But Christ greets with hopeful assurance the very men and women who cause us discouragement. In them He sees qualifications that will enable them to take a place in His vineyard. If they will constantly be learners, through His providence He will make them men and women fitted to do a work that is not beyond their capabilities; through the impartation of the Holy Spirit He will give them power of utterance.

Many of the barren, unworked fields must be entered by beginners. The brightness of the Saviour's view of the world will inspire confidence in many workers, who, if they begin in humility, and put their hearts into the work, will be found to be the right men for the time and place. Christ sees all the misery and despair of the world, the sight of which would bow down some of our workers of large capabilities with a weight of discouragement so great that they would not know how even to begin the work of leading men and women to the first round of the ladder. Their precise methods are of little value. They would stand above the lower rounds of the ladder, saying: "Come up where we are." But the poor souls do not know where to put their feet.

Christ's heart is cheered by the sight of those who are poor in every sense of the term; cheered by His view of the ill-used ones who are meek; cheered by the seemingly unsatisfied hungering after righteousness, by the inability of many to begin. He welcomes, as it were, the very condition of things that would discourage many ministers. He corrects our erring piety, giving the burden of the work for the poor and needy in the rough places of the earth to men and women who have hearts that can feel for the ignorant and for those that are out of the way.

The Lord teaches these workers how to meet those whom He wishes them to help. They will be encouraged as they see doors opening for them to enter places where they can do medical missionary work. Having little self-confidence, they give God all the glory. Their hands may be rough and unskilled, but their hearts are susceptible to pity; they are filled with an earnest desire to do something to relieve the woe so abundant; and Christ is present to help them. He works through those who discern mercy in misery, gain in the loss of all things. When the Light of the world passes by, privileges appear in all hardships, order in confusion, the success and wisdom of God in that which has seemed to be failure.

My brethren and sisters, in your ministry come close to the people. Uplift those who are cast down. Treat of calamities as disguised blessings, of woes as mercies. Work in a way that will cause hope to spring up in the place of despair.

The common people are to take their place as workers. Sharing the sorrows of their fellow men as the Saviour shared the sorrows of humanity, they will by faith see Him working with them.

"The great day of the Lord is near, it is near, and hasteth greatly." Zephaniah 1:14. To every worker I would say: Go forth in humble faith, and the Lord will go with you. But watch unto prayer. This is the science of your labor. The power is of God. Work in dependence upon Him, remembering that you are laborers together with Him. He is your Helper. Your strength is from Him. He will be your wisdom, your righteousness, your sanctification, your redemption. Wear the yoke of Christ, daily learning of Him His meekness and lowliness. He will be your Comfort, your Rest.

- **Power from on High**

As the divine endowment—the power of the Holy Spirit—was given to the disciples, so it will today be given to all who seek aright. This power alone is able to make us wise unto salvation and to fit us for the courts above. Christ wants to give us a blessing that will make us holy. "These things have I spoken unto you," He says, "that My joy might remain in you, and that your joy might be full." John 15:11. Joy in the Holy Spirit is health-giving, life-giving joy. In giving us His Spirit, God gives us Himself, making Himself a fountain of divine influences, to give health and life to the world.

As God so liberally bestows His gifts on you, remember that it is in order that you may return them to the Giver, multiplied by being imparted. Bring into the lives of others light and joy and peace. Every day we need the discipline of self-humiliation, that we may be prepared to receive the heavenly gift, not to hoard it, not to rob God's children of His blessing, but to give it in all its rich fullness to others. When more than now shall we need a heart open to receive, aching, as it were, with its longing to impart?

We are in duty bound to draw largely from the treasure house of divine knowledge. God wants us to receive much, in order that we may impart much. He desires us to be channels through which He can impart richly of His grace to the world.

Let sincerity and faith characterize your prayers. The Lord is willing to do for us "exceeding abundantly above all that we ask or think." Ephesians 3:20. Talk it; pray it. Do not talk unbelief. We cannot afford to let Satan see that he has power to darken our countenances and sadden our lives.

Pray in faith. And be sure to bring your lives into harmony with your petitions, that you may receive the blessings for which you pray. Let not your faith weaken, for the blessings received are proportionate to the faith exercised. "According to your faith be it unto you." "All things, whatsoever ye shall ask in prayer, believing, ye shall receive." Matthew 9:29; 21:22. Pray, believe, rejoice. Sing praises to God because He has answered your prayers. Take Him at His word. "He is faithful that promised." Hebrews 10:23. Not one sincere supplication is lost. The channel is open; the stream is flowing. It carries with it healing properties, pouring forth a restoring current of life and health and salvation.

To every teacher is given the sacred privilege of representing Christ. And as teachers strive to do this, they may cherish the reassuring conviction that the Saviour is close beside them, giving them words to speak for Him, pointing out ways in which they can show forth His excellence.

Teachers meet with many trials. Discouragements press upon them as they see that their efforts are not always appreciated by their pupils. Satan strives to afflict them with bodily infirmities, hoping to lead them to murmur against God, to forget His goodness, His mercy, His love, and the exceeding weight of glory that awaits the overcomer. Let them remember that by trial God is leading them to more perfect confidence in Him. His eye is ever upon them, and if in their perplexity they look to Him in faith, He will bring them forth from the furnace refined and purified as gold tried in the fire. He permits trials to come to them to draw them nearer to Him, but He lays on them no burden greater than they are able to bear.

And He declares: "I will never leave thee, nor forsake thee." Hebrews 13:5. He is always ready to deliver those who trust in Him. Let the hard-pressed, sorely tried teacher say: "Though He slay Me, yet will I trust in Him." "Although the fig tree shall not blossom, neither shall fruit be in the vines; the labor of the olive shall fail, and the fields shall yield no meat; the flock shall be cut off from the fold, and there shall be no herd in the stalls: yet I will rejoice in the Lord, I will joy in the God of my salvation." Job 13:15; Habakkuk 3:17, 18.

Students, co-operate with your teachers. As you do this you give them hope and courage. You are helping them, and at the same time you are helping yourselves to advance. Remember that it rests largely with you whether your teachers stand on vantage ground, their work an acknowledged success.

In the highest sense you are to be learners, seeing God behind the teacher, and the teacher co-operating with Him.

Your opportunities for work are fast passing. You have no time to spend in self-pleasing. Only as you strive earnestly to succeed will you gain true happiness. Precious are the opportunities offered you during the time you spend in school. Make your student life as perfect as possible. You will pass over the way but once. And it rests with you yourself whether your work shall be a success or a failure. As you succeed in gaining a knowledge of the Bible you are storing up treasures to impart.

If you have a fellow student who is backward, explain to him the lesson that he does not understand. This will aid your own understanding. Use simple words; state your ideas in language that is clear and easy to be understood.

By helping your fellow student, you help your teachers.

And often one whose mind is apparently stolid will catch ideas more quickly from a fellow student than from a teacher.

This is the co-operation that Christ commends. The Great Teacher stands beside you, helping you to help the one who is backward.

In your school life you may have opportunity to tell the poor and ignorant of the wonderful truths of God's word. Improve every such opportunity. The Lord will bless every moment spent in this way.

We are living in a time when Satan is working with all his power to discourage and defeat those who are laboring in God's service. But we must not fail nor be discouraged. We must exercise greater faith in God. We must trust His living word. Unless we have a firmer hold from above, we shall never be able to cope with the powers of darkness that will be seen and felt in every department of the work.

Earth's cisterns will often be empty, its pools become dry; but in Christ there is a living spring from which we may continually draw. However much we draw and give to others, an abundance will remain. There is no danger of exhausting the supply; for Christ is the inexhaustible wellspring of truth.

The ethics inculcated by the gospel acknowledge no standard but the perfection of God's mind, God's will. All righteous attributes of character dwell in God as a perfect, harmonious whole. Everyone who receives Christ as his personal Saviour is privileged to possess these attributes. This is the science of holiness.

55. Consideration for those Struggling with Difficulties

For years a lack of wisdom has been shown in dealing with men who take up and carry forward the Lord's work in difficult places. Often these men labor far beyond their strength. They have little money to invest for the advancement of the work, and they are obliged to sacrifice in order to carry the work forward. They work for small wages and practice the strictest economy. They make appeals to the people for means, and they themselves set an example of liberality. They give God the praise for what is done, realizing that He is the Author and the Finisher of their faith, and that it is by His power that they are enabled to make progress.

Sometimes, after these workers have borne the burden and the heat of the day, and by patient, persevering effort have established a school or a sanitarium, or some other interest for the advancement of the work, the decision is made by their brethren that some other man might do better, and therefore that he is to take charge of the work they have been doing. In some cases the decision is made without giving due consideration and due credit to those who have borne the disagreeable part of the work, who have labored and prayed and striven, putting into their efforts all their strength and energy.

God is not pleased with this way of dealing with His workers. He calls upon His people to hold up the hands of those who build up the work in new, difficult places, speaking to them words of cheer and encouragement.

In their ardor, their zeal for the advancement of the cause, these workers may make mistakes. They may, in their desire to get means for the support of needy enterprises, enter into projects that are not for the best good of the work. The Lord, seeing that these projects would divert them from what He desires them to do, permits disappointment to come upon them, crushing their hopes. Money is sacrificed, and this is a great grief to those who had fondly hoped to gain means for the support of the cause.

While the workers were straining every nerve to raise means to help them over an emergency, some of their brethren were standing by, criticizing, and surmising evil, putting a prejudicial construction on the motives of the heavily burdened laborers, and making their work more difficult. Blinded by selfishness, these faultfinders did not discern that their brethren were sufficiently afflicted without the censure of men who had not borne heavy burdens and responsibilities. Disappointment is a great trial, but Christian love can turn the defeat into victory. Reverses will teach caution. We learn by the things we suffer. Thus we gain experience.

Let care and wisdom be shown in dealing with workers who, though they have made mistakes, have manifested an earnest, self-sacrificing interest in the work. Let their brethren say: "We will not make matters worse by putting another in your place, without giving you opportunity to retrieve your mistake, and to stand on vantage ground, free from the burden of unjust criticism." Let them be given time to adjust themselves, to overcome the difficulties surrounding them, and to stand before angels and men as worthy workers. They have made mistakes, but would those who have questioned and criticized have done better? To the accusing Pharisees Christ said: "He that is without sin among you, let him first cast a stone." John 8:7.

There are those who are premature in their desire to reform things that to them appear faulty. They think that they should be chosen to take the place of those who have made mistakes. They undervalue what these workers have done while others were looking on and criticizing. By their actions they say: "I can do great things. I can carry the work forward successfully." To those who think they know so well how to avoid mistakes, I am instructed to say: "Judge not, that ye be not judged." Matthew 7:1. You might avoid mistakes on some points, but on other things you are liable to make grave blunders, which would be very difficult to remedy and which would bring confusion into the work. These mistakes might do more harm than those your brethren have made.

The instruction given me is that the men who lay the foundation of a work, and who, in the face of prejudice, fight their way forward, are not to be placed in an unfavorable light in order that others may take their places. There are earnest workers who, in spite of the criticisms of some of their brethren, have moved forward in the work that God said should be done. Should they now be removed from their position of responsibility, an impression would be made that would be unjust to them and unfavorable to the work, because the changes made would be looked upon as a justification of the unjust criticisms made and the prejudice existing. The Lord desires that no move shall be made which would do injustice to those who have labored long and earnestly to build up the work given them.

- **Unwise Changes**

Many changes are made that might better never be made. Often, when workers become discontented, instead of being encouraged to stay where they are and make a success of their work, they are sent to another place. But they take with them the same traits of character that in the past have marred their work. They will manifest the same un-Christlike spirit, for they have not learned the lesson of patient, humble service.

I plead for a different order of things. Changes must be made in the groups of workers in our conferences and institutions. Men of efficiency and consecration must be sought for and encouraged to connect with the burden bearers as helpers and colaborers. Let there be a harmonious union of the new and the old, in the spirit of brotherly love. But let not changes of management be made abruptly in such a way as to bring discouragement to those who have labored earnestly and successfully to bring the work to a degree of progress. God will not sanction anything done to discourage His faithful servants. Let the principles of justice be followed by those whose duty it is to secure the most efficient management for our publishing houses, our sanitariums, and our schools.

- ### A Call to Service

God calls for workers. The cause needs men who are self-made, who, placing themselves in the hands of the Lord as humble learners, have proved themselves workers together with Him. These are the men that are needed in the ministry and in the school work. Let those who have shown themselves to be men move out and do what they can in the Master's service. Let them step into the ranks of workers and by patient, continuous effort prove their worth. It is in the water, not on the land, that we learn to swim. Let them fill with fidelity the place to which they are called, that they may become qualified to bear still higher responsibilities. God gives all opportunity to perfect themselves in His service.

He who puts on the armor to war a good warfare will gain greater and still greater ability as he strives to perfect his knowledge of God, working in harmony with the plan God has laid down for the perfect development of the physical, the mental, and the spiritual powers.

Young men and young women, gather a stock of knowledge. Do not wait until some human examination pronounces you competent to work, but go out into the highways and hedges, and begin to work for God. Use wisely the knowledge you have. Exercise your ability with faithfulness, generously imparting the light that God gives you. Study how best to give to others peace and light and truth and the many other rich blessings of heaven. Constantly improve. Keep reaching higher and still higher. It is the ability to put to the tax the powers of mind and body, ever keeping eternal realities in view, that is of value now. Seek the Lord most earnestly, that you may become more and more refined, more spiritually cultured. Then you will have the very best diploma that anyone can have—the endorsement of God.

However large, however small, your talents, remember that what you have is yours only in trust. Thus God is testing you, giving you opportunity to prove yourself true. To Him you are indebted for all your capabilities. To Him belong your powers of body, mind, and soul, and for Him these powers are to be used. Your time, your influence, your capabilities, your skill —all must be accounted for to Him who gives all. He uses his gifts best who seeks by earnest endeavor to carry out the Lord's great plan for the uplifting of humanity, remembering always that he must be a learner as well as a teacher.

As young men go out into this work and, in spite of many difficulties, make a success, let not propositions be made that they take up another work and that the work they have started be given into the charge of men who are older and more experienced. As our young men struggle with difficulties, they may make mistakes; but if they press forward perseveringly, their defeats will be turned into victories.

My fellow workers, persevere in the work that you have begun. Keep at it until you gain victory after victory. Educate yourselves for a purpose. Keep in view the highest standard, that you may accomplish greater and still greater good, thus reflecting the glory of God.

God has endowed some of His servants with special talents, and no one is called upon to disparage their excellence. But let none use their talents to exalt self. Let them not regard themselves as favored above their fellow men, nor exalt themselves above other sincere, earnest workers. The Lord looks upon the heart. He who is most devoted to God's service is most highly esteemed by the heavenly universe.

Heaven is watching to see how those occupying positions of influence fulfill their stewardship. The demands upon them as stewards are measured by the extent of their influence. In their treatment of their fellow men they should be as fathers, just, tender, true. They should be Christlike in character, uniting with their brethren in the closest bonds of unity and fellowship.

Section 6: Counsels to Burden Bearers

56. A Wise Distribution of Means

The perplexing question of means has troubled many. Again and again, by his deceitful, alluring projects, Satan has blocked the way against advance. The church has not stood in dependence upon God, but, yielding to the temptations of the enemy, has tried to carry out plans that called for means far exceeding her revenue. Much money has been invested in a few places. This has deprived missionary fields of the help they should have received. In building up the work in their part of the field, men have followed selfish plans and have drawn means from the Lord's treasury, forgetting that all the revenue is the Lord's and that other parts of His vineyard must be supplied.

For reasons that they will not be pleased to meet in the judgment, they closed their eyes to the needs of their fellow workers. Thus destitute fields have been left unworked. By rushing on to erect large buildings, without counting the cost, without taking into consideration how much would be needed to build the tower, men have brought debt, discouragement, and confusion upon the cause. The way of progress in new fields has been hedged up.

A kind of frenzy has taken hold of the minds of some, leading them to do that which would absorb means without any prospect of afterward producing means. Had this money been used in the way the Lord signified it should be, workers would have been raised up and prepared to do the work that must be done before the coming of the Lord. The misappropriation of means shows the need of the Lord's warning that His work must not be bound about by human projects, that it must be done in a way that will strengthen His cause.

By working on wrong plans, men have brought debts upon the cause. Let not this be repeated. Let those at the head of the work move cautiously, refusing to bury the cause of God in debt. Let no one move recklessly, heedlessly, thinking, without knowing, that all will be well.

Undue excitement and interest in the work in one place contribute nothing to the advancement of the work as a whole. When plans are laid to erect a building in one place, give careful consideration to other places that are in just as great need of money for the erection of needful buildings. Time is short, and while buildings must be erected, let this be done with due consideration for all parts of the Lord's vineyard. Let the one who has charge of the building be a man of sound, sanctified mind, not one who, in his anxiety to erect a fine piece of architecture, will bring perplexity upon the work by expensive investment. God is not the author of confusion, but of order and progress. Let those who desire to advance His kingdom make haste slowly and build intelligently. Let no one rush on with a stumbling supposition that means must be invested to make a display. Thus saith the Lord: "Means must not be so expended, for it is at the expense of souls."

The result of selfish management stands before us today as a representation of the wisdom of men whose minds and hearts needed the guidance of the Holy Spirit. The Lord has many ways of trying and proving those who claim to be Christians. With unmistakable accuracy He has traced the results of human wisdom, showing those who have thought they were doing great things that they need to review the past; that they need to see that they were not actuated by the Holy Spirit, but that in many things they refused the counsel of the Lord. Had they taken up this self-examination at the beginning of their work, as the Lord directed them to do, years of God-dishonoring service would have been changed into a service of love.

Every heart in every household needs to take up the work of self-examination, else some will find, as did Saul, that they are appointed to destruction. Especially is this applicable to men in positions of responsibility. Saith the Lord: "I will not serve with any selfish devising." Everyone needs now to seek the Lord. God's people will not endure the test unless there is a revival and a reformation. The Lord will not admit into the mansions He is preparing for the righteous, one soul who is self-sufficient. Under no circumstances should our people in any land put all their means into one great, expensive medical institution. To bring together a large number of people in one place is not favorable to the securing of the best results in physical or in spiritual restoration.

And besides this, to establish such an institution would be to rob other places where health institutions should be established. Wherever we work, some will desire to secure as much means as possible, in order to erect a large building; but this is not the wisest plan. When planning for an institution in one place, we should keep in mind the needs of other places. Let economy be practiced so that it will be possible to give the people in other sections of the country similar advantages.

57. Our Aged Pioneer Workers

To the aged pioneer laborers who have been connected with the work of the third angel's message almost from its beginning, whose experiences in it dates nearly from the passing of the time in 1844, the Lord says: "Your help is needed. Do not take upon yourselves loads that others who are younger can carry. It is your duty to be careful in your habits of life. You are to be wise in the use of your physical, mental, and spiritual strength. You who have passed through so many and such varied experiences are to do all that it is possible for you to do to preserve your powers, that you may labor for the Lord as long as He permits you to stand in your lot and place to help to advance His work."

With John, these burden bearers can say: "That which was from the beginning, which we have heard, which we have seen with our eyes, which we have looked upon, and our hands have handled, of the Word of life; (for the life was manifested, and we have seen it, and bear witness, and show unto you that eternal life, which was with the Father, and was manifested unto us;) that which we have seen and heard declare we unto you, that ye also may have fellowship with us: and truly our fellowship is with the Father, and with His Son Jesus Christ...This then is the message which we have heard of Him, and declare unto you, that God is light, and in Him is no darkness at all. If we say that we have fellowship with Him, and walk in darkness, we lie, and do not the truth: but if we walk in the light, as He is in the light, we have fellowship one with another, and the blood of Jesus Christ His Son cleanseth us from all sin." 1 John 1:1-7.

The cause needs the help of the old hands, the aged workers, who have had years of experience in the cause of God; who have watched the development and the progress of the message in its various lines; who have seen many go into fanaticism, cherishing the delusion of false theories, resisting all the efforts made to let the light of truth reveal the superstitions that were coming in to confuse minds and to make of none effect the message which in these last days must be given in its purity to God's remnant people.

Many of the tried servants of God have fallen asleep in Jesus. Let the help of those who are left alive to this day be appreciated. Let their testimony be valued. The good hand of the Lord has been with these faithful workers. He will uphold them by His strong arm, saying: "Lean on Me. I will be your strength and your exceeding great reward." Those who were in the message at its beginning, who fought bravely when the battle went hard, must not lose their hold now.

The most tender interest should be cherished toward those whose life interest is bound up with the work of God. Notwithstanding their many infirmities, these workers still possess talents that qualify them to stand in their lot and place. God desires them to occupy leading positions in His work. They have stood faithful amidst storm and trial, and are among our most valuable counselors. How thankful we should be that they can still use their gifts in the Lord's service!

Let not the fact be lost sight of that in the past these earnest wrestlers sacrificed everything to advance the work. The fact that they have grown old and gray in the service of God is no reason why they should cease to exert an influence superior to the influence of men who have far less knowledge of the work and far less experience in divine things. Though worn and unable to bear the heavier burdens that younger men can and should carry, their value as counselors is of the highest order. They have made mistakes, but they have learned wisdom from their failures; they have learned to avoid errors and dangers, and are they not then competent to give wise counsel? They have borne test and trial, and, though they have lost some of their vigor, they are not to be pushed aside by less-experienced workers, who know very little about the labor and self-sacrifice of these pioneers. The Lord does not thus lay them aside. He gives them special grace and knowledge.

When John was old and gray-headed, he was given a message to bear to the persecuted churches. The Jews made several attempts to take his life, but the Lord said: "Let him live. I who created him will be with him and will guard him." Constantly this aged disciple bore testimony for the Master. In beautiful language, with a musical voice, speaking in a way that impressed the hearts of all who heard him, he told of the words and works of Christ. He was sent as an exile to Patmos, but Christ visited him in his exile, and communicated to him the grand truths found in the Revelation.

As those who have spent their lives in the service of God draw near the close of their earthly history, they will be impressed by the Holy Spirit to recount the experiences they have had in connection with His work. The record of His wonderful dealings with His people, of His great goodness in delivering them from trial, should be repeated to those newly come to the faith. The trials also that have been brought on the servants of God by the apostasy of some once united with them in labor, and the working of the Holy Spirit to make of none effect the falsehoods told against those who were holding the beginning of their confidence firm unto the end, should be related.

The old standard-bearers who are still living should not be put in hard places. Those who served their Master when the work went hard, who endured poverty and remained faithful to the truth when our numbers were small, are ever to be honored and respected. I am instructed to say: Let every believer respect the aged pioneers who have borne trials and hardships and many privations. They are God's workmen and have acted a prominent part in the building up of His Work.

The Lord desires the younger laborers to gain wisdom, strength, and maturity by association with the aged laborers who have been spared to the cause. Let the younger men realize that, in having such laborers among them, they are highly favored. Let them show great respect for the men of gray hairs, who have had long experience in the development of the work. Let them give them an honored place in their councils. God desires those who have come into the truth in later years to take heed to these words.

May the Lord bless and sustain our old and tried laborers. May He help them to be wise in regard to the preservation of their physical, mental, and spiritual powers. I have been instructed by the Lord to say to those who bore their testimony in the early days of the message: "God has endowed you with the power of reason, and He desires you to understand and obey the laws that have to do with the health of the being. Do not be imprudent. Do not overwork. Take time to rest. God desires you to stand in your lot and place, doing your part to save men and women from being swept downward by the mighty current of evil. He desires you to keep the armor on till He bids you lay it off. Not long hence you will receive your reward."

58. Care for Workers

Some provision should be made for the care of ministers and others of God's faithful servants who through exposure or overwork in His cause have become ill and need rest and restoration, or who through age or loss of health are no longer able to bear the burden and heat of the day. Ministers are often appointed to a field of labor that they know will be detrimental to their health; but, unwilling to shun trying places, they venture, hoping to be a help and a blessing to the people. After a time they find their health failing. A change of climate and of work is tried, without bringing relief; and then what are they to do?

These faithful laborers, who for Christ's sake have given up worldly prospects, choosing poverty rather than pleasure or riches; who, forgetful of self, have labored earnestly to win souls to Christ; who have given liberally to advance various enterprises in the cause of God, and have then sunk down in the battle, wearied and ill, and with no means of support, must not be left to struggle on in poverty and suffering, or to feel that they are paupers. When sickness or infirmity comes upon them, let not our workers be burdened with the anxious query: "What will become of my wife and little ones, now that I can no longer labor and supply their necessities?" It is but just that provision be made to meet the needs of these faithful laborers and the needs of those who are dependent on them.

Generous provision is made for veterans who have fought for their country. These men bear the scars and lifelong infirmities that tell of their perilous conflicts, their forced marches, their exposure to storms, their suffering in prison. All these evidences of their loyalty and self-sacrifice give them a just claim upon the nation they have helped to save—a claim that is recognized and honored. But what provision have Seventh-day Adventists made for the soldiers of Christ?

- **Workers Neglected**

Our people have not felt as they should the necessity of this matter, and it has therefore been neglected. The churches have been thoughtless, and, though the light of the word of God has been shining upon their pathway, they have neglected this most sacred duty. The Lord is greatly displeased with this neglect of His faithful servants. Our people should be as willing to assist these persons when in adverse circumstances as they have been willing to accept their means and services when in health.

God has laid upon us the obligation of giving special attention to the poor among us. But these ministers and workers are not to be ranked with the poor. They have laid up for themselves a treasure in the heavens that faileth not. They have served the conference in its necessity, and now the conference is to serve them. When cases of this kind come before us, we are not to pass by on the other side. We are not to say, "Be ye warmed and filled" (James 2:16), and then take no active measures to supply their necessities. This has been done in the past, and thus in some cases Seventh-day Adventists have dishonored their profession of faith and have given the world opportunity to reproach the cause of God.

- **Providing Homes for Workers**

It is now the duty of God's people to roll back this reproach by providing these servants of God with comfortable homes, with a few acres of land on which they can raise their own produce and feel that they are not dependent on the charities of their brethren. With what pleasure and peace would these worn laborers look to a quiet little home where their just claims to its rest would be recognized!

The duty we owe to these persons has been referred to again and again, but no decided action has been taken in reference to it. As a people we should feel our responsibility in this matter. Every church member should feel an interest in all that concerns the human brotherhood and the brotherhood in Christ. We are members one of another; if one member suffers, all the members suffer with him. Something must be done, and the conference should have spiritual discernment, that they may understand the privileges and comforts that these worn-out workers need and deserve.

• Our Sanitariums a Refuge for Workers

Often these ministers need special care and treatment. Our sanitariums should be a refuge for such and for all our worn workers who need rest. Rooms should be provided where they can have a change and rest, without continual anxiety as to how they are to meet the expense. When the disciples were worn with labor, Christ said to them: "Come ye yourselves apart, ... and rest awhile." Mark 6:31. He would have arrangements made whereby His servants now may have opportunity to rest and recover strength. Our sanitariums are to be open to our hard-working ministers, who have done all in their power to secure funds for the erection and support of these institutions, and at any time when they are in need of the advantages here offered they should be made to feel at home.

These workers should not at any time be charged a high price for board and treatment, neither should they be regarded as beggars, or in any way made to feel as such by those whose hospitality they receive. To manifest liberality in the use of the facilities God has provided for His worn and overworked servants is genuine medical missionary work in His sight. God's workers are bound to Him, and when they are received it should be remembered that Christ is received in the person of His messengers. He requires this, and is dishonored and displeased when they are treated indifferently or dealt with in a small or selfish manner.

God's blessing will not attend close dealing with any of His chosen ones. Among the medical fraternity there has not always been a keenness of perception to discern these matters. Some have not regarded them as they should. May the Lord sanctify the perception of those who have charge of our institutions, that they may know who should have true sympathy and care.

That branch of the cause for which these worn-out laborers have worked should show an appreciation of their labor by helping them in their time of need, thus sharing largely with the sanitarium the burden of expense.

Some workers are so situated as to be able to lay by a little from their salary, and this they should do, if possible, to meet an emergency; yet even these should be welcome as a blessing to the sanitarium. But most of our workers have many and great obligations to meet. At every turn, when means are needed, they are called upon to do something, to lead out, that the influence of their example may stimulate others to liberality and the cause of God be advanced. They feel such an intense desire to plant the standard in new fields that many even hire money to help in various enterprises. They have not given grudgingly, but have felt that it was a privilege to work for the advancement of the truth. By thus responding to calls for means, they are often left with very little surplus.

The Lord has kept an accurate account of their liberality to the cause. He knows what a good work they have done, a work of which the younger laborers have no conception. He has been cognizant of all the privation and self-denial they have endured. He has marked every circumstance of these cases. It is all written in the books. These workers are a spectacle before the world, before angels, and before men, and they are an object lesson to test the sincerity of our religious principles. The Lord would have our people understand that the pioneers in this work deserve all that our institutions can do for them. God calls upon us to understand that those who have grown old in His service deserve our love, our honor, our deepest respect.

• A Workers' Fund

A fund should be raised for such workers as are no longer able to labor. We cannot be clear before God unless we make every reasonable effort in this matter, and that without delay. There are some among us who will not see the necessity of this move, but their opposition should have no influence with us. Those who purpose in their hearts to be right and to do right should move steadily forward for the accomplishment of a good work, a work that God requires to be done. There are many who are at their ease, who have postponed the work of doing good with their substance; but shall it be so longer? Shall we love money so well that we will bury it in the earth?

God calls for the co-operation of all in this enterprise. The affluent should give of the abundance; but if they give grudgingly, longing to have every dollar to invest in some worldly enterprise, they will receive no reward.

The humble gift from the poorer class is not, in the sight of God, inferior to the larger offerings of the more wealthy. The Lord will add His blessing to the gift, making its errand of love fruitful in accordance with the wholehearted cheerfulness with which it is bestowed. The mites from every source should be carefully cherished.

The ardor of the youth is now needed. They should put away vanity and restrict their wants. I would urge upon them and upon all our people that the money usually invested in unnecessary things be put to a higher, holier use. Do what you can toward creating a fund for the aged ministers, worn out with constant labor and care. Consecrate all that you have to the Lord. Do not use your money to gratify self. Put it into the Lord's treasury. Do not allow means to pass out of your hands merely to gratify the wishes of yourselves or others. In your expenditure consider that it is the Lord's money which you are handling and that you must render to Him an account of its use.

To the aged, who are losing their hold on this life, I appeal to make a right disposition of your Lord's goods before you fall asleep in Jesus. Remember that you are God's stewards. Give back to the Lord His own while you live. Do not fail of attending to this while you have your reason. As age comes upon us, it is our duty to make a disposition of our means to the instrumentalities that God has established. Satan is using every device to divert from the Lord's cause the means so much needed. Many are binding up their talent of means in worldly enterprises, when the cause of God needs every dollar to advance His truth and glorify His name.

I ask: Shall we not lay up for ourselves treasure in heaven, in bags that wax not old? I would especially urge the aged who are soon to make a disposal of their means to remember those who have ministered faithfully in word and doctrine. Place your means where, should health and life fail, they can be invested in the cause of God. Thus they will be put out to the exchangers and be constantly accumulating.

I call upon the church as a whole, and upon its members individually, to render to God His own entrusted capital with interest. Thus you will have treasure in heaven. Let your hearts be true to Jesus. Although you may feel that you are the least of all saints, yet you are members of Christ's body, and through Him you are identified with all His human agencies and with the excellence and power of the heavenly intelligences. None of us liveth to himself. To each is assigned a post of duty, not for his own narrow, selfish interests, but that the influence of each may be a strength to all. If we really believed that we were individually a spectacle to the world, to angels, and to men, would we not as a church manifest a very different spirit from that which we now manifest? Would we not be a living, working church?

The small and the larger streams of beneficence should ever be kept flowing. God's providence is far ahead of us, moving onward much faster than our liberalities. The way for the advancement and upbuilding of the cause of God is blocked by selfishness, pride, covetousness, extravagance, and love of display. The whole church is charged with a solemn responsibility to lift in every branch of the work. If its members follow Christ, they will deny the inclination for display, the love of dress, the love of elegant houses and costly furniture.

There must be far greater humility, a much greater distinction from the world, among Seventh-day Adventists, else God will not accept us, whatever our position or the character of the work in which we are engaged. Economy and self-denial will furnish many in moderate circumstances with means for benevolence. It is the duty of all to learn of Christ, to walk humbly in the self-denying path in which the Majesty of heaven trod. The whole Christian life should be one of self-denial, that, when calls for help are made, we may be ready to respond.

As long as Satan works with unremitting energy to destroy souls, as long as there is a call for laborers in any part of the wide harvest field, so long will there be a call to give for the support of the work of God in some one of its many lines. We relieve one need only to make way to relieve another of like character. The self-denial required to obtain means to invest in that which God values most highly will develop habits and a character which will win for us the approbation, "Well done," and make us fit to dwell forever in the presence of Him who for our sake became poor, that we through His poverty might inherit eternal riches.

Men in positions of responsibility are in danger of becoming crushed under the many burdens that they bear, but the Lord does not press on anyone burdens too heavy to be borne. He estimates every weight before He allows it to rest upon the hearts of those who are laborers together with Him. To every one of His workers our loving heavenly Father says: "Cast thy burden upon the Lord, and He shall sustain thee." Psalm 55:22. Let the burden bearers believe that He will carry every load, great or small.

Jesus consents to bear our burdens only when we trust Him. He is saying: "Come unto Me, all ye weary and heavy-laden; give Me your load; trust Me to do the work that it is impossible for the human agent to do." Let us trust Him. Worry is blind and cannot discern the future. But Jesus sees the end from the beginning, and in every difficulty He has His way prepared to bring relief. Abiding in Christ, we can do all things through Him who strengthens us.

Because of unconsecrated workers, things will sometimes go wrong. You may weep over the result of the wrong course of others, but do not worry. The work is under the supervision of the blessed Master. All He asks is that the workers shall come to Him for their orders, and obey His directions. All parts of the work —our churches, missions, Sabbath schools, institutions — are carried upon His heart. Why worry? The intense longing to see the church imbued with life must be tempered with entire trust in God; for "without Me," said the great Burden Bearer, "ye can do nothing." "Follow Me." He leads the way; we are to follow. Let no one overtax his God-given powers in an effort to advance the Lord's work more rapidly. The power of man cannot hasten the work; with this must be united the power of heavenly intelligences. Only thus can the work of God be brought to perfection.

Man cannot do God's part of the work. A Paul may plant, and an Apollos water, but God gives the increase. In simplicity and meekness man is to co-operate with divine agencies, at all times doing his best, yet ever realizing that God is the great Master Workman. He is not to feel self-confident, for thus he will exhaust his reserve force and destroy his mental and physical powers. Though all the workmen now bearing the heaviest burdens should be laid aside, God's work would be carried forward. Then let our zeal in labor be tempered with reason; let us cease our efforts to do that which the Lord alone can accomplish.

www.ingramcontent.com/pod-product-compliance
Lightning Source LLC
Chambersburg PA
CBHW070136080526
44586CB00015B/1719